D1561418

What Is
Archaeology?

Paul Courbin

What Is Archaeology?

An Essay on the Nature of
Archaeological Research

Translated by
Paul Bahn

The University of Chicago Press
Chicago and London

PAUL COURBIN, a prominent French archaeologist, is a professor at the Ecole des Hautes Etudes en Sciences Sociales in Paris.

Originally published as *Qu'est-ce que l'archéologie? Essai sur la nature de la recherche archéologique* (© 1982) by Payot, Paris

The University of Chicago Press, Chicago 60637
The University of Chicago Press, Ltd., London

97 96 95 94 93 92 91 90 89 88   54321

Library of Congress Cataloging in Publication Data

Courbin, Paul.
   [Qu'est-ce que l'archéologie? English]
   What is archaeology? : an essay on the nature of archaeological research / Paul Courbin : translated by Paul Bahn.
      p. cm.
   Translation of: Qu'est-ce que l'archéologie?
   Bibliography: p.
   Includes index.
   ISBN 0-226-11656-5. ISBN 0-226-11657-3 (pbk.)
   1. Archaeology.   I. Title.
CC165.C6613 1988
930.1'01—dc19   88-1727
                                                     CIP

Contents

Preface to the English Translation · ix
Translator's Preface · xvii
Introduction · xxi

1 The "New Archeology" · 3
    The Founding Fathers
    A Prehistoric and Americanist Archaeology
    Traditional Archaeology as Seen by the New
        Archeology
    The New Archeology Compared with the "Old"
    The Philosophical Foundations of the New
        Archeology
    The Theoretical and Scientific Environment of the
        New Archeology
    The Objective of the New Archeology

2 The Hypothetico-deductive Method · 18
    The Hypothetico-deductive Method
    The Validation of Hypotheses
    Protracted Amazement: The Nonvalidation of
        Hypotheses
    Pits and Pots
    Against Braidwood
    Against Bordes
    The American Disciples
    The English
    Renfrew and the Cyclades
    Traditional Validations
    Pseudovalidations
    Validations

Contents

3 Laws   45
        Laws
        Variations
        No Laws
        Mickey Mouse Laws
        Schiffer's Laws
        Critique
        Waste Products Law
        South's Law
4 Theories   62
        Theories
        Central Theory, Middle-Range Theory
        Read's Theory: Area of Habitation and Population
        Critique
        Binford and the Nunamiut Eskimo
        Against Yellen
        Critique
5 The Old Archaeology and the New:
   A Comparison of Results   75
        An Epistemological Failure
        The Essential Conclusions
        Their Character
        Their Solidity
        Their Interest
        The Results of Conventional Archaeology
        The Example of Nichoria
6 The Spirit and the Letter   84
        The State of Mind
        Sects
        Days of Contempt
        The Motivations
        Form
        References and Illustration
        A Cloud of Smoke
7 The Conned   98
        The "Conned" and Followers
        Critical Faculty
        Variability
        The Motivations

8   An Attempt at an Assessment   104
      An Acknowledgment of Failure
      Logical Reasons
      Philosophical Reasons
9   What Is Archaeology?   110
      What Archaeology Alone Can Do
      The Establishment of Facts
      Facts and Approaches to Problems
      Toward an Open Approach to Problems
      Against the Manipulation of Facts
      The Difficulties of Identification
      Archaeological Demonstration
      Induction
      A Return to the Facts
10 The Territory of Archaeology   133
      New Fields and New Problems
      Excavation
      Experimental Archaeology
      Archaeometry
      The Elaboration of Data
      Description
      Classification
      Quantification
      Processing by Computer
11 The Frontiers of Archaeology   150
      Anthropology or History?
      History and Liberty
      The Distribution of Roles

      Conclusion   157
      Abbreviations   163
      Notes   165
      Index   189

Preface to the English Translation

As a confirmed admirer of English and American archaeology in the Mediterranean and the East, I cannot but appreciate the publication of an English translation of an essay that calls into question one aspect of Anglo-Saxon archaeology: the New Archeology and its later successors. So first of all I would like to thank those who took the initiative to have it done—first and foremost the late Glyn Daniel. In principle, what could be more straightforward than a translation? In practice, however, things did not go quite so smoothly, and a first English version was completely distorted by its publisher during editing and was rejected by the original French publisher. I would like to thank those who brought the present edition to fruition, and especially the editorial staff at the University of Chicago Press.

When all is said and done, this translated edition constitutes the most positive reaction there has been to this little book that is already six years old. Because, while it brought me numerous letters from archaeologists—those who do research and fieldwork and who, even so, make progress without ceasing to think (despite what the New Archeologists believe, ingenuously)—and while many were delighted to see what they had thought to themselves for so long being said out loud at last, some impressed upon me, for example, that the book came a bit late, that "in Chicago nobody takes the New Archeology seriously anymore," that it was "hounding something that no longer exists," in short, that I was flogging a moribund horse.

When one wants to step back a little to gain perspective, there is obviously a risk of appearing to be behind the times. But so many of those who reacted immediately were mistaken—greatly mistaken. And where the New Archeology is concerned, their view is neither charitable nor correct. Moribund? Hardly; in fact, the New Archeology is more active than ever, as one can see from reading its output, which has by no means been discontinued and is always of the same ilk, even if it shields itself under different names.

Others pointed out to me that my criticisms had for the most part already been made. Of course, there's never anything new under the sun. I quoted a certain number of people who took up positions against the New Archeology, but I was neither able nor willing to read everything written on the subject (and I regret this, since authors like Jacquetta Hawkes, for example, were involved; I became acquainted with their articles only afterward). But many of the criticisms that had been published previously were hedged about with so many qualifications, and mingled with so many eulogies, that one could legitimately wonder whether their authors were for or against: rather than aiming for scrupulous balance, they give the impression of hedging their bets and finding it safer to run with the hare and hunt with the hounds. This is not to mention those who said one thing one day and the opposite another, even if this meant returning to their first opinions later: amid recantations and U-turns, turnarounds and repentance, at what point were they to be believed? Of course, only fools never change: but change alone doesn't make one intelligent.

Others objected that I hadn't really made the task difficult for myself in aiming at such easy targets. But it seemed to me that I had studied the fundamental texts, and those of the leaders, not just the stooges. And dare I remind the reader that the article by Dwight W. Read and Steven A. LeBlanc in *Current Anthropology* (1978) had been sent to fifty scholars, and that among the twenty or so who thought it helpful to send in an opinion *not one* saw the fallacious nature of the calculations? Everything looks easy once it has been done.

I was also told: "All this is well and good, but what else should one do, what can one put in its place?" An admirable and disarming objection, because what use is it to cling to an error under the pretext that there is no alternative solution? Besides, is this really the case? As David Ridgway said so well, I thought I'd suggested one direction: you might find it banal, retrograde, not very exalting—but what results has New Archeological "progress" produced? And I said at the start that I especially didn't want to pull a new "innovation" out of my hat—but in that case you have to look for a different solution. Nothing justifies falling back into the rut.

My book amused a lot of people, more than I would have believed. But some found my criticisms severe, aggressive, murderous—in short, exaggeratedly polemical. If that is the case, I regret it: to the same degree that the compliments of the New Archeology toward unbelievers have always been, as we all know, exquisitely gracious, decidedly courteous. There are plenty of examples, some of them very recent. Observations of this sort, however, would carry more weight if those who made them had ever risen up against the jibes of the New Archeology. But no doubt in their eyes vigor is admissible only in a single direction: the right one. Theirs, not someone else's. This unilateralism is well known and typically "rightist"; it forms part of the system and, at the same time, must be fought against. That said, what I really wanted to do above all, with a subject like this, was to try as best I could to avoid being boring.

As for the reviews that I have seen, if I restrict myself to those written by partisans of the New Archeology, one can understand the mixed response; indeed, it is admirable that their feelings are merely mixed. Anthony Snodgrass considered my book "the one really extended treatment of the problem" (*American Journal of Archaeology,* 1985). In a palliative way, Jean-Claude Gardin tried to create a smokescreen and, for the requirements of his demonstration, did not hesitate to invent false arguments that were totally imaginary (*Revue Archéologique,* 1985). Along with a number of hacks, Alain Gallay tried to attribute statements to me that were the exact opposite of what I'd actually written (*L'archéologie demain* [Paris: Belfond, 1986]). The most serious and interesting reviews, albeit critical ones, seemed to me to be those by Colin Renfrew (*Antiquity* 1982), by Ulpiano Bezerra de Meneses in *Revista de Historia* (São Paulo, 1983), and by Stanislaw Tabaczynski in the Italian journal *Archeologia Medievale* (1984).

I could say a lot about these reviews, but I shall limit myself to two things that struck me. The first is that the reviewers all admit (to differing degrees, but very broadly) the exactness of my critique: it is irrefutable, unanswerable, fully admissible, says Bezerra, for example. The second is that, in perfect unity, they immediately return—as if nothing had happened—to their first loves! Imperturbably. How can one admit that a criticism is well founded and then return immediately to the position that has been so justly criticized? It's one more New Archeological mystery. Thus, concerning the chapter on theories—in which I tried, with a few examples, to demonstrate mathematically their illusory nature—all three reaffirm straightaway the indispensable nature of theories, their at least potential existence: for Tabaczynski, for example, theories must exist, even if we've never yet found any, because they are necessary; in other words, there must be some because we need them. *Perseverare diabolicum.* They stick to their guns, like that commentator who, though noting the death of this immortal doctrine, insists that "whether one likes it or not" (an admirable formula) "the New Archeology has made a contribution." I suppose one should always try to look on the bright side.

What's the reason for this? No doubt it is that the characterization of archaeology I have proposed—the establishment of facts—seems to them a sad disappointment, a disheartening platitude of extreme naïveté.* (But *who* is naive? Only Tabaczynski ends by suspecting *in fine* that my proposition is perhaps less simplistic than it appears.) And each in turn, very seriously, using a German philosopher in support (preferably one whose name begins with an H), reminds me that "facts" are "theory laden," that they are already "interpretative options," that "raw facts" don't exist. A fundamental criticism, one might think.

The funny thing is that this is exactly my point of view. It's what I have always thought; it's what I say and write. This is a typical New Archeological procedure: breaking down an open door, preaching to the converted—the well-known conjuring tricks and spreading of confusion that, once again, would make one doubt its seriousness, if any more proof were needed. It's very curious to see oneself opposed like this with one's own point of view.

So did I explain my views so badly? If I say that the proper procedure of archaeology is the establishment of facts, this is precisely because they *have to be established.* Like everyone, probably, I think that they are never "given," that they are, as the word indicates, made, fabricated, at the most elementary stage of observation on which all the rest depends. And a fortiori at all successive levels of interpretation. To take just one example, when one determines whether the traces visible on the bear bones from the Grotte des Furtins in Bourgogne were made by man (as one of my students began to do in 1976), this is exactly what I mean by the establishment of facts.

I am in no way suggesting that the archaeologist's role should be reduced to this establishment of facts: I suggest that it is the *proper* task of archaeology, that which belongs and can belong only to archaeology. But I said repeatedly that archaeologists changed themselves in most cases—and in any case could change themselves—into historians or anthropologists in order to interpret their finds without leaving the thinking to others: I simply believe that at that stage they are no longer behaving as archaeologists sensu stricto but as anthropologists or as historians—in the same way as historians and anthropologists, without being archaeologists in any way, use archaeology for their own ends. And this doesn't reduce archaeology to an auxiliary of history or

---

* At the end of his review, Colin Renfrew perpetrated a Greco-Latin hybrid, "retro-archaeology," of uncertain meaning, which he mistakenly attributed to me, and finally applied to me. In fact, I had criticized "l'archéologie *rétro,*" that is, the archaeology of the first half of this century, a quite different meaning. I therefore cordially render him his child.

anthropology; otherwise the word would have been done away with, which it never has been. Is this such a subtle distinction? Isn't it something that happens and can be observed every day? And at this stage of "transition" all the "theories" of the New Archeologists can take their place again perfectly well, but this time rid of their pseudo-epistemological hodgepodge. That should console them.

Since the French edition came out in 1982, of course, many things have happened in the archaeological sphere, and notably in its epistemology. But—since it has become an obsession for some people—what is *new* among all these "novelties"?

On some fronts there is little change, it must be said. I had joked about the mania the New Archeologists have for periodically republishing their own work. The least one can say is that they have not proved me wrong: books that collect recent and easily accessible articles have not ceased to appear. I had been amused by the incense that was wafted about. They have gone one better: Lewis Binford has even been called—with the utmost seriousness—"the greatest [archaeological] thinker . . . of this century." No, don't laugh. The thing that is most foreign to archaeology is an awareness of its comical dimension, and yet it's here that it achieves greatness! I also raised the problem of the New Archeology's strange language: this applies more than ever; as Richard Atkinson has said recently: "Jargon [is treated] as a substitute for thought."

As for content, I indicated that the New Archeology was oriented toward ethnographic analogy, focused on the relations between present behavior and remains (but that was scarcely a great change), systematized where necessary by experimentation and rebaptized ethnoarchaeology: this is certainly what has continued to happen, and it has sometimes taken a paleontological direction. But ethnoarchaeology—despite the mass of new observations it has brought us, which constitute its positive contribution—doesn't always make more legitimate the inference from the present to the past: this is its congenital defect. Binford himself recently questioned—not without paradox—the usefulness of ethnoarchaeology (*Man,* 1987). As a reaction against "processual" archaeology, structuralism, sometimes termed "French," was on the way. It's now here in the work of Ian Hodder, with a perspective that is linguistic, even semiotic, but—if I understand it correctly—"post–Lévi-Straussian," and even "Marxist." It was accompanied by the rediscovery of the role of symbols. This is conceptual archaeology, "of the mind," "cognitive." The new incarnation of mental archaeology?

Coming after the astonishing rehabilitation, in 1977, of the individual and even of style by James N. Hill and Joel Gunn, this supplementary step brings us a little closer, it seems, to *terrae* that are scarcely
incognitae any longer. The rediscovery of the moon is more than ever
the order of the day. In reality, the newest aspect (if indeed it's new)
might perhaps be the relationship of archaeology with the period when
it arose and with the social class that was then dominant (its sociology,
in short): this is what seems to be fashionable at the moment. As I
noted in the book, true innovations are found in the questions asked,
in the approaches to problems, and in original observations rather
than in epistemology.

As far as methodology is concerned, hypothetico-deductive reasoning (which was already in a bad way, though less so than laws) has
suffered a new attack: Hodder (in *Antiquity,* 1984) noticed that the
famous "validation of hypotheses" couldn't base itself on new "facts"
since the latter are themselves theories; archaeology couldn't be a science!

But the coup de grace has just been delivered: after everything that
was written about the absurd piling up per se of facts cut off from any
set problems, it was with a certain admiration that one recently observed (in the United States and before a typically New Archeological
society) a leader of the New Archeology, a processual archaeologist,
deliver a vibrant plea (already begun in 1980 in actual fact) for the
publication in bulk of the masses of data produced by Cultural Resource Management. In short, for the accumulation of "raw" facts?
Or even for . . . the establishment of these facts? We have really come
full circle. In the New Archeological game of snakes and ladders, it's
well and truly a return to square one.

As one of our best present-day pompous windbags in France said,
"When one has made a silly mistake, one has to know how to go into
reverse, if it's the right maneuver to carry out." This is obvious; unless
one finds a shortcut allowing one to rejoin the road one had lost . . .
and this is what we've been witnessing for some time already, and
probably we'll see it happening a little more every day, though on tip-
toe, because the New Archeologists need to save face. One can only
rejoice in this return to wisdom, but what a lot of effort has been
wasted! Not in everyone's case, it's true—not for those who bet on the
New Archeology, and on the incompetence of the powers that be, to
build their careers. But these characters will turn their coats one more
time (while claiming the opposite, of course)—and, as Kent V. Flannery said so well in his imperishable parable of the Golden Marshall-
town (*American Anthropologist,* 1982)—will continue to consider

archaeology as "a means to an end," as "a vehicle" to the (administrative) "top."

What a curious time when, in order to rival technology's prodigious leap forward, archaeologists wanted not to find something new (which would have delighted everyone) but to do something new, at all costs, and especially something new in the epistemological line, with scarcely any success. It's an episode that will leave in the history of archaeology, as Glyn Daniel said a few years ago, the image of an "extravagance." In another period, the sex of the angels also caused a lot of ink and saliva to flow. It seems to me—and this again is an epistemological point of view—that there are better things to do at this moment than epistemology, especially if it has to be of the kind we've just experienced. What archaeology needs most today, in my opinion, is *professionalism*—a professional archaeology. What is comforting is that this is certainly what is happening; and a whole generation of young archaeologists has abandoned the false prophets and everywhere is working seriously and with discretion. This is where archaeology's future lies, as well as its hope.

I couldn't end without offering my congratulations to Paul Bahn: he did not content himself with a translation, albeit one that is more successful than I would have thought possible, up to and including the French puns; he also revised the text on many points and, above all, checked the references and usefully rectified a good number of them; thus, thanks to his pitiless exactness, the present edition is a clear improvement on the original. He has my warmest thanks.

Paul Courbin

Translator's Preface

I accepted with pleasure the invitation to translate this book, not only because of the challenge the project represented, but also because I had read and admired the work when it was first published and had hoped it would eventually reach a much wider, anglophone readership.

There has been need of a book like this for a long time, and it was something of a surprise when it appeared in France rather than in Britain or America: it was generally assumed that most French archaeologists had little knowledge of or interest in the New Archeology. Yet Courbin has a deep and detailed acquaintance with the subject, and his analysis of the basic New Archeological literature in the first part of the book is a model of serious and reasoned argument, though presented with clarity and humor. His only anglophone equivalent in the debunking field is Kent V. Flannery, although their styles are very different.

Courbin makes extensive use of direct quotations from the New Archeologists, who are thus hanged with their own rope; but he cannot be accused of distortion by taking selected sentences out of context. In preparing this translation I have had to return to the original texts to obtain precise wording, and it is indisputable that Courbin's analysis provides an objective and faithful representation of the views expressed.

His approach bears some resemblance to Terry Arthur's, in his valuable but little-known *Ninety-five Percent Is Crap*,[1] which shows, by means of numerous quotes from the culprits, how many of our politicians' solemn pronouncements are meaningless, self-contradictory, or hypocritical. Indeed, the political analogy is an apt one, since the mock battles of the "New Archeologists" against the "traditionalists" resemble nothing so much as the black-and-white world of party politics—rallying to the flag and denigrating everything said and done by one's opponents. I have drawn attention to the repeated use of "isms" and "ists" in the literature of the past two decades,[2] so that archaeological articles read like manifestos: as George Watson said in a stimulating article, "Like nationalism, theory calls for loyalty rather than analysis. . . . Theory, being personal, is a badge of personal freedom. You have chosen your theory, after all, as you might choose a party or church. . . . [This] means enlisting with a group, and theories nowadays have groupies much as pop-stars do."[3] The New Archeologists formed an "in-group"—but, by definition, as soon as one creates an "in-group" someone else is inevitably relegated to an "out-group"; hence the vociferous condemnation of the principles and practice of the "traditionalists," despised primarily for their alleged lack of theory and their unscientific approach. Yet, as Stephen Jay Gould has pointed out, silence about theory does not connote an absence of theory;[4] the angry young New Archeologists failed to grasp that there are different ways of doing archaeology, all of which are legitimate and to some extent valid, and their scientific aspirations revealed them to be suffering from what has been called "physics envy."[5]

Perhaps the two features of the New Archeological literature that caused the most offense were its opinionated and patronizing arrogance and its obscurity of language: both were unfortunate, since they masked a basic, desperate sincerity and considerably lessened any influence the positive aspects of the work might otherwise have had. Leaving aside the overstatements and the application of double standards, the sheer pomposity alienated the reader: for example, the library copy of *American Antiquity* I consulted to obtain the precise wording of Fritz and Plog's "We all want our discipline to contribute to the knowledge of laws of human behavior" had "Speak for yourself, mate" penciled in the margin at this point! And the intemperate boasting and bullying caused hilarity when the crunch came: it is always funny to see a show-off fall flat on his face, and as Courbin's book shows clearly, the New Archeologists have spent a great deal of time in that position.

Their language can be violent out of proportion to the cause, but it is its misuse that is at issue here. Indeed, some would say that they do not just express ideas poorly, they simply have nothing to express in the first place, and thus incompetence is passed off as innovation. As Lady Wootton said recently of sociology, "It is using a lot of words to cover up rather obvious remarks." Excessive verbiage hides a basic lack of real information.[6] George Orwell firmly believed that anything important could be conveyed in language comprehensible to the common man and that if most intellectuals and bureaucrats did not express themselves simply, it was because they did not wish to, since incomprehensibility is a means of control (this is what he was mocking with his invention of Newspeak); and of course poor grammar and nonexistent words distract attention from the content or lack of content. The real culprits here are the handful of publishing houses that have produced so much of this kind of literature over the past twenty years: one New York/London publishing house in particular has emitted enough hot air to keep the Albuquerque Balloon Fiesta in operation for years.

The main thrust of Courbin's attack is aimed, quite understandably, at Lewis Binford, a man who has dished out enough in his time to take a little once in a while. Indeed, his treatment at Courbin's hands barely matches the aggression that characterizes his own work. Binford bears not a little resemblance to Claude Rains's portrayal of Professor Challenger in *The Lost World*, both in physique and in temperament—Lev Klejn has referred to his "irascible nature" in his writing,[7] and Glynn L. Isaac has compared him obliquely to a "rutting male antelope";[8] but perhaps the best analogy is to see him as archaeology's Norman Mailer. Mailer, a much-married, pugnacious, controversial writer, was part of the "New Journalism." He has a combative manner; he is egotistical—Woody Allen joked in *Sleeper* that Mailer had donated his ego to science, and Richard A. Gould has stressed the "high level of ego-involvement" in some of Binford's work;[9] both men have a tendency to produce large, verbose books, and both republish collections of their articles. Both make stimulating observations and criticisms, but one has to do a lot of spadework to find the nuggets, and in a discipline with an ever-growing literature, conciseness is a great virtue.

Moreover, just as certain physical anthropologists love to create new species, almost for the sake of it—as Stephen Jay Gould has said, "Taxonomists often confuse the invention of a name with the solution of a problem"[10]—so Binford rarely lets slip an opportunity to propose new "special terms"; in virtually every book and major article he has presented some new vocabulary for us to conjure with. Such terms are occasionally wrong (see the recurrent "surficial" in *Bones*), but more often they are simply unnecessary: for example, he has stated that his obscure term "middle range theory" is "essentially identical" to Clarke's "interpretive [*sic*] theory" and, apparently, equal to Schiffer's "behavioral archeology," so one cannot but wonder why he felt we needed yet another term for the same thing.[11]

In the years since Courbin's book was published, Binford has produced no fewer than four books—just when you thought it was safe to go back into the bookshops—including his second recycled album of greatest hits and golden oldies, *Working at Archaeology*, and his first truly readable volume, *In Pursuit of the Past*. The latter is something of a revelation in his apparent contrition about some of the aspects of the monster he did so much to unleash.[12] Courbin deals briefly with some recent literature in the Preface written specially for this translation.

There were several reviews of the original French edition of this book; one must discount the shoddy, unsigned effort in a French journal of popular science that, scandalously, publishes anonymous reviews and refuses to disclose the authors' identities: in the words of J. B. Priestley, "I see no justification in anonymous reviews; embittered dons lurk in those thickets, knife in hand." The genuine reviewers seem to admit the perspicacity and accuracy of the first part of the book but dismiss the second part as reactionary. It is for the author to counter this charge, and he does so in the Preface.

This book is very different from an earlier tome of the same name, which was simply an introduction and a contemporary definition of the subject.[13] Courbin is at pains to avoid offering a definition; instead, his aim is to isolate the deadwood in the tree and the many useless suckers and creepers attached to it and expose them for what they are.

Can it be coincidence that the "flagships" of the New Archeology (one written by David Clarke, the other edited by the Binfords) appeared in that annus mirabilis of 1968, when the "New Left" manned the barricades and sought to transform society? Twenty years later, it is clear even to those who jumped on the bandwagon to take part in the widespread protests that nothing revolutionary happened, and the cherished ideals of excited and rebellious youths have inevitably matured into the pragmatic realism of middle-aged consumers: "Almost the universal dénouement of 1968" was "business as usual."[14] Life has changed, of course—we now have ubiquitous personal computers and many other manifestations of New Technology—but this kind of progress has nothing to do with the events of 1968; it has occurred despite, rather than because of, that angry outburst. The parallels with what happened within archaeology are obvious.

The story of the New Archeology is a modern version of "The Pied Piper of Hamelin" or, even more aptly, "The Emperor's New Clothes"; and for a while it was possible, in some circles, to get away with having no clothes as long as you were wearing "designer nude." A lot of time, effort, and paper have been wasted on many pointless aspects of the New Archeology, and since even Binford has now decided that it made a lot of mistakes, it seems like a good time to write it off as a bad job. Would the last person to leave please turn off the lights?[15]

Paul G. Bahn

Introduction

Have no fear: my purpose here is not to put forward yet another new definition of archaeology, one that is more subtle or more comprehensive than all the others or that encompasses the discipline's latest developments more fully than all previous definitions; nor is it my intention—and this is a solemn pledge—to put forward a new theory of archaeology that is even newer than the others but qualified, like them, with a simple or composite adjective ending in -ic, -al, -logical, or -tic and that is destined to replace or definitively eliminate all those which have been in use up to now—until the next one comes along. No, the problem I have set myself is nothing like that.

Archaeologies

The present situation can be seen as follows: for the past twenty years or so archaeology has witnessed all kinds of developments; it has proliferated in all sorts of directions, putting forth "pseudopods" into domains that were barely explored, or even unknown, before then. Certainly there had always traditionally been tensions between, for example, archaeology and the history of art, between archaeology and philology (especially epigraphy), or between archaeology and history, archaeology and anthropology. But there has now been an explosion: it is no longer a question of archaeology but of *archaeologies*.

This eruption has found expression in a flourish of composite words, prefixes, suffixes, new epithets, complementary names—in short, it first swung into action in the grammatical sphere. One can mention—though here, as elsewhere in the book, I cannot hope to be exhaustive—"behavioral" archaeology, conventional, ecological, environmental, ethnological, ethological, evolutionist, experimental, general, industrial, Marxist, nautical, new, political, quantitative, rural, spatial, structural, systemic, theoretical, traditional, urban, and so forth, and I'm sure to have forgotten some. Occasionally the word has a prefix: bioarchaeology, ethnoarchaeology, geoarchaeology, pata-archaeology.[1] Often, a complement expresses a different connection: archaeology of behavior, of the landscape, of habitat, and so forth, not to mention archaeological administration, archaeological "management," archaeological careerism, archaeological politics or the archaeology of politics. In short, the new archaeology (not to be confused with the *New Archeology*, any more than archaeology with archeology) has become a category of mind: Michel Foucault writes of the archaeology of knowledge, the journalist L. Sciascia calls one of his articles "The archaeology of the Moro affair," Lucien Bodard talks of the archaeology of the heart, and so forth.

A Revolution

These lexicographic manifestations are merely the expression of a much deeper convulsion which goes back to the 1960s. It was then that, more or less simultaneously, though apparently quite independently, events occurred in England and the United States which could be (indeed have been[2]) described as a revolution, although the use of the word was regretted later. What is meant is an epistemological revolution, the birth of the "new archaeology" or *New Archeology*.[3] The sort of archaeology that had been prevalent until then, labeled "traditional," faced scornful criticism from the American Lewis R. Binford, writing in a crashing, arrogant, extraordinarily violent way, and from the Englishman David L. Clarke, writing in a more discreet and more technical but no less firm manner. Each critic, followed by his retinue, proposed renewed and ambitious objectives, a logic previously unknown, and revolutionary methods. Whatever one's final judgment of this attempt, one must begin by saluting the prodigious breadth of vision, the epic stamina, the radical desire for renovation, the firmness of thought. We had never seen anything like it. It meant nothing less than tearing the old archaeology away from its congenital mire, its undetermined objectives, its obsolete methods, its detailed and absurd catalogs, its fanciful and always untested assumptions, and its historical tendencies, and helping it at last to attain the much demanded status of a true science, like any other discipline, in which hypotheses would be validated by adequate tests, examined statistically and with the help of computers, using the means and techniques of present-day science—all this with a view to resolving vast problems which would be set out precisely and explicitly at the start in a resolutely anthropological perspective. Of course, the traditional archaeologists would fight a few vague, rearguard actions for the sake of honor, but they would be swept aside. We were going to see what we were going to see, and that no one can stop progress.

A Failure

The strange thing is that we did not see very much—at any rate, not what we were expecting. After the initial taking up of positions, that song of glory, that hymn to the future, and of course the associated curses aimed at the (few) contradictors, we expected that after a reasonable interval (though certainly soon, in view of the invocation of these powerful new concepts and modern methods) we would see results which would be spectacular, to say the least—not in the traditional sense of fantastic discoveries of objects or outstanding ruins, but in the sense of the New Archeology itself. We could legitimately hope that old problems would at last find the solution which had been deferred for so long; that questions which had never been asked before would now be asked and solved in their turn; in short, that our understanding of the human past would have new and lasting light thrown upon it. All it needed was a little patience.

Almost twenty years have now gone by; and if at the beginning it was perfectly justifiable to give credit, today—with the perspective of time—the most one can say is that far from fulfilling the promise of the blossoms, the fruits have remained very dry. The disappointment is bitter. Certainly, the New Archeologists have published (and republished) a great deal, especially theoretical works (theory has evolved considerably) but also case studies which are of great value, though nothing out of the ordinary, so to speak. New hypotheses have been put forward about important problems new and old, but they are in no way different from those put forward before, and they don't seem much more solidly proved than their predecessors. The revolution of the New Archeology has not been followed by a revolution in knowledge.

The Permanence of Traditional Archaeology

On the other hand, "traditional" archaeology has not been cast into outer darkness as had been promised. First—and this may be its most characteristic feature—far from putting up any sort of a fight, with certain exceptions the old archaeology in fact rejected confrontation: this is, as is well known, a formidable defense. For a long time it proudly ignored the New Archeology. Second, instead of wilting and seeing its production dry up little by little, it has pursued its course as before and imperturbably continued to line up publications, volume after volume, which are not devoid of interest—far from it—even for the New Archeology. Things have not turned out as prophesied, and the New Archeology, which undertook to "predict" the past, has made a big mistake about the present or the immediate future.

What Is Archaeology?

This unexpected situation can only plunge archaeologists—be they laymen, amateurs, professionals, or even the sincere New Archeologists—into disarray: we no longer know what to think or do, or whether what we do still has any meaning. Was the old archaeology right? This doesn't seem very probable, at least where the caricature of it that has been presented is concerned. But is the new concept of archaeology solidly based? If yes, then how can one explain that error of judgment and the relative but undeniable failure of its own point of view? And if not, then what, definitively, is archaeology? How should the archaeologist exercise his profession, from the beginning of his work to the end, from the posing of problems to the formulation of conclusions, from the search for data to their use, via their processing?

Outline of the Book

In an attempt to answer these questions which are really one and the same, I propose to start with a critical examination (though one that is as impartial as possible) of the New Archeology: the men, their motives, the objectives, then the principles, the methods—logical or otherwise—and then their implementation and the results. Finally, the balance sheet can be drawn up. It is out of the question, of course, to write another history of archaeology, or even just of the New Archeology; nor will this be an attempt at an exhaustive analysis of the doctrine and its products. Such an enterprise is discouraged by the sheer immensity of the literature, despite its repetitions, and by its nature, which, it must be said, is mostly indigestible; even the archaeologist Lev Klejn, admired by his critics for the impressive extent of his reading,[4] is the first to admit that he has failed to get to know everything that has appeared. No, I shall content myself—and in this I will in fact be conforming to one of the leitmotivs of New Archeology—with a sample (representative, I hope) of a certain number of soundings taken in this enormous mass. But I think it is useful to go back to the beginnings of the New Archeology, although its theoreticians—especially those who were perhaps in too much of a hurry to fall into step—are today displaying a marked propensity for casting a veil over the immediate past. For, as one of the best New Archeologists, Kent V. Flannery, has said, quoting Clarke, it is difficult to understand a system without knowing its history and its trajectory.[5] The New Archeology has certainly evolved a great deal, and that is perfectly natural and healthy, but the direction and the interest of this evolution must be measured and compared with the initial declarations. As will be seen, this examination will lead me to ask whether New Archeology's most serious mistake, whatever it may say, was not the very fact that it ventured dangerously far outside archaeology.

I will then have to put my money where my mouth is by setting out an analysis of what, in my view, proper archaeology fundamentally *is*. I will try to divulge its specific character in comparison with other, closely connected disciplines; to show what distinguishes it from everything which is not "it." With this aim, I shall use a method based on a certain image of the work of the archaeologist, on his "praxis," or what could be called the specifically archaeological act.

That done, I shall draw inferences from it for the continuation of the intellectual procedure. Even though the topic crops up with great frequency here and there, I by no means wish to present a systematic and specialized outline of techniques (of surveying, excavation, statistical and computerized processing, "scientific" analysis, or dating) or of methods (of reasoning, demonstration, interpretation, theorization, etc.). But it will be seen that, in the perspective to be defined here, I shall reintegrate the most recent methodological "conquests" of present-day archaeology and the new ways of asking questions.

This book took shape little by little in my seminars at the Bureau d'Etude des Méthodes Archéologiques, in which all these questions were freely debated day after day—with no eye to publication—with my colleagues and my most advanced students, and in the course of my teaching at the Ecole des Hautes Etudes en Sciences Sociales, where, from the autumn of 1974 onward, an extra hour's class provided the opportunity and the setting for reflections inspired on the one hand by the reading of New Archeology and on the other by the uninterrupted practice of archaeological research in the field. It therefore owes much to the varied reactions—sometimes visceral, often critical, always friendly—of my site collaborators or my successive students, both French and foreign, on whom I "tested" my "propositions," thus applying the precepts of New Archeology in this, at least. I wish to thank them above all.

What Is
Archaeology?

I The "New Archeology"

The Founding Fathers

Where and when was New Archeology born? Although precursory signs had already appeared before the Second World War,[1] it was in 1968 that there appeared the two really fundamental works, *Analytical Archaeology* by David L. Clarke (in London) and *New Perspectives in Archeology*, edited by Sally R. and Lewis R. Binford (in Chicago). Which was first? The question has about as much importance as who invented the radio. Before publishing these books, their authors had in fact each produced other, preliminary works, here again in the same year, 1962.[2] I do not know if Clarke ever claimed any sort of priority, but Binford lays claim to it without beating about the bush, and it is true that whereas Clarke quotes Binford several times, Binford's book ignores Clarke's name. Clarke "cited much of my work," says Binford, declaring himself the first to have envisaged the application of "systems theory" to archaeology. One can accept that Binford did not know Clarke's work, and that each worked independently in the beginning: the dates of 1962 and, especially, 1968 are all the more significant for this, as is the fact that the locations of this double birth are both Anglo-Saxon. In any case, the sobriquet of "Binclarke" applied to these more-or-less twin brothers shows the extent to which the two are linked.[3]

Straightaway the points of view put forward by both met with opposition—and I shall return to this subject—but both also found immediate emulators. The latter were perhaps fewer and less rapid for Clarke in England—one could mention Colin Renfrew (although, while approving the new approach, he did at first call it "pata-archaeology"[4]), James E. Doran, or, more recently , for example, Ian Hodder. Binford immediately surrounded himself with what has been called his "Mafia": William A. Longacre, James N. Hill, Robert Whallon, Jr., Kent V. Flannery, Stuart Struever, and so forth, soon followed, toward 1970, by a "second wave"—John M. Fritz, Fred T. Plog—and then the next: Stanley South, Michael B. Schiffer.[5] Some, like Flannery, would distance themselves later; on the other hand many "epigones," usually young, would appear fairly quickly, more or less everywhere, this time outside the Anglo-Saxon world.

A Prehistoric and Americanist Archaeology

One of the most striking characteristics of the New Archeology—in England as much as in the United States—is that it concerns prehistory first and foremost. Certainly the historical periods have, relatively recently, been touched by grace: in his preface to South's book, *Method and Theory in Historical Archaeology,* Binford welcomed "historic sites archaeology to the science of archaeology."[6] But Lev S. Klejn, for example, has been reproached for calling his analysis of New Archeology "a panorama of theoretical archaeology" and not a panorama of prehistoric archaeology.[7] It is clear that in the beginning it was the pre- and protohistoric periods which were the main subject of study.

Another characteristic, no less clear, is that New Archeology deals mainly with America (North, South, and Central). Of course, the English have taken an interest in Great Britain: one of Clarke's first studies deals with the Beaker pottery of the British Isles, and his contribution to *Models in Archaeology* (1972) includes a study of an Iron Age village, Glastonbury in Somerset. And Binford himself has dealt with the "French" Mousterian, Sally Binford worked in Israel, Patty Jo Watson at Tell Halaf, and one could mention other examples, such as those concerning Iran in particular.[8] It is nevertheless true that the center of interest has been North America, including Alaska very recently, and essentially the United States, especially the southwestern states with their Indian *pueblos,* or the colonial settlements of the East Coast. The University of Minnesota's expedition to Nichoria in Greek Messenia remains an apparent exception. Even though Africa and Australia have been studied as well, New Archeology retains a distinctly North American tonality.[9] Even Clarke's second volume, *Models in Archaeology,* includes a fair number of American articles, of which a significant proportion concern the New World. Robert C. Dunnell calls his recent annual reviews "Americanist Archaeology."[10]

So the New Archeology—essentially "Americanist" and prehistoric—was born of criticism of archaeology as it was earlier practiced in America. But, as we shall see, this criticism is even clearer in Clarke's work.

Traditional Archaeology as Seen by the New Archeology

The image that the New Archeology developed and presented of the archaeology that preceded it—labeled "traditional"[11]—was apocalyptic, at least in the beginning. The New Archaeologists could not find words harsh enough to describe it. If one tries briefly to summarize their criticisms, traditional archaeology first sets out—tacitly and perhaps even unconsciously—a humanist, liberal philosophy as a matter of course. It has no defined method of asking questions; one digs for the sake of digging, aimlessly and haphazardly: we'll see what we find, and then, when we've found it, the main thing is to describe and then classify the material for purely chronological purposes, or almost just for the pleasure of classification. That done, traditional archaeology either stops and hands over to others the hazardous task of interpreting these results, or else it ventures into interpretations or generalizations which it doesn't bother to prove. Its conclusions could never be believed to be true; science and the knowledge of the past did not progress one inch. But the condemnation is much more detailed, and it is renewed periodically.

A good example—and one of the first—of the New Archeologists' reaction to traditional archaeology can be seen in the review which Binford wrote for *American Anthropologist* in 1968 (and republished in 1972 in *An Archaeological Perspective*) of Robert F. Heizer and John A. Graham's manual, *A Guide to Field Methods in Archaeology,* revised and augmented edition published in 1967. For Binford this work has the unpardonable fault of approaching fieldwork only from the perspective of excavation procedure, with little attention to the problem of data collection as such: certain types of observations are declared "important" without any discussion of why they might be important or what relevance various types of information may have to investigation of the past. At the root is the mistake of believing that archaeology has accomplished its aims when it has collected enough remains to permit empirical generalizations, after which one is free to draw inferences about the conditions which modeled these remains, and the job is finished. No attention is paid to the scientific problems of confirmation and verification; no mention is made of the control of data quality, although it is needed in hypothesis testing. In short, as a guide, it is mainly a guide for nonscientific research!

Binford continues to rain blows, using quotations chosen to ridicule the authors. How do you decide which artifacts to keep? Above all, with regard to your ease of transport! Stratigraphic analysis is preferred to the horizontal location of artifacts, recorded in whatever way suits the diggers. The authors did not even take into account the chapter on sampling by Sonia Ragir that was added to the new edition. The use of test excavations can never provide a representative sample of the differential distribution of implements or of activity areas. Excavation by arbitrary levels cannot measure culture change. The sum total is that Heizer and Graham's 1967 book is "very poor." It conveys the misleading impression that archaeology can be restricted to "cookbook directives": photography, surveying, identification of artifacts, and even—shock horror!—careful manual work, when in fact what is necessary is a research design, the control of data quality, and sampling. Apart from Ragir's addendum and the bibliography, it will be of little use to students—and amateurs would do better to use another manual, for which Binford kindly supplies the reference.[12]

Everything is there, the substance and the tone. Binford, whose style is still readable at this period, does not stoop to explaining his reasons, and he proceeds by allusion and affirmation. It is worth remembering this attitude when we come to examine his own publications in their turn.

His pupils hammer the point home in a more philosophical and more precise way. Hence, John M. Fritz and Fred T. Plog, criticizing in 1970 an article by B. K. Swartz published three years before in the same journal (*American Antiquity*), define "traditional" research as an approach which they label "empiricist" or "narrow inductivist"[13] and which was described by their mentor, the philosopher Carl Hempel—who is going to crop up several times later—as (1) the observation and recording of all facts; (2) their analysis and classification; (3) the induction of generalizations; and (4) further testing of these generalizations. In fact, the ideal model for research proposed by Swartz is the following sequence of phases: first, the preparation, which includes the bibliography of the subject, and notably preparation for the technical problems of fieldwork; then the "mechanical" acquisition of data, followed by the analysis of these data, which are thus situated in time and space; then the "interpretation," which shows how, in this time and place, an assemblage of artifacts was made and used. Then comes either what he calls the "integration"—that is, both the reconstruction of a given group's way of life and what he calls the "synthesis" which describes bigger cultural units—or, alternatively, the comparison with interpretative data. Finally there is the abstraction from observed regularities of the laws or general principles which are the ultimate goal of the preceding phase.

Traditional archaeologists would no doubt recognize at least the first of these phases in their work, though not perhaps all of them. But supposing the aim to be the formulation of laws, Fritz and Plog believe that the empiricist method does not permit archaeologists to achieve it: for want of a preliminary hypothesis, both the classification and the analysis remain blind, as was well said by Hempel. It is the pursued aim—namely, the explanation—which must organize the research. Relevant data as well as their analysis and classification must be defined not after but *before* the start of the research. While empiricists naively suppose that they collect *all* the facts of use to all the explanations which may present themselves later (which no one does, or could do), in reality they only collect the data they have been taught to perceive—and these will allow them to solve only a small number of the problems which may turn up after the event.

Furthermore, empiricists suppose that facts speak for themselves, and that explanations or laws are summaries of facts: all one needs to do is collect, analyze, and classify data in sufficient abundance, then juggle with them properly, and the explanations or laws simply propose themselves. But it isn't so: since Aristotle, philosophy of science has taught that formulated hypotheses derive only from the creative capacity of scientists.

In short, traditional archaeology has remained at the "prescientific" stage: its propositions, its "explanations" may perhaps be true or plausible; they may have been accepted, but they have not been tested; their "truth" has not been established, and it is quite possible that they are wrong. They cannot be taken as true.

Of course, no example is quoted; but, if I understand them correctly, everything remains to be done.

In 1972 in Clarke's second book, *Models in Archaeology,* James N. Hill, one of the most likable and honest New Archeologists, takes up Fritz's critique and amplifies it.[14] Every epistemology is based in a metaphysic, and that of "current" archaeology is none other than the empirical philosophy of Hume, Mill, and Bacon; "empiricism" believes that every object has an inherent significance which simply needs to be discovered. One of the consequences of the "narrow inductive view" is that archaeologists go into the field without a specific problem in mind; as a consequence, all the facts seem significant to them, all are worthy of being recorded—in any case, as many data as possible should be recovered. This is the vacuum cleaner technique: the simple accumulation of data will speak to us, it will present problems and then solve them. For Hill, this is unrealistic and impossible. If our inferences are about the data themselves, they cannot deal with the "intangible" realities such as the processes of operation and change of prehistoric societies. Archaeology is restricted to describing, dating, and comparing; analysis becomes pure description, "taxonomy"; assemblages are *pigeonholed* into chronological sequences—Walter Taylor was already complaining about this in 1948. This is natural history in the nineteenth-century sense; all of this is "relatively uninteresting."

Another consequence is that because data can be gathered "prior to and separate from problem or hypothesis formulation," they can be gathered by people with no interest in the issue, and thus fieldwork can be separate from analysis and interpretation. This is inadmissible, or, to quote Hempel again, "untenable."

Of course, a few pages earlier, Clarke himself had poured a bit of water into this wine. I shall return shortly to his opinion of traditional archaeology, which he said in 1968 had contributed nothing—or almost nothing—of fundamental importance since Montelius (who died in 1921) and was still "writhing" at the stage of piling up different data.[15] By 1972 he is declaring that the opposition between old and new is artificial, and he concedes that both approaches have their advantages and their drawbacks; in reality, they are complementary. The "new" archaeology will grow old in its turn; and the old will continue. In any case, he adds, the "traditionalist" style is more acceptable to those he calls "nonscientists."[16] One cannot but praise this moderate tone, so different from the usual arrogance, even though it is not entirely free of condescension.

Binford's disciples, however, did not disarm. Certainly Michael B. Schiffer, a representative of the new wave of New Archeologists, showed in 1976 that he regretted the fact that the New Archeology had not been able to "integrate" the old (which he gives the more accurate name of "archeology . . . preceding the 1960s") and that it had not reconciled the two approaches despite an attempt by Clarke in this field.[17] But the following year Stanley South—who, as I said above, extended the principles of New Archeology to the historic and even modern periods—took up the same criticisms of the archaeology of the preceding fifteen years, accusing it of being "humanistic," "particularistic" or particularizing, "idiographic," that is, of only being interested in individual cases, not in the search for "laws." He concedes that it gathers data carefully, but it nevertheless immerses itself in a blind empiricism. By devoting itself to antiquarianist work it disdains the "hypothetico-deductive" method, opposes science (which it sees merely as help by experts) and anthropology, and rejects quantification. Its only goal is the "reconstruction" of the past; data serve only to confirm or, if need be, complete what is known from texts. In this way it leads only to certainties which are already known. It can be summarized by the following formula (in the United States at least, and for the modern period): "*a* sponsor, with *a* heritage goal, regarding *a* site, on which is *a* ruin, from which *a* group of artifacts is recovered for exhibit in *a* museum"![18] Although South displays a certain imagination, expressed in humorous diagrams (a "halberd" represents archaeology; a snail represents the emerging trend), his attitude differs little from that of Binford, whom he quotes and whose earlier criticisms he summarizes.

Even quite recently Colin Renfrew—who, in 1976, deplored the interest taken in stratigraphy as a simple sequence, in destructions followed by reconstructions, for example, with no concern about what might have caused them[19]—repeated once again, during the celebration of the centenary of the American Archaeological Institute, that traditional archaeology might seem to accumulate data mindlessly, with no clear purpose in mind; that it describes these data with more enthusiasm for neatly ordered classification than for novelty of ideas; that its only goal is the reconstruction of the past; and, in these circumstances, that it can only answer yesterday's questions, and even then not all of them: it cannot answer those we ask today.[20]

I could easily supply many more examples, but I have said enough about the poor esteem—sometimes even blatant contempt—in which the New Archeology holds its precursor. To summarize: traditional archaeology is based on a philosophy which is humanistic, empiricist, outdated; it has no working hypothesis, no preliminary formulation of a problem or plan of research; it piles up a maximum of data, but does so blindly, with no rules for sampling—data are gathered on occasion by simple technicians, in stratigraphic test pits of insufficient horizontal extent; it describes data haphazardly, classifies them in typologies whose only possible goal is chronology; it compares them, dates them, so that in the best cases it can induce (in the primary or narrow sense of the term) empirical generalizations which it neither confirms, tests, nor demonstrates; its objective is to reconstruct, not to determine the processes in operation or the causes of change, let alone the laws of human behavior. Blind, prescientific, nonscientific, with no basic truth, it is, in a word, indefensible.[21]

Besides, it is destined to disappear in disgrace. The New Archeologists enthusiastically adopted the theory of a physicist, Thomas Kuhn, which was published in 1962 and entitled *The Structure of Scientific*

Revolutions; they apply it without hesitation to traditional archaeology. Thus in 1973, James Fitting—after having indicated that an attachment to old problems (such as "finding out what is there") is or should be penalized by refusal of all funding—dwells complacently on the "many personal tragedies" which eventually strike traditional archaeologists reduced to changing their field of research, or ordinary archaeologists who try desperately to transpose the new paradigms into traditional terms, merely arousing the hostility of the holders of these paradigms. The new paradigms are readily accepted by the young generations, who grew up with them. But for those who preceded them there is no way out at all, even (and especially) if they try to find one. They are entangled in their outmoded concepts. To reject the new paradigms is antiscientific; to accept them in part and try to make a synthesis of the old and the brand-new is equally disastrous: they are forced to rewrite what they knew, and thus lose their primary role. So . . . should they accept the innovation and immerse themselves in it? Even that wouldn't save them: their contribution is negligible. No, their productive career is finished; they are simply reduced to the role of "anticipators." Only one road is still open to them—that of writing reviews (favorable ones, of course) of the new works. Fortunately this absurd opposition will cease with their death.[22] A heartening prospect. Hara-kiri is not suggested, however.

To what degree is this virulent criticism applied, in its authors' minds, to American and Americanist archaeology first and foremost? This would be an interesting point to specify by examining the literature quoted.[23] If, as seems pretty clear, it is equally directed at Old World archaeology, then is it aimed not only at the archaeology practiced before the Second World War but also at that which came afterward?[24] If so, to paraphrase the well-known saying, it would be worse than unfair: it would be incorrect. That, at least, is what I shall try to demonstrate later on.

Poor old "traditional" archaeology! It certainly has its faults. But one really wonders how it can still have the nerve to show its face—on a few excavations, in a few rare labs, in a few published works (no doubt out of force of habit), and in series of volumes which were famous in the past but have now clearly had their day—when there is so much better to be done, and when the New Archeology has just thrown wide open the doors onto a radiant scientific future.

For in the end, beyond all these fundamental points of disagreement, the New Archeology does not content itself with purely negative and sterile denigration: each time, it puts forward propositions which are substantial, positive, radically different, and completely new, and which it always makes sure it illustrates with rigor and coherence. At least, that is what the New Archeologists assert.

The New Archeology Compared with the "Old"

Every archaeologist of the new tendency has taken pleasure in contrasting the two conceptions of archaeology. A good example can be found in Clarke's introductory article for *Models in Archaeology*.[25] Whether it be in the attitude of mind, the mode of expression, or the type of approach—in short, the philosophy—traditional archaeology and the New Archeology clash. Where traditional archaeology is based on a historical view of things, the New Archeology is experimental. The former's approach is qualitative and "particularizing," the latter's is quantitative and generalizing. The old archaeology expresses itself in a "literary" manner, the new in a symbolic manner; the one is narrative, the other uses a jargon. Finally, where traditional archaeology is "isolationist," the new is "condisciplinary"; where the former is naturally authoritarian, the latter is anarchic, if anything. All this was written by Clarke in 1972, no matter how strange some of these points may appear.

Binford has on many occasions expressed his opinion about what separates the new and old conceptions of archaeology, and I shall return to his view at some length. But his disciples are perhaps more lucid, and they clarify the points mentioned by Clarke. Thus, Hill, already introduced above, using in part an unpublished work by Fritz dating from 1968, presents the difference between the two methods as follows. All research—archaeological or otherwise, but more particularly archaeological—arises in a preliminary theoretical framework, be it implicit or explicit; these theoretical premises guide the choice of problems, and the problems must be clearly defined before everything else because only these problems can specify the "data" which must be gathered. Traditional archaeology, on the other hand, is wrong in its belief that one can collect a large body of "basic data" and then use it to solve any problem which might later present itself. In addition to having problems in view, it is necessary to have formulated hypotheses about their possible solution because these hypotheses further specify the data to look for: they are bridges between problems and data, they will provide a framework for interpretations, as well as a means of evaluating objectively the research results. These hypotheses can only be deduced from the problem, so the method is "hypothetico-deductive"—there, the cat's out of the bag!—whereas traditional archaeology imagines that it can confine itself to the simple induction of hypotheses from the data alone.[26]

These, then, are the essentials: the logic of the method and its theoretical basis. Certainly the New Archeology's theory has variations, and it has evolved through time, as we shall see. But even in 1977 South is still saying the same thing: "Explicitly"—another master word!—"scientific" (ditto) archaeology examines past events in order to test hypotheses about cultural "processes" (ditto), unlike "antiquarians" like Franz Boas, who gather data and then try to deduce something from them. The best hypothesis is the one that proves the most reliable, the most capable of "predicting" (another fundamental term) verifiable consequences; it is the one any trained researcher could discover independently by repeating the same procedure.[27] And thus he quotes Binford, according to whom, if our (archaeologists') ultimate aim is to understand the events and the people that are originally responsible for the archaeological record and the processes that cause "cultural change," then archaeology has to be scientific—that is to say (and here, we reach the heart of the problem) it must be an archaeology that puts forward "laws," a "nomothetic" archaeology. Whereas the empiricists, literally blind, are "immersed in a sea of facts," and while those who are "armchair speculators" construct hypotheses with only occasional reference to the data, the new scientific archaeology puts the emphasis on trial solutions, potential explanations whose value is estimated not from their plausibility alone but by predicting consequences and by testing these hypothetical consequences with the help of new, independent data (in order to avoid a vicious circle).[28] And South makes a prophecy: dramatic changes will occur in the coming decades; the "particularists" will find themselves faced with a body of scientific analyses and reports far less vulnerable than those of today.

The Philosophical Foundations of the New Archeology

It is obvious that every methodology, every epistemology, rests on a "philosophy," whether conscious or not, visible or not, spoken or tacit. It is curious that the New Archeologists, those champions of the explicit, have not been more explicit about this fundamental question, at least at the start—in this, they have behaved exactly like the traditional archaeologists they reproach for the same thing. Unless I am mistaken, Clarke doesn't even allude to this issue and begins straight off with systems theory, not with what it presupposes. Binford spoke only in passing of his philosophy—and then almost in anecdotal form—in connection with his university entanglements with Robert Braidwood.[29] It is perhaps Hill, once again, who sets out the problem most clearly: "The epistemology of any science is based in a particular metaphysic," and the New Archeology is "positivist." And, curiously, he immediately gives us a vision of this positivism which seems idealistic: "the metaphysic is that artefacts . . . and so forth do not have inherent meanings. . . . It is our own perception of them that gives them meaning." [30]

Be that as it may, it is clear that the New Archeology's philosophy is materialist: "I argued . . . a materialist's philosophy of history," says Binford.[31] It is a determinist materialism, of course, and a determinism that is rather "primary," at least at the start. Binford was the pupil of Leslie White, for whom cultural evolution is marked out by the appearance of successive energy sources: hunting and gathering, agriculture and stock rearing, fossil fuels (coal, oil), the atom[32]; and for whom, as for V. Gordon Childe, stages are linked to these successive innovations. Summarizing the arguments of European prehistorians during the last hundred years, Binford describes their relatively "mechanistic" approach as "completely compatible with a materialistic . . . approach." [33] In 1976, Schiffer sets out once more the "basic cultural-materialist principle that the nature of a [social] organization is determined by (or at least is closely related to) the tasks it carries out." [34]

Evolutionism is an essential aspect of materialist dynamism and a fundamental assertion of the New Archeology. Binford had used the word at the beginning, and South came back to it insistently in 1977: every method implies a theory, a conceptual framework, a system of reference, and this can only be evolutionist: "When we look deep within the hub of systems for causes of change, we are addressing ourselves to the concept of cultural evolution." [35] In 1980, Renfrew stated that evolutionist archaeology is the "now dominant" school "in American archaeology," and Dunnell, in his annual review, put the emphasis on studies by evolutionists.[36]

Finally, since ideas, mentalities, kinship systems, and social organization are not directly perceptible through archaeology, the New Archeology puts emphasis on observable and measurable traces of behavior—traces which used to form part of a "behavioral" system in action, as Schiffer reminds us, and which have reached us at the end of a "chain" which is also "behavioral." [37] The stress placed on this concept of behavior shows the degree to which certain of the New Archeology's conceptions refer to Anglo-Saxon behaviorism, and to the philosophy of behavior.

Materialism, determinism of greater or lesser sophistication, positivism, evolutionism or neo-evolutionism, human ethology or behaviorism—all of them make up a rough, incomplete outline of the innermost philosophy that supports the New Archeology—consciously or not, implicitly or explicitly, but always in snatches: never, it seems, systematically. At the end of this first section I shall return to what one can think, and perhaps what one must conclude, about this ensemble of assertions, of presuppositions—in short, of postulates and convictions—which are hammered home with far more conviction than demonstration: a deep and passionate conviction.

The Theoretical and Scientific Environment of the New Archeology

The New Archeology has made enough appeals for ecological considerations for one to feel at liberty to look at New Archeology itself from that viewpoint. While one cannot pretend to provide a "panorama" of the theories and scientific techniques that have been in the limelight during the past two decades, it may perhaps be useful, as will be seen later, to have a look at them, no matter how cursory this examination might be.

At the beginning of *Analytical Archaeology*, Clarke looks back to 1950 and gives a list of theories that are external to archaeology and yet have repatterned it: the study of systems, games theory, set and group theory, topology, information theory, cultural ecology, the locational analysis of the new geography, and analytical and inductive statistics.[38] This list has been extended over the years—economy, modern architecture, and so forth have also been made use of, to say nothing of course of ethnography—but Clarke's list remains essentially valid. It was after the Second World War that a whole series of scientific disciplines developed rapidly and spectacularly: one might mention the new mathematics, astrophysics, atomic physics, molecular biology and the theory of the genetic code, the renewal of evolutionism, neo-Darwinism or, rather, the "new synthesis" of evolutionary theory, ethnography, ethnology, cultural and structural anthropology, linguistics, and so forth.

Determinist materialism best expresses itself in "systems theory" or "systemism," which the New Archeologists have discovered and adopted with a real feeling of ecstasy. For Binford—who borrowed this from White in 1965, his quotation being reused by Clarke in 1968—it is a self-evident truth that "culture is . . . the system of the total extrasomatic means of adaptation. Such a system involves complex sets of relationships among people, places, and things whose matrix may be understood in multivariate terms."[39] For Clarke, systems theory or cybernetics assumes that cultural systems are "integral whole units: all the cultural information is a stabilized but constantly changing network of intercommunicating attributes forming a complex whole—a dynamic system." In a less abstruse style, Renfrew specifies that systems are an ensemble of subsystems (technical, economic, religious, social) which interact and thus avoid the useless search for the starting mechanism, the "cause of the cause." [40]

Evolutionary theory has "a systemic relationship [with] the ecosystem concept," [41] and the ecological approach is a stock in trade of the New Archeology: man has a systemic relationship with his environment, and more specifically with his ecological "niche"; culture is only a mediation between man and his surroundings, to which it adapts itself and which condition it but do not, as was believed in the nineteenth century, determine it: there is interpenetration, interdependence, complex interaction between culture and the "ecosystem." [42]

Turning now to technical applications, let's remember the progress made by electronics, the prodigious leap of computer hardware and software, and the extension they give to statistics: all of them are summarized in the conquest of space and man's first steps on the moon, the secret importance of which for New Archeology can never be overestimated. The New Archeology grabs handfuls of everything that comes within reach and that looks, rightly or wrongly, as if it can be borrowed or transposed. It was in this context that it was born and developed—one should never forget that—and this "explains" quite a lot of things. Because even if it is true that, as has been said, science progresses through its fringes, certain influences are not necessarily beneficial, and borrowings from one discipline to another have to be handled with caution. The classification of models, as proposed by Clarke in his introductory article for *Models in Archaeology*, is borrowed directly from Peter Haggett and Richard J. Chorley, two geographers: Clarke states this himself, and it comes as no surprise to see the planispherical look given to the archaeological "world." [43] This is not to say that archaeology can derive nothing from the theories of geomorphology—indeed, this had already been done long beforehand for stratigraphy. But many scientists have directed the attention of archaeologists to the danger of these borrowings. Charles G. Morgan deplores the fact that archaeologists should have "incorporated" certain debatable analyses of logical positivism in matters of explanation. [44]

The Objective of the New Archeology

New Archeology's aim, its destination in the broadest sense, is very banal. If you consider its content, it is that of all previous archaeology:

it is purely and simply the knowledge of the past,[45] primarily of the human past but also of everything nonhuman which man confronts. Or rather, it is the increase of that knowledge: to ensure "the expansion of our knowledge of the past," Binford said in 1968, to "learn something about the past" he repeated in 1972,[46] and, in 1977, "the way in which the world works" or again "why the world is the way it appears to be."[47] It is "understanding past lifeways," South said at the same moment.[48] Who would not subscribe to this view? It is practically a platitude.

It is the *form* of this improved knowledge (or understanding) of the past which is new and original: archaeology must become a science. The great word has been uttered, and it is a true leitmotiv. As early as 1968, Binford was stressing that henceforth they were going to attempt to explain variability "scientifically"[49]; the subtitle of the well-known book *Explanation in Archeology,* by Patty Jo Watson, Steven A. LeBlanc, and Charles L. Redman, is *An Explicitly Scientific Approach;* at a conference in 1972, Binford was acting the prophet yet again: "Insofar as we agree that our goals in . . . archaeology are understanding of the events and the people . . . such understanding will not be forthcoming until a science of archaeology is developed"[50]; Flannery's famous article is entitled "Archaeology with a Capital S"[51]; in his preface to South's book, Binford ended by bidding historical archaeology welcome to the "science of archaeology," and in the book itself South repeats the demand for a "scientific archaeology": "Explicitly scientific archeology . . . is a science examining data from the past."[52] One could find innumerable such quotations, because this determination not to let archaeology lag behind when the sciences are progressing in such a spectacular fashion, this will to raise it to the status of a real science[53] is at the root of all the New Archeology. And this does constitute the least debatable of its innovations, for even though previous archaeology had for a long time been calling on the assistance of the sciences and imagining itself to have "scientific" procedures, it apparently had never had the pretension of placing itself among them. It confined itself instead to the subordinate role of an auxiliary to history—which is not even a science.

With the New Archeology, the objective is marked out. But there remains the task of mapping out the path to be followed: How can archaeology become a science?

But first, what is a science? Or rather, what is the New Archeologists' idea of a science? A science, apparently, can be defined as a "body of theories" organizing an ensemble of "laws," imagined or "created" by scholars, whose logical consequences have been "tested"—or rather, have not been disproved; these allow one "to explain," and thus understand, the observed data. Traditional archaeology never accomplished these ends as we all know, even though it occasionally deluded itself that it had.

2 The Hypothetico-deductive Method

The Hypothetico-deductive Method

The answer is quite simple: if archaeology is to become a science, it has to do what sciences worthy of the name do, it must copy their procedures, whether it be their explicit objectives or their method. Now, what is the scientific method par excellence? It means never being satisfied with unproved assertions, it means rigorously demonstrating every proposition that is put forward. How does it carry out this demonstration? By applying a method of logic, the hypothetico-deductive method. It is this method that has made progress possible in the most "classical" sciences, whether physics or medicine; and the relatively new sciences such as biology only began to make substantial progress from the moment they adopted it.[1]

The hypothetico-deductive method of the logician Carl Hempel is at the center and the starting point of the New Archeology. All of its adherents have dwelt on this fact and hammered it home on many occasions. What essentially does this method consist of? In contrast (as we are unceasingly reminded) to the empiricist or narrowly inductivist method, it takes a proposition about the data being studied and extracts from it other propositions which are involved, and it draws from the initial proposition certain inferences which are logical but the correctness of which is not yet known. In short, it deduces from a proposition some hypotheses which, in a way, are secondary to the starting hypothesis/proposition. It is in this sense that the method is hypothetical and deductive—deductive of hypotheses, hypothetico-deductive.[2] The whole secret of the only valid type of "explanation" (because at the outset everything revolves around the notion of explanation) lies in these few words.

In his famous article "Archaeology as Anthropology," written in one night in 1962 and later republished in *An Archaeological Perspective* in 1972, Binford tackled the copper objects found in the eastern

United States, which, curiously, seem utilitarian in the "archaic period" but nonutilitarian in the following period. Already at this time he was searching for "adequate explanatory hypotheses," and he ends by putting forward the "suggestions which must be phrased as hypotheses," according to which these objects had both a technological significance (he says "technomic" with a straight face) and also a social significance ("sociotechnic").[3] In 1965, at the Denver symposium (the acts of which were to be published in 1968 under the title *New Perspectives in Archeology*) he presents, from the outset, the method he considers correct: referring to the geographical break in the distribution of rock paintings and engravings between southern Africa and the Sahara, he "proposes," despite their great similarities of style, that they are the product of two independent cultures. And then from this initial "proposition" he immediately derives a "deduction": the apparent similarity of style is merely the result of parallel but independent developments. So there you have a first deduction from the hypothesis. But the procedure has multiple stages; he deduces another hypothesis from the first, this time under the form of a "prediction": if this is so, then we should observe a similar break in the form or the decoration of other objects (beads, projectile points, bone objects). From there, by means of a "bridging argument,"[4] namely, that these formal characteristics vary as a function of style and tradition, he derives a final hypothesis: the data under consideration will exhibit an interrupted distribution.[5] Even though this last hypothesis seems to duplicate the above-mentioned "prediction," the principle is clear: it is the hypothetico-deductive, or logico-deductive, method.

Binford returned to the method in 1967,[6] in 1968,[7] and on many other occasions. Clarke, for his part, ended his first big book in the same period by presenting the successive stages of the recommended procedure: once the problem has been defined, the data collected, the "strategic" variables located and their relation to one another analyzed and duly experimented with, then the fifth point is expressed as follows: "Formulate a set of hypotheses, or construct a model, organizing the results of these experiments within the frame of the selected problems."[8] I shall return to the later stages of the method. As usual, Binford's pupils take over the theme. Fritz and Plog, mentioned in the previous chapter, chime in with their own mini Ten Commandments. The first two are (1) to acquire a hypothesis, and (2) to formulate its implications.[9] Two years later, Hill (quoted earlier) devoted a whole section of his paper on the "methodological debate" to the necessity of hypotheses because the definition of a problem is not enough: we must "refine our *a priori* ideas to the point of generating specific hypotheses or other testable propositions." Just as the presentation of the problem of cancer did not enable us to solve it, Hill states, in the same way archaeology needs "tentative solutions"—or hypotheses. "Hypotheses . . . are necessary," and these hypotheses will provide the "deductive consequences," the useful predictions. He quotes E. B. Wilson, Jr.: "Logic does not enter science until this stage is reached." [10] It is a stock argument.

The Validation of Hypotheses

The power of the hypothetico-deductive method comes not from the fact that it deduces hypotheses but that it "validates" or invalidates them. Certainly, if hypotheses that have been deduced logically from the initial proposition are confirmed by the data, then the proposition must be true—or, if you like, the proposition is not absurd if the inferences drawn from it are not contradicted by reality. In short, you judge a tree by its fruits and a proposition by the value of its implications. It is therefore essential not to restrict yourself to the derivation of hypotheses, but to proceed to their verification.

That is why all the New Archeologists rightly dwell upon this indispensable requirement of the method. Every single one of the authors quoted in the preceding pages mentions—immediately after the requirement of hypotheses—the necessity of "testing" them. [11] With Binford, the insistence becomes something of an obsession. In some papers in *An Archaeological Perspective* the refrain reappears almost on every page: "It is only through the testing of hypotheses logically related to a series of theoretical propositions that we can increase or decrease the explanatory value of our propositions." On the next page he repeats it: "Our knowledge is sound to the degree that we can verify our postulates scientifically. . . . Scientific verification for archaeologists is the same as for other scientists; it involves testing hypotheses systematically." [12]

It is especially in the well-known field of the "ethnographic parallel" that the validation is feasible, because it enables one to transform hypotheses into something other than unfounded conjectures. "[Ethnographic] data may be used for testing hypotheses for which information on one or more of the relevant variables is not obtainable through archaeology." On the next page, Binford continues: "Ethnographic data . . . serve as resources for testing hypotheses." [13]

But the procedure is much more general: "The basic form of archaeological argument, or of any argument which seeks to formulate general propositions, should be logicodeductive. From a set of premises,

we can frame testable hypotheses whose confirmation will lend support to the postulates and assumptions (premises) on which the hypotheses are based" The following year, in 1968, he returned to the
charge: archaeologists must "begin to test the validity of explanatory
principles currently in use and attempt to refine or replace them by
verified hypotheses." [14] And so on.

But how does one verify hypotheses? Obviously by confronting
them with the "data": "Successful explanation and the understanding
of process . . . both proceed dialectically—by the formulation of hypotheses . . . and the testing of their validity against empirical data." [15]
At this point, there arises a very important consideration of method:
these data must not be the same as those which led to the formulation
of the propositions to be demonstrated: otherwise the data to be explained would be used for their own explanation, and thus there
would be a vicious circle. [16] This is a point that Binford's pupils have
particularly stressed. Fritz and Plog, for example, in the article mentioned above, itemize the procedure which follows the formulation of
the hypotheses to be verified, the test implications: after settling on the
right sampling technique, one has to acquire these data—which are
therefore "new"—then analyze them, process them, and thus succeed
in confirming or weakening the hypothesis. [17] In the same way, in 1971,
the three authors of *Explanation in Archeology*, quoting Hill, empha-
size that propositions must be tested with data independent of those
used in the formulation of these propositions, and they point out that
it is always—or nearly always—possible to find independent data
with which to test them. Hill shows clearly that it is the list of test
implications that indicates what relevant data must be gathered at this
stage. [18] Clarke was no less clear in 1968: the sixth and seventh points
in the procedure he recommended were the choice and carrying out of
new experiments, appropriate sampling of corresponding data, and
only then the testing of the models or hypotheses in the light of these
new results. Binford echoed this in the same year: "The main point of
our argument is that *independent* means of testing propositions about
the past must be developed." [19]

In any case, it is clear that for the New Archeology the validation of
hypotheses is the only path to salvation, no matter what the problem.
If it is the reconstruction of culture history, "we must develop means
for using archaeological remains as a record of the past and as a source
for data for testing propositions which we set forth regarding past
events"; if it is the reconstruction of the ways of life of past sociocultural systems, what is required is "the rigorous testing of deductively
drawn hypotheses against independent sets of data"; if it is the mea-

surement of "the accuracy of our knowledge," the "yardstick of measurement is the degree to which propositions . . . can be confirmed or refuted through hypothesis testing"; or if it is the accessibility of the "nonmaterial" aspects of culture—as opposed to just material culture—we can achieve it "in direct measure with the testability of propositions being advanced about them." [20] The same idea, almost in the same wording, is hammered in from page to page, paper to paper, book to book.

"The changes in archaeology . . . are more than simply new methods and new theories; the changes consist of theories and methods developed in the context of a new epistemological perspective." [21] As David H. Thomas states without beating about the bush, at the beginning of an often-quoted paper on Great Basin Shoshonean subsistence and settlement patterns, "Untested theories cannot compete for serious attention in the arena of modern science" because "an unverified hypothesis has the epistemological status of a daydream." [22] Things could not be put more clearly.

Protracted Amazement: The Nonvalidation of Hypotheses

The moment has come when we cannot be satisfied with setting out the theoretical positions of the New Archeology as objectively as possible and with a minimum of comment. It is time to offer a first appraisal.

After what one has just read (and it could be extended almost ad infinitum), one certainly might expect that, at the very least, the New Archeologists' first concern—their most constant and scrupulous care, in all their work, whether masters or disciples—would be this testing of hypotheses that has been so vaunted, so tirelessly called for, and presented as the touchstone of the new concept, in contrast to the disheartening archaeology that preceded and, alas, accompanied it.

Well, now, what one finds is astounding. Contrary to what one was expecting in all innocence, one has to bow to the facts—which are that, apart from a very few exceptions to which I shall return later, the New Archeologists almost never test their hypotheses! The reader will agree that this is enough to leave one flabbergasted and that it is pretty hard to swallow.

Nevertheless, that is just how things are, as true today as it was at the beginning; and not only among the disciples but first and foremost among the leaders. As the question here is no longer that of the assertion of principles but rather that of putting them into practice, we must study the practices of the New Archeologists in their application of principles and no longer in their theoretical writings.

Binford, one might say, sets the example—a bad example. In "Archaeology as Anthropology," the 1962 article quoted previously, he does it blatantly: after having pointed out that his suggestions about the "technomic" and "sociotechnic" significance of the copper objects "must be phrased as hypotheses" and that these hypotheses must be "tested against ethnographic data," he hurries on, in his utterly characteristic way, to do nothing of the kind—at the very moment when any reader would expect to see him actually carry out the testing; and he conceals this pretty surprising about-face behind boasts that are all the more bombastic: "*Nevertheless,*" he continues, "it is hoped that this discussion *is sufficient* to serve as a background against which an explanatory hypothesis concerning the Old Copper materials can be offered as an example of the *potential* utility of this type of approach."[23] There follows a series of paragraphs, each one more bewildering than the last, which begin with expressions such as "I suggest," "I propose," "I have suggested," and "it is my opinion," or which point out that some fact or other "should be explicable," or is "most certainly explicable" through his theory, and which end in a series of arrogant injunctions: "Archaeology must accept a greater responsibility"; "archaeologists should be among the best qualified to . . . directly test hypotheses [*sic*]"; "the lack of theoretical concern . . . must be modified"; "we cannot afford to keep our theoretical heads buried in the sand"; "we must shoulder our full share of responsibility"; and so forth. Not that the set of hypotheses Binford puts forward is uninteresting, but he in no way proves them: he contents himself with pointing out that population increase is "generally demonstrable in terms of the increased number of archaeological sites," that the shift to aquatic resources is "demonstrable" in fish remains and the choice of suitable sites—but this is not "demonstrated." Or else he contents himself with mingling unproven assertions with references to other authors on very general points. And he has the effrontery to conclude, "This explanatory 'theory' has the advantage of 'explaining'" the different points which he has in no way "explained" in the sense he himself means!

The indiscretions of youth, you think? Not at all. This is very much Binford's usual behavior. He does exactly the same thing with the rock art of the Sahara and of southern Africa in 1965 (see p. 19): "If the hypothesis were confirmed, . . . the existence of cultural boundaries would have been established by independent data. If the hypothesis were refuted . . ."; but of course it is neither refuted nor confirmed, by him at any rate. But this does not prevent him stringing together methodological assertions for the benefit of the scholarly world.[24]

Pits and Pots

An astonishing example of this class of ideas is the often-quoted Binford article of 1967, republished in *An Archaeological Perspective*, on smudge pits and hide smoking in the Mississippi valley around A.D. 1000. These little oval pits contained, among other things, corn cobs without kernels, and they had been filled intentionally. They had been interpreted as cereal caches, as ceremonial, as "postmolds," or, finally, as smudge pits with the smoke being used to control mosquitoes, an idea which now seems hilarious to Binford. Depending on ethnographic analogies observed among the Indians of the southeastern United States between A.D. 1700 and 1950, and thus in a period not very remote, "relatively speaking," from that of the pits, he proposes a revolutionary interpretation: these pits were used to smoke hides suspended over hearths. Besides offering some thoughts on the correct usage of the ethnographic parallel, Binford points out how one could refute his proposition or, on the other hand, increase the probability that it is valid. In order to determine if the smoking occurred in a particular place and at a certain period of the year, if it was linked to other activities such as the manufacture of clothing, or if similar pits were used for other purposes, it would be advisable to test whether hide smoking—a female activity—varies with other female activities (e.g., ceramics); whether these pits occur only in the base camps after the hunting season and before winter; and, finally, since the pits imply a specialized activity, whether their incidence is independent of the site population and the duration of occupation. An excellent program, except that, as usual, Binford carefully abstains from actually proceeding to carry it out. Nevertheless he cannot—again, as usual—refrain from moralizing and reminding us that "the final judgement of the archaeological reconstruction presented here must rest with testing through subsidiary hypotheses drawn deductively." [25]

The biggest joke is that two years later, in 1969, another attempt at interpretation (sorry, "explanation") of the smudge pits was made by Patrick J. Munson, and it led to very different conclusions although it explicitly respected the procedure Binford recommended. [26] As a matter of fact, by basing his work on observations made among the Cherokee at more or less the same very recent period, Munson proposes to see these pits as installations used for smudging pottery. "Peaux" or "pots"? The French pun is the joke's punchline. Crestfallen but honest, Binford is forced to acknowledge that, in a way, his argument has been "refuted," even though he makes the most of the fact that it is a single, recent, and somewhat debased example that goes against his thesis. But the most interesting thing, from the point of view that concerns us at the moment, is that he acknowledges the undeniable fact that he has not verified his hypotheses, any more than has Munson: "Neither proposition has been tested." [27] What do you think he infers from this? Incredible but true, he starts yet again to assure us that "the accuracy of a proposition can only be determined by the testing of deductively drawn hypotheses against independent data." And what do you suppose he does? Test his hypotheses? Not a bit of it. Let's recall that in the preceding paper he was lamenting that the previous interpretations "all must be considered as conjecture." No doubt his "decisions as to how to invest research time in hypothesis testing" must have been negative. [28]

Against Braidwood

One could at least hope that things would be different later on, since problems of really great importance are involved. Alas! In the paper written in 1966, published in 1968 and republished unaltered in 1972 on post-Pleistocene adaptations, in which he criticizes and ridicules (in his own eyes at least) both Robert Braidwood and, to a lesser extent, V. Gordon Childe, Binford makes much of one aspect of an idea borrowed from Leslie White. According to this notion, agriculture arose not through a mere concentration of population caused by desiccation (Childe's "oasis" theory), nor through increased knowledge of the environment (Braidwood's theory), but through a demographic disequilibrium, a population increase caused by the "immigration" of neighboring peoples, and, consequently, a diminished food supply (here he links up again with Childe). [29] This crisis situation favors "the development of plant and animal domestication," assuming that the animal and plant forms are "amenable to manipulation" (which, incidentally, is a return to Braidwood's thesis). [30] His theory is interesting although it is not as "radically" original as he claims, but that is not what is at issue here. What is in question is the way Binford puts it forward. Rediscovering the world, as usual, he successively contrasts the "functional" differences and the "structural" differences between ecological niches by means of purely theoretical considerations, devoid of any supporting examples; he then contrasts "closed" and "open" population systems, the latter being subdivided into "donors" and "recipients"; and from all sides, from North America to Australia, or from Polynesia to South America, he takes ethnographic "parallels" which he doesn't question for a moment (no doubt because his thesis is meant to be valid for the whole world at the end of the Pleistocene). It's not clear exactly why he introduces, in passing, the fundamental idea that one circumstance favorable to his theory would be an increased dependence on seasonal "aquatic" resources (fish and migratory birds): no doubt it is his background as a student in forestry and wildlife conservation showing through. Assertions follow each other at a headlong pace: "The shift to the exploitation of highly seasonal resources such as anadromous fish" (salmon, sturgeon, etc.) "and migratory fowl, did not occur until the close of the Pleistocene"; it was probably caused by worldwide changes in sea level. Linked to an increased sedentism, it "established for the first time conditions leading to marked heterogeneity in rates of population growth and structure of the ecological niche of immediately adjacent sociocultural systems" and thus "in turn, conditions favoring improved subsistence technology" (agriculture).[31] It is a vision, a novel: and why not? All that the reader asks for, in the very perspective of New Archeology, is a demonstration. Binford reminds us of this himself, in case we had forgotten: "If the model presented here has value above and beyond that of a logical exercise, it must be tested by the formulation of hypotheses and the collection of data."[32] Binford then formulates three "predictions": the beginnings of animal and plant domestication will come from the Near East, in "areas adjacent to those occupied by relatively sedentary forager-fishers"; next they will appear in European Russia and south-central Europe, near areas with exploitation (of salmon and wild ducks); finally, evidence for independent and parallel innovations will appear around the world, alongside neolithization. In support of the first prediction Binford cites Jean Perrot's excavation at Mallaha (but hadn't he already used it to put forward his thesis beforehand? And as a demonstration it is a bit short). Where the other two are concerned, however, we do not find the slightest trace of a verification, or even of any further particulars: we might have expected Binford to go and see or to study what occurred on the shores of the Black Sea and to give us examples of parallel innovations other than those which gave rise to his "prediction," but we wait in vain. Binford's conclusion is outspoken: "It is hoped that the theoretical perspective offered here will serve to generate a new series of questions, the answers to which may increase our understanding of the major cultural changes which occurred at the close of the Pleistocene."[33] Let us indeed hope so. However, may I remind you of Binford's ejaculatory proclamations in that same year of 1968: "Hypotheses about cause and effect must be explicitly formulated and then tested. Only when this is done are we in a position to judge what facts might be relevant; only then can we objectively evaluate the implicit propositions which underly [*sic*] 'plausible' historical interpretations"; "if we omit any of these steps . . . we can have little confidence in the historical reconstruction offered."[34]

Against Bordes

Certainly the paper by Binford which was published four years later, in 1972, in both *An Archaeological Perspective* and *Models in Archaeology*, and which he said was a "frontal attack on the traditionalists' theory,"[35] can be envisaged—at least, in its central part—as the first (or so it seems) effective, though nonexplicit, application of the new method, with the formulation of a general hypothesis, the deduction of implications, and their verification. I shall return to this point (p. 39). This time Binford is going for François Bordes, the Leakeys, and to a lesser extent Clarke, in connection with the interpretation of the variations observed in Mousterian assemblages. According to Binford, this variability can in no way be explained by the presence of distinct cultural traditions mutually influencing or replacing each other; making use, as usual, of the idea of another prehistorian, J. Desmond Clark, he intends to demonstrate that in reality the material results from different activities, carried out at different seasons, in different places, and for a variety of purposes (butchery, tool making, etc.) by people of different ages and sex: "We should expect that, other things being equal, the composition of tool assemblages would vary directly in accordance with the tasks performed."[36] This thesis is both banal and interesting, although its demonstration, through a laborious, interminable, and unreadable factor analysis, leaves one very skeptical. Whatever its final value, it ends with a series of declarations that begin (as I have already pointed out) with phrases such as "I submit that," "I suggest," "it is my impression that," "I am convinced that," and so on, over and over again; these show that even if man in the Lower and Middle Pleistocene was physically different from modern man, and if the variability of assemblages does not measure cultural "distance," so to speak, or "ethnic" distinctiveness, and even if the latter phenomena did not exist during most of the Pleistocene and did not appear before the Upper Paleolithic, nevertheless these ideas—so stimulating mentally—are only ideas; and their implications were not explicitly deduced, let alone tested, contrary to doctrine.[37]

In 1978 things do not seem to have changed. Although Binford is now doing very significant work in the ethnographic field or, more exactly, in "ethnoarchaeology" rather than simply archaeology, and taking an interest in the present-day "Nunamiut" Eskimo of Alaska (and, consequently, interpretation has given way to direct observation), when it comes to producing a theory we find yet again the old phrases—"I am suggesting," "I have suggested"; moreover, at the end they are remarked upon as follows: "Hints, ideas *to be explored in hopes* of recognizing or inventing variables *that could be used to explore* causal relationships between activities and their organization in space." [38] But Binford prefers to heap advice on his reader rather than tackle this effective exploration.

If Binford himself can be considered a champion of the nonvalidation of hypotheses, what can be said—with certain exceptions—of his pupils or his more remote disciples?

The American Disciples

Sally R. Schanfield (Binford), for example, in her paper on the Levallois Mousterian of the Near East, published in 1968 in *New Perspectives in Archeology*, supports the thesis which was to be taken up and developed in 1972 in the above-mentioned article by Binford: the variability observed between tool assemblages is explained not by migrations or by "mutations" of the lithic material with "transitions," but by the different functions for which they were used. It is true that she first finds confirmation that the site of Shubbabiq in Israel is a "base-camp" in the fact that it is very sheltered, well lit, and has a floor space of three hundred square meters, whereas the site of Jabrud in Syria is a temporary work camp, as shown by its floor space of just over half that size and the fact that it is a relatively open site. [39] On the other hand, when it comes to interpreting the change from specialized hunting and butchering tools to less specialized tools for the same function—that is, to deciding whether it is a stylistic change—she leaves it to faunal analyses still in progress. Above all, when she "suggests" that variability in the same broad culture type must be investigated functionally and concludes that "*if* structural change can be demonstrated . . . then we have the basis for developing processual models for understanding changes," [40] she acknowledges that her hypothesis has not yet been demonstrated: it is the same attitude as Binford's, and almost the same wording.

Kent V. Flannery, who parted company with Binford and his group quite early, though he was to receive the master's approval a long time afterward, [41] does verify in "Social and Economic Systems of Central America," a paper he wrote with Michael D. Coe for the same volume, that Marshall Sahlins's Polynesian model for villages living in "symbiosis" (which he makes his hypothesis) is attested in Mesoamerica. But his paper ends with a list of seven methodological "suggestions" for archaeologists interested in the reconstruction of pre-Columbian social organization; these call to mind very strongly the usual, never-tested hypotheses.[42]

Yet another example: Thomas Cook published part of the excavation by Stuart Struever (one of Binford's first companions) at Koster, Illinois; the heading of his last paragraph is "Testing the Archaic Stage Model"; and there he explains, very honestly, that he is not in a position to carry out most of the tests, which must therefore be put off till later.[43]

If we now turn to more recent examples, like that of Schiffer in 1976, we find that although he makes an effort to test his "synthetic model" (but we shall see how, see p. 42) or to verify his hypotheses about the "spatial transformations" of objects into archaeological remains (but this is done with the help of *simulated* data), on the other hand he puts forward "stipulations" or "hypothetical laws" (such as "with increasing site population [or perhaps site size] and increasing intensity of occupation, there will be a decreasing correspondence between . . . use and discard locations") which he himself acknowledges are untested. Moreover, Schiffer adds that assertions of this kind "seem never to be tested"![44]

South shows the same contradictory attitude in his 1977 book on historical archaeology. While it is true that he controls very conscientiously his "Carolina artifact pattern,"[45] on the other hand, quite frequently, he once again puts off till later the explanation of his hypotheses through verifications.[46] No one would dream of holding it against them, but it is astonishing that they don't reproach themselves for it, given the insistence with which the New Archeologists, and especially their leader Binford, have made the testing of hypotheses a sine qua non condition of scientific procedure. Permit me to recall Thomas's words with which I closed the earlier part of this chapter: "An unverified hypothesis has the epistemological status of a daydream."

The English

But what about the English New Archeology, you may ask? One is forced to state that it proceeds in the same way. And here again, this is the doing of the master, the initiator: David L. Clarke. Clarke is best known for his theoretical writings, but besides his studies of the Beakers of Great Britain[47] he also published, for example, "A Provisional

Model of an Iron Age Society and Its Settlement System," a paper that dates to 1972. He did not excavate the site himself: he takes up the old publication (1911, 1917) of an excavation carried out between 1892 and 1907 at Glastonbury in Somerset by Arthur H. Bulleid and Harold St. George Gray (the New Archeologists adore rewriting the work of their predecessors). It was a "lake village," dated by the excavators to a period from circa 150 B.C. to the beginning of our era. Given the dates of the excavation and the publication, it is not surprising that, some eighty years later, Clarke can make certain clarifications. Where the excavators saw only an agglomeration of huts with clay floors that was if not "amorphous," then at least "with no definite or discernible arrangement,"[48] Clarke, basing his work on the analysis of a correlation matrix, has the indisputable merit of putting forward a completely new view of things: far from corresponding to our modern orthogonal plans, the village of Glastonbury had concentric groups of "building units" which were themselves circular and subdivided into two halves: on the one hand two houses facing each other, separated by a courtyard and surrounded by outbuildings; on the other a "minor" house linked to a byre and stocked with "technical" huts[49] (fig. 1). Whatever the accuracy of this presentation—because in at least one case the pattern is not respected, but in that very case he draws important inferences (headman's house)—there remains the fact that this is at least a structured working hypothesis, a great advance in our understanding of the site. But from the point of view which interests us at the moment, one cannot fail to notice that many essential points are put forward with no demonstration, although surrounded or encumbered with an impressive display of preliminary "assertions." They are untested hypotheses, in the New Archeology's own terms. For example, the house which is an exception to the rule is attributed to the "headman": however, it is noted that it left a mound which, while bigger than the others, seems to have been little frequented; the pottery is no different from that of the other houses, and the only notable particularity is that of less than ten weaving combs.[50] Or again, the identification of the "guard huts," outhouses, stables, pigsties, and kennels is based on nothing other than the presence of the corresponding animal bones inside or nearby: But did these animals live there, or did they die there? While Bulleid and Gray's final date is reduced to 50 B.C.—quite rightly, it seems—on the basis of recent typologies of fibulae, and while the period of occupation is divided into four probable phases on the basis of vertical and *horizontal* stratigraphy, the population estimate (lower than that of the original authors) rests only on

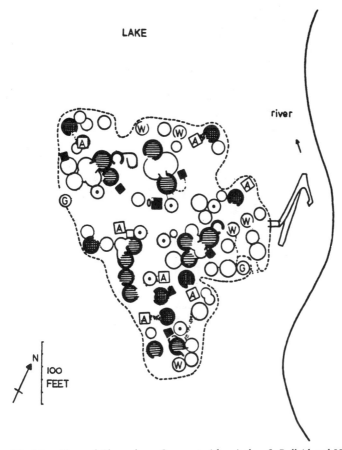

Fig. 1. The lake village of Glastonbury, Somerset. After Arthur S. Bulleid and Harold St. George Gray, *The Glastonbury Lake Village* (Glastonbury: Glastonbury Antiquarian Society, 1911–17), and David L. Clarke, ed., *Models in Archaeology* (London: Methuen, 1972), 834, fig. 21.5 (phase 4).

ethnographic analogies whose relevance, contrary to the great principles, does not seem to have been verified in any way.[51]

Given this background, Clarke then puts on a show for us which, coming from a New Archeologist, is quite bewildering. To confine comment to the point under consideration at present, this is a real novel, a series of more or less gratuitous accounts, of hypotheses that are never tested and, moreover, may perhaps be untestable. Judge for yourselves: Clarke has "a strong impression" that there was no headman, strictly speaking, but a primus inter pares, who nevertheless lived in a richer house (see above, however), and who—we discover out of the blue—is ancestrally linked to the houses that are owned or inherited "jointly."[52] The presence, in his house, of fibulae of the various types found in the other dwellings leads Clarke to put forward the idea that "perhaps" the women from these other dwellings came to work there. This simple hypothesis rapidly becomes a reality: a "levy" of female weavers. In the same way, the principal half of each unit housed the family, the other half housed the females.[53] The special nature of the objects found in each assemblage "probably" reflects marriages; "it may be tempting" to see finger rings, which are not found in the "poor quarter" of the north, as wedding rings, symbols of the endogamous and exogamous marriages of a certain social class, because one has "an impression" that lineages were exogamous, or, rather, linked by endogamy, balanced with exogamy. In short, Clarke posits a patrilocal extended family of fifteen to twenty persons, comprising the patriarch, his wife or wives, his unmarried children, his married sons and their wives and children. The three generations lived together, apparently; a house of female servants was attached to the two major familial houses.[54] The village was abandoned when it had exactly doubled its population from sixty to 120 people and thus had ceased to be viable.

I do not claim that all of this is wrong or without interest, but these inferences are never accompanied by any validation.

And Clarke presses on, imperturbably. The imports "suggest" that the northern quarter had connections with the southern region, while the village's central and southern quarters had ties with the North. Relying on David P. S. Peacock's mineralogical analyses, Clarke concludes that there were exchanges of stone objects and ores with the region of present-day Maesbury, situated within a radius of sixteen kilometers—that is, accessible in a day, whether on foot, on horseback, in a cart or by canoe—but the radius of activity could reach thirty-two or even 130 kilometers.[55] In such a context one can understand, Clarke tells us, the choice of sheep as livestock, and the activity of female weavers in polygynous families whose men were shepherds.[56]

Barley (for beer) must have been planted in the dry area near the village, wheat and beans farther away, cereals alternating every five years with fallow for pasture; ashes must have provided from one hundred to two hundred cubic meters of fertilizer; manure can be estimated at one hundred tons. There was "a high return for high risk." As for ditches and embankments, a large part of the labor must "certainly" have been devoted to them.[57] And so on and so forth. In summer, the sheep must have grazed in the drained flat areas, in the lambing season; harvesting also occurred in the summer. When the one thousand sheep were shorn, everybody lent a hand. In the spring, the people were short-handed, but afterward they could net shoals of fish. In the autumn, obligatory works were undertaken. In winter the canoes came out again, and women made 100 to 500 kilograms of wool into forty to two hundred pieces of weaving, including the "cloaks fit for heroes" which may have been the principal output of ancient Glastonbury. "It is tempting" to identify the winter mining camps with the "hill forts" distributed along the hills.[58]

Let's cut this short, because Clarke finishes off his "painting" in the same vein, with interregional exchange. The picture is vivid if not colorful, idyllic and precise if not literary, and not lacking in charm. All the same, the reader will agree that it comes as a surprise from the pen of this theoretician. "All in all, an idealized model . . . can be assembled, and, as with ideal gas models, although it may be unreal it provides a basis for prediction, and thus for testing the degree of its reality or unreality."[59] Words of wisdom: but why doesn't he proceed to the testing stage? Why does he confine himself to the most traditional archaeology you can imagine? His conclusion is appropriately disarming: "This provisional procedure usefully exposes the full consequence of the cumulative chain of assumptions for further testing, but it is in no way a substitute for the necessary testing between models."[60] One could not put it better: but why doesn't he do it? He suggests the possible tests, but leaves to other people the trouble of carrying them out.[61] This is the man who adopted in his own name the procedure to which I've already referred, in which the testing of hypotheses or models appears twice, not as a simple possibility but as an indispensable stage in scientific procedure.

Renfrew and the Cyclades

Clarke opened up the way: What about his successors? Have his followers perhaps gone farther and reached that stage of validating inferences? This scarcely seems to be the case, and as an example I'll take Renfrew's important book *The Emergence of Civilisation,* published in that same year of 1972. Presenting the problem of the appearance of civilization in the "Greek" Cyclades and the Aegean Sea in the third millennium B.C., he rejects the idea that the changes perceptible in agriculture, technology, social organization, art, religion, trade, and population owe almost everything to the Orient, as the "diffusionists" believe.[62] He proposes a "systemic" explanation, in the sense of cybernetics, in which feedback alone—be it positive or negative—does not explain the change: the latter only occurs if a modification in one of the subsystems (means of subsistence, technology, society, symbols, communication) favors one in another subsystem. This is what he calls the "multiplier" effect.[63] After a very careful and complete study in the first two long sections of his book of the sequence of post-Neolithic cultures in Crete, on the mainland, and in the Aegean; of their successive phases; and then of the functioning of his five subsystems within the systems which these regions make up (a quite positive piece of work, even from the most traditional point of view), at the end—in his final chapter—he comes to the solution of the initial problem. Broadly speaking, the birth of the Early Bronze Age Cycladic civilization was caused by vine cultivation, which develops the manufacture of drinking vessels and, at the same time, benefits religion, or it was caused by the production of daggers combined with the "invention" of better boats, the longships.[64] One will agree that these factors are not particularly original, apart from the (equally banal) emphasis placed on their interaction. But that is not the problem.

Because it is at this stage that one would expect his proposition to be properly demonstrated, in the sense agreed on by Binford and Clarke, the theoreticians of the New Archeology, to whom Renfrew refers by name.[65] For after all, at the end of his three introductory chapters Renfrew himself stresses, in connection with his subsystems and the positive feedback they exercise on each other, that "if they lead us to formulate new hypotheses *which can be tested* in the archaeological record—to posit, for instance, a correlation between one observable factor and another in a given culture—then they are fruitful constructs."[66] Now what does he do? He certainly derives a few "predictions" from his hypotheses: for example, that "regions rich in copper or tin ores should be outstandingly wealthy." But he immediately notes that this prediction will not be testable until a "clearer picture ... of the original mineral resources available" is produced. And he adds at once that the predictive tests "are not obvious."[67] Far from presenting us with new, independent data, as in the official doctrine, he refers us back to the documentation that he provided earlier and that is the ultimate source of his propositions—a circular argument if ever there was one. His two explanatory models (on the redistribution of the means of subsistence, and on wealth brought about through metallurgy and trade) are declared—shock, horror!—to be "plausible," a term and a concept spurned by Binford.[68] The testing—very much as usual—is put off indefinitely: "the evidence available is not yet sufficient to try [these predictions] effectively. Further work will test their validity"!⁶⁹

Let's stop there: it would be easy to add any number of examples. There are, I repeat, counterexamples, and I shall return to them soon: they are not as decisive as might be thought at first sight. Nevertheless, the fact remains that, on a point of methodology presented as fundamental by the New Archeologists themselves—Hempel's hypothetico-deductive reasoning—practice contrasts with the theory that has been repeated a thousand times, and this applies even more to the leaders than to their followers. It has to be admitted that there is some cause for surprise here, and not for the last time: as a general rule, the New Archeologists do not test the implications of their hypotheses or, therefore, their hypotheses themselves. It appears that they put off the task until later, if not onto other people. It is as though the important thing is for the implications to be testable rather than tested; for the possibility rather than the reality of the test to exist. Thus, for example, Binford praises Childe—in connection with his oasis theory, mentioned earlier—for having been the first to provide a "set of testable propositions"; and he commends Braidwood (just this once) for having "actively sought . . . field data to test Childe's propositions."⁷⁰ It's a bit like having a share-out of roles; some people first formulate hypotheses or models, other people undertake to try them out or put them to the test. This is so clear that Gardin was able to write: "It follows that [the author of the provisional hypothesis] could leave the bother of testing these predictions to others . . . that is to say, to the people who will be able to find *new* data which will confirm (or weaken) the explanation."⁷¹ We can do away with the conditional tense: although the New Archeologists more often than not (but not always, as we have just seen with Renfrew) deduce the secondary hypotheses, they themselves do not test them.⁷²

In this they are doing precisely what they reproached the "traditional" archaeologists for in such acrimonious terms. Out of a wide field, let's recall Fritz and Plog: "Prescientific knowledge might be defined as a set of statements which are plausible and accepted, but which have not been tested."⁷³ Or again, "current archaeological theory is prescientific. It has not been tested" because in fact—even supposing that traditional archaeology doesn't test its hypotheses, a claim we are going to examine shortly—its propositions are at least as testable as those of the New Archeology, when the latter forgoes validation of their implications or puts off this formality until later. One cannot see any difference between a traditional untested implication and an untested implication in New Archeology. It is said that traditional archaeologists do not explicitly formulate the consequences which could be tested, that they do not make the implications plain; but here again, even supposing this to be true, there is nothing to prevent someone doing it in their place—deducing from their conclusions the hypotheses which should be tested, and then testing them. The possible veracity of a thesis is independent of its verification, even if it is the verification which establishes it. But then, what if the objection is raised that these hypotheses, these implications, are unlikely to be tested, are not verifiable, in the present state of our knowledge? This may (or indeed may not) be the case: but isn't this also what occurs with the New Archeology—which finds, in this very situation, an excuse for putting off the testing?

Traditional Validations

But the most outrageous part is that the New Archeology's claim is not even correct—and it is an insult to traditional archaeology to reproach it for never testing its hypotheses. Of course, it does not always formulate hypotheses and sometimes contents itself with setting out data: in that situation it cannot be accused of not testing hypotheses it never formulated. Certainly, when it puts forward "working" hypotheses, traditional archaeology often refrains from testing them, especially when they are fanciful, and this is the case not only with amateur archaeologists, local scholars, or Sunday diggers, but also, all too frequently, with professional archaeologists (and not necessarily the older ones)—we have just seen that the New Archeologists are their equals in this. But it is not always this way: leaving aside the fact that hypothetico-deductive reasoning is not the only type of sound reasoning, when it *is* used in traditional archaeology it is accompanied by testing far more regularly than the New Archeology's theoreticians believe. In fact, it is a classic procedure of traditional archaeology, after arriving at a provisional conclusion, to look for further confirmation of it— that is, with new and independent data. Because, to take one example, what other logical significance can there be in what are usually called (in the most conventional archaeology) "check-excavations," the verificatory excavations that follow a preliminary excavation? The latter leads to the formulation of a theory, a thesis, an "interpretation"; and, after the event, the excavator checks that he has not made a mistake, resumes the excavation, extends it: in short, he tests his extrapolation.

Let's take a more particular field, one that is abhorrent to a whole present-day category of archaeologists—or self-styled archaeologists—one that is disparaged, ridiculed as being repetitive, useless, representative of the intolerable "classic" archaeology: architecture. When some specialist or other in ancient architecture is convinced that no architecture, beyond a certain stage, can have been erected without a system of measurement, he looks for what the ancient "foot" or whatever might have been, its submultiples, its multiples, the standard unit in a construction, and so forth. When he takes his measurements and then breaks them down, divides, multiplies them, combines them in different ways, what else is he doing but trying to test his hypotheses, and then his more precise hypothesis (that the foot used had a certain value)? Even if he does not express it in the same terminology, he is validating (or invalidating) the implications of his assumption.[74] When, in a Peloponnesian site, one discovers the remains of a furnace of an unusual type which, instead of the usual sort of solid central support, possesses something that seems, on the contrary, hollow and noncontinuous; when, confronted with this anomaly, one looks for its explanation; when the idea comes to mind (through a mechanism that I shall have to come back to) that it might be something other than a bread oven or a potter's kiln (the most frequent type), and may, for example, be a metal-working furnace; when one takes part of it, has it analyzed, and thus finds that the content of this sample is abnormally rich in silver; when one then concludes, at least provisionally, that it is not only a metal-working furnace, but more exactly a furnace for the cupellation of silver—then what else has one done but make observations, use them to formulate a hypothesis, deduce possible consequences from it, and test those consequences? And yet the New Archeology was still unborn, in limbo.[75] Turning now from the field of the most concrete data to that of theories: when—to take one example among many others one could invoke—Leonard Woolley, before the Second World War, tried to elucidate the possible relationship between Crete and the Near East, explored the Syrian coast looking for sites which could provide data on this problem, chose Al Mina and Alalakh, dug them, and discovered that at Al Mina there were no Cretan remains of the Late Bronze Age but Euboean exports of the ninth to eighth centuries B.C., then what else did he do but present a problem, formulate a hypothesis, test the predictions he could deduce from it, and find that they were wrong—that is, invalidate them? That was in 1938–40.[76] When Heinrich Schliemann, passionate—*horresco referens*—about Homeric antiquity, resolved to rediscover the town made famous by the war between Greeks and Trojans, went to northwestern Asia Minor and decided to excavate the tell of Hissarlik, what else was he doing but testing a hypothesis? How is this possible? After all, this was 1871, and Binford was not yet born. More recently, in a different field, when André Leroi-Gourhan, confronted by the mysterious "signs" accompanying the animals on Magdalenian cave walls, considered the possibility that they had a sexual significance and then deduced statistical consequences from this and tested them, what else was he doing, yet again? [77] It has been said that the New Archeology "suddenly . . . is everybody's archaeology," and with good reason—on this point, it had never ceased to be so! [78]

It would be tedious to add more examples. Even though traditional archaeology has indisputably failed to carry out the hypothetico-deductive procedure in many cases, it was not as ridiculous as the New Archeologists believe. In fact one might well end up by concluding, paradoxically, that it is traditional archaeology that tests its hypotheses, without constantly making a song and dance about it, and the New Archeology that doesn't test its suppositions, contrary to its ceaseless declarations of principle.

There is a reason for this. It is a very curious and significant fact that all the New Archeologists act precisely as if the hypothetico-deductive method, their battle cry, had been invented by Carl Hempel and Paul Oppenheim between 1965 and 1968, that is to say, at the time when the New Archeology was being formed. They refer to it almost ritually. [79] And yet Europeans may remember hearing, during their secondary studies, about something which seems to have pretty close similarities: the hypothetico-deductive reasoning of Claude Bernard and Auguste Comte. This takes us back to the discovery of the glycogenic function of the liver (1849) and, in a more general way, to the experimental method. [80] "Deduction, useful as a method of testing hypotheses"—this definition, which one might think comes from some New Archeologist or other, and to which the New Archeology tends to lay claim as its own property and as the transference to archaeology of a discovery by Hempel, in fact appeared in dictionaries in 1913, and probably in much earlier works. [81]

Pseudovalidations

Thus when the New Archeologists happen by chance to test their hypotheses and for once put their money where their mouth is, they are not doing anything that is very original or that was not done by the archaeology that they hold in contempt. Because, amazingly enough, a few New Archeologists have been known to test their propositions— it's the very least they could do. Furthermore, one should note, the disciples do it more often than the masters. What is striking is that these verifications often have no regard for the essential clause of their validity—that is, the call for data that, if not new, should at least be "independent," different from those that specifically gave rise to the hypothesis.

When Binford—in the "Models and Paradigms" article already mentioned above—formulates what is, in a way, his hypothesis (if the associational relationships between prehistoric tools are not covariant relationships, the traditionalist "paradigm" is false)[82] and then tries to test it by means of thirty-two assemblages from seven sites in East Africa, it looks as if he is applying his method and confronting his theory with independent data. But in reality he has done nothing of the sort because this theory did not originate in the study of initial data; at all events, no source is cited.[83] The argument seems completely theoretical, with no reference to a given archaeological situation (the starting point is undoubtedly ethnographic). And so the material used in the demonstration (from Olorgesailie in Kenya, Isimila and Kalambo Falls in Tanzania) is not different, independent material—it is the only material that crops up in the demonstration, and it is from its composition (we shall see how the latter is handled) that he draws his conclusions (I've already said how—see above p. 27). It seems to me that it is the conclusion that should have been tested with other data at this stage if the method was being applied rigorously, especially as some effort was being made in this direction for once! Instead, we have the series of unproven "suggestions" to which I have already referred.

In general, however, the New Archeologists use a collection of observed data as their starting point. But when, once in a blue moon, they aspire to testing their hypotheses, most often they do it by confronting the hypotheses with the very data which gave rise to them rather than with original data. As a general rule, this is what happens with Clarke who, apart from calling on more recent typologies of fibulae (for dating purposes) or on Peacock's mineralogical analyses of 1969, uses essentially the data recorded by the Glastonbury excavators.[84] This is not to say that the approach is illicit or uninteresting, but it is contrary to the doctrine as set out by Clarke.[85]

Renfrew's case is even clearer: at the end of his *Emergence of Civilisation* he points out that the "consequences" implied and predicted by his model are documented . . . in previous chapters![86] Things could not be clearer, and this is by no means the exception that proves the rule in his work. In the article "Social Organisation in Neolithic Wessex," published the following year, 1973, in *The Explanation of Culture Change*, he proposed an interpretation of the succession (from the early to late Neolithic of long barrows and causewayed camps on the one hand, and then megalithic "henges" on the other) based on Polynesian chiefdoms, and he interpreted the very long earthworks in terms of the social organization of the Creek and Cherokee Indians. ("It is not stretching the limits of proper ethnographic comparison too far," he adds.)[87] In reality, all the factual data were known from the start (and in any case they are far from verifying all the model's points). "Fresh" data are never used. The validations are contained "in the monuments themselves" or are the logical result of previous validations, which comes to the same thing, or are contradicted—but always by the same initial data. We are far from the demands of theory.

Hill is indisputably one of the most readable, intellectually most honest, in short, most conscientious of the New Archeologists. In his study of the Broken K Indian "pueblo" he really tried to "test his hypotheses," a fact that deserves mention because of its rarity. This work, often cited as the classic example of the application of the New Archeology's method and harshly criticized no less often, even by New Archeologists,[88] is indeed quite characteristic. In his study of this surface site, located in eastern Arizona and occupied continuously from A.D. 1150 to 1280, Hill dug part of it—chosen by an elementary sampling technique—but nevertheless completed the work with eight additional rooms because he felt the necessity to do so; he isolated the material found on the floors, and systematically sieved the fill. That done, he distinguished three categories of rooms: large ones, small ones and "special" ones—which bear a strong resemblance to ceremonial rooms or kivas—characterized by different architectural criteria: he didn't hesitate to use a χ^2 test to make sure that if a single hearth out of twenty-three occurs in a small room, the likelihood is less than one in a thousand that this is due to chance—a point which one is happy to grant him. These differences between the rooms, this "variability," corresponds, of course, to different functions; "the activities [performed in the large rooms] required more space than those carried out in the small rooms." And he got the idea that this ancient pueblo could be similar to modern pueblos: the least one can say is that this is a quite natural idea; and as a matter of fact, it is indeed correct.[89] He therefore unhesitatingly put forward the proposition that the variability of the rooms at Broken K can be placed in the same behavioral context as in modern pueblos, and that the different types of room are functionally equivalent.[90]

But Hill did not want to rest content with this, as is all too often the case. Rather, as a good New Archeologist, he wanted to test his proposition: and not with the same data as served to formulate the proposition but with "additional" data, independent of the architectural categories already used. One can recognize here the perfectly justified principle of the method. And, as a matter of fact, he went on to reexamine modern pueblos by taking an interest this time in the activities taking place in the different rooms, in the utensils and the raw materials that they worked with (metates, cereals, etc.). From this he deduced—like rabbits out of a hat—no fewer than sixteen "expectations" if the ancient rooms had the same function as the modern ones (for example, the big rooms should contain more varied material, since one can suppose that a greater number of different activities took place in them). Then he moved on to test his predictions by confronting them with the corresponding archaeological data from Broken K. It comes as no great surprise, it has to be said, to find that twelve out of sixteen are verified, but Hill, very honestly, admits that two of them are only partly verified, and the last two are not verified at all: however, he doesn't make a song and dance about it, since these exceptions can be explained and do not outweigh the far more numerous verifications.[91] Conclusion: "It is thus demonstrated that the three major room types at Broken K Pueblo were the general functional equivalents of the three major kinds of room in present-day Pueblo villages."[92]

At first sight the application of the method seems (and has seemed to many people) impeccable because the hypothesis formulated from the architectural variability is verified by the material, that is, by data of a different kind. The logic appears rigorous.

And yet . . . Where do these "additional" data come from, as if by magic? Did Hill know nothing about them at the time he formulated his hypothesis? Did he, in a way, collect them afterward, for the requirements of his demonstration? It seems clear that the answer is no, except perhaps, naturally, for the pollen analyses—and here again, he could have had them at his disposal in the course of his research. But it is evident that he discovered all his material in the rooms he dug and that these rooms were not found empty, that they didn't first yield their architectural characteristics and then, subsequently, their pots, their grains, and so forth. In other words, Hill knew from the start, at least *grosso modo*, that a certain kind of room contained such and such a type of pottery and utensils, while another kind contained other types. This is so true that the "special" rooms are identified straight off as kivas, and that there is not, in a way, a "return" to the site or the material (he expresses regret at one point that no one had thought of looking to see whether certain pottery bore traces of fire).[93] Of course, his thinking certainly progressed as the study advanced; groupings which had not been clear at first, associations which had escaped his attention, subsequently appeared; statistical tests were carried out: but all this happened before the validation. In short, it is hard to escape the impression that from the start Hill compared the ancient pueblo with what he knew about modern pueblos, and that—even if he progressively refined this comparison—the conclusion was known in advance. The "demonstration" seems to be merely a trick of presentation intended—as he says at the beginning of his article—to validate the "methodological approach" of the New Archeology.[94]

In a different style Schiffer offers us a curious example of pseudo-validation of a hypothesis. He advocates a "model" of "archeological knowledge" which, in contrast with other models, he calls a "synthetic" model. This model is based on the realization—which would be hard to dispute—that the remains of a past society have not reached us intact: in the course of time they have undergone "transformations"—either "c-transforms" (*c* for cultural—they were discarded, transported, etc.) or "noncultural" (with the stupefying initial of "n-transforms"—for *n*oncultural—which Binford accepts as a matter of course[95]), caused, for example, by wind, water, rodents, and so forth. According to Schiffer these transformations relate the variables of human behavior (e.g., the procedures used to make a flint tool) to the variables which characterize objects as they are found, or their *final* spatial distribution. To these "assumptions" he adds "stipulations" which differ from assumptions in that they aim at "specific inference justification" (for example, that "population remained constant during site occupation"), but the inference is independently testable. As I understand it, this is Schiffer's "synthetic model," and he immediately proposes to test it.

One might therefore expect him to deduce from the model a number of implications (to be tested) which are contained in the assumptions that one has just read, and which have some bearing on the content of these implications. But what implications does he deduce? Formal ones, in a way, which concern not the content of his assumptions but, on the whole, the way archaeologists use them! The three implications are as follows: (1) that inferences may or may not be justified; (2) that occasionally one may find explicit instances of one's assumptions; (3) that many independent inferences reveal the use of a single principle. It is really hard to see the connection, or how these implications confirm the "c" and "n" transforms. Of course, examination of excavation reports gives him confirmation of these implications. And he boldly concludes, "the synthetic model has held up under testing."[96] One is left flabbergasted.

Validations

All the same, there are examples of hypothesis validation which seem to conform to the method. Although South, as I have already pointed out, sometimes postpones his verifications, he does have the merit of immediately testing what he calls his "Carolina artifact pattern."[97] This pattern compares not the absolute quantities of such and such a type of artifact found in the historic sites of Carolina—that would be meaningless—but rather the percentages of the groups of these objects (in the total of objects found). He is dealing with mean percentages and their range: this gives a minimum and maximum percentage, between which lies the proportion of the group of objects under consideration. To take an example, tailoring objects (because one of the houses dug at Brunswick Town was a tailor shop) normally represent a stable percentage, somewhere between 0.6 percent and 5.4 percent (sic). If the observed percentage is higher, then one has good reason to think that one is dealing not with a private house but with professional premises. These percentages are calculated for kitchen utensils, bones, arms, furniture, architectural elements (wooden architecture), and so forth. It is the ensemble of these percentages that constitutes the Carolina artifact pattern. If it has any meaning, then one must find these same percentages elsewhere: that is South's implicit hypothesis.

In order to test it, South applies—very vigorously, at least in its principle—the validation method by means of additional, independent data: he compares his percentages with those one can find on a Newfoundland site where three different sectors had been dug by Edward Jelks.[98] One could say much about the way in which the test is carried out: without going as far as "simulating" all the data needed for the test, as Schiffer did, he allows himself—when he does not have the necessary data—to "extrapolate" them . . . from his own data! But the fact remains that, for once, one sees the theoretical validation actually carried out. And it confirms his pattern, once it's been given a nudge—that is, providing that South carries out one of those data "adjustments" to which he is so accustomed[99]; but still, let's admit that the Carolina artifact pattern has been formally tested.

However, its "applicable range" is not very great; as soon as one leaves Carolina for the "frontier" region, the pattern is no longer applicable: two percentages are inverted! At Brunswick itself, a different house corresponds to neither pattern. It looks as if the validation of hypotheses may not have all the virtues attributed to it. The validation of a consequence shows that it is possible but does not necessarily mean that the proposition from which it is derived is true. As Karl Popper showed, it is only if a consequence is invalidated that the truth of the initial proposition can be questioned: only a negative demonstration counts. To be validated, a proposition has to be confirmed many times. Already in 1971 the three authors of *Explanation in Archeology* were discussing the problem of how a hypothesis could be considered "adequately" confirmed. They proposed—in order to remove the handicap of unconfirmed points—that implications had to be "necessary" (if the large jars expected to be found in the small rooms of a pueblo are not found there, the implication was not necessary: it does not mean they had never been there, they may have been removed).[100] In 1974, Plog returned to this question: the solution is not to pile up validations of one single hypothesis but to vary the *type* of hypotheses that one tests.[101]

The New Archeologists, in their turn, are coming up against a problem that is as old as the hills, one which only their congenital naïveté had concealed from them until now: that of reasoning.

But it does not matter very much because the validation of hypotheses—and we have seen how they have carried it out—is only a minor objective; behind it lurks an aim of a higher order. What they really want to attain is not so much explanations confirmed by hypothesis testing, but laws which explain the explanations.

3   Laws

Laws

For the New Archeology, the notion (the concept) of laws is central. Binford declared this right from the start, without beating about the bush: "We were searching for laws."[1] In 1968: "Our ultimate goal is the formulation of laws"; in 1972: "insofar as ... our goals ... are ... understanding of the events and the people which are responsible for the production of the archaeological record," we need a "nomothetic" archaeology (that is to say, one which establishes laws).[2] Again in 1978: "If we accept the goal of explaining our observations, then what is needed? We clearly need ... *laws.*"[3] I could give many other examples. The disciples are not backward in coming forward: "[We] have made the formulation ... of laws our goal"; and they add, "There are sound reasons for believing that such universal laws exist" in archaeology; and "if laws are our goal ..."[4] In the same way, the three authors of *Explanation in Archeology,* Patty J. Watson, Steven A. LeBlanc, and Charles L. Redman, start with a fanfare: "A basic goal of scientific archeology is ... to establish general laws."[5] Where Hill seems to be an exception to the rule and scarcely uses the word "law" (although nothing in his work gainsays this concept; indeed, on the contrary, this notion actually underlies his procedure),[6] in Schiffer's work on the other hand the concept is omnipresent. The different "strategies" that he distinguishes involve the notion of law, and the integration of previous archaeology into the new "depends on making explicit the multiple roles of laws in archeological research."[7] I shall return to this idea and examine it at some length. In 1977, South is still upholding exactly the same point of view; "The explanation of why these lawlike regularities exist is the goal of archeology," he states, and his Carolina artifact pattern, already mentioned above, is finally expressed by a "law."[8]

In a significant way the concept of law seems to play a less important role in English New Archeology, between the "models" on the one hand and general theory on the other, whether it be in the work of Clarke[9] or (especially) of Renfrew.[10] But, as we shall see, it only *appears* to be absent from this work, since the theory implies it, and a validated model can be considered a law.[11] Moreover, it is understood that if archaeology must become scientific, then scientific laws must be its pillars: the demonstration of laws is linked to the progress of science.

The search for laws is closely tied to the hypothetico-deductive or "logico-deductive" method and its testing of hypotheses: in a sense, they are one and the same, because the testing of a hypothesis transforms it, in a way, into a law. As Binford says in his 1967 reply to an article by K. C. Chang, "it is in the testing of hypotheses ... that we can raise our hypotheses to the level of general laws of culture."[12] And reciprocally, it is laws that allow one to explain observations scientifically because they enable one to see an isolated phenomenon as a particular example of a more general phenomenon: archaeology subsumes "particular explanations under universal laws," say Fritz and Plog; "Explanation ... means subsumption of a phenomenon under a general law," chorus the authors of *Explanation in Archeology*.[13] One finds in all this not just the influence but the actual presence of Carl Hempel's ideas—indeed, he is cited by name on innumerable occasions, and his work is sometimes summarized in detail. As we know, for this logician, one of the principal types of explanation, which he calls "deductivo-nomological [*sic*]" and which is as valid for a law as for a particular fact "to be explained" ("explanandum"), involves a *law* on the one hand and, on the other hand, particular specific and observed *conditions,* these two terms "explaining" ("explanans") what has to be explained.[14] Hempel states it more clearly himself: "The explanation of the occurrence of an event of some specific kind ... amounts to the statement that, according to certain general laws, a set of events of the kinds mentioned is regularly accompanied by an event of kind E" (E for "effect"); or again: "the fact under consideration can be inferred from certain other facts by means of specified general laws."[15] Whatever is or has been thought of these assertions, they were received by the New Archeologists as gospel and accepted as primary truths. This is their cross and their banner. Consequently, it follows that if a scientific explanation worthy of the name requires the use of a general law, then laws are indispensable.

Variations

The idea the New Archeologists formed of the concept of law seems to have evolved markedly through time. At the start they appear to have been satisfied with any constant, recurrence, or "regularity," any configuration that is evident or disclosed in observations, providing that it be duly validated: the terms "law" and "law-like proposition" often appear to be equivalent. Thus Hill, in connection with his excavation in the Santa Monica mountains of California, seems to equate "scientific law" and "law-like answers."[16] Again, in 1972, Binford, commenting on his analysis of a "mortuary complex" at Galley Pond, evokes "the assumptions or statements which function in the logic as 'laws.'"[17] Others, like Albert Spaulding, more or less assimilate laws and empirical generalizations—something Binford has always refused to do, even though others call them "experimental laws" and Hempel himself calls them "empirical laws."[18] On this point, as usual, he has been followed by his disciples.[19]

But it seems clear that the definition has varied: on the one hand, Binford submits that the validation of a hypothesis makes it a law: "Once hypotheses are explicitly stated, . . . if validated, such hypotheses would be raised to the status of laws."[20] The "level," be it high or low, of the hypothesis and thus of the law matters little; it is its validation that distinguishes it from an "empirical generalization" which will never be a law. On the other hand, Binford then proceeds to uphold a point of view which appears completely different, according to which, far from being reduced to a duly validated hypothesis, a law in reality is the logical consequence of a theory.[21] In this, he seems to join Clarke's position of 1972: hypotheses arise not from observed data but from a model which is "but one simplified . . . expression of a theory"[22]—thus, in a word, from a theory. Here perhaps we have not so much a contradiction as a distinction between two types of law: "empirical" laws (experimental), and "theoretical" laws.[23] Generalizations are only inductions; they are the implicit and often even unconscious laws of traditional archaeology.[24] It is these which have to be validated.[25]

One gets the impression that, for certain New Archeologists, these laws are frankly determinist. Indeed it is here that one can bring in the concept, or rather the term (so important in the eyes of New Archeology) of *process*, of the "processual" angle, however horrible the word may be—that is (if I understand it correctly), the functioning of a system, the "dynamic relationships . . . operative among the components of a system or between systematic components and the environment."[26] Moreover, these relationships are from cause to effect;[27] and the "laws of cultural dynamics,"[28] ultimate goal of the New Archeology, explain the effect by its cause, by what it has produced or "determined"—if not mechanically then at least in a way that is almost automatic, definite, calculable.[29]

And yet, right at the start, Spaulding had clearly distinguished—within the nomological or covering-law explanation, the "only . . . kind of serious explanation"—the deductive category, which "admits of no exceptions"; the causal type, in which antecedents are "sufficient to produce that which is to be explained"; the complete type (that of universal laws); and, on the other hand, the "probabilistic-statistical" (or inductive) laws, which have "the form of a frequency distribution"; noncausal laws of coexistence (for example, Mariotte's law, pendular law); and finally, partial laws, which do not account for a particular phenomenon. And for him, the laws which are valid for archaeology as he understands it are clearly partial and probabilistic-statistical laws rather than deductive and complete laws.[30] In the same way, for Clarke, among mathematical analogue models (capable of being tested and thus transformed into laws), which are symbolic, the proper mathematical and determinist models, which assume that all known data and factors can be expressed exactly, contrast with statistical models which take account of fluctuations, of variations in the results of an experimental test or in a sample, by including an error component. They contrast especially with "stochastic" (conjectural) models which incorporate a specific random process capable of fully reproducing multiple factors which otherwise are nonspecifiable (to a value *A* corresponds only a probable value of another variable) and which are therefore particularly well adapted to archaeological situations.[31] That said, once an alternative has been decided upon, determinism comes into force.[32]

It is certainly the case that the laws that are demanded and sought for explicitly scientific explanation in archaeology are not any old laws: they are not mathematical theorems, nor the laws of physics or astrophysics, nor even the laws of biology, let alone historical or even sociological "laws": they are anthropological laws and, more precisely, the laws of past human behavior. For the American New Archeologists this goes without saying, and it is a choice they rarely think of justifying in an explicit way, though at first sight it shocks Europeans whose prejudices toward English "behaviourism" or American "behaviorism" are well known.[33] The declaration by Gordon R. Willey and Philip Phillips in 1958, "American archaeology is anthropology or it is nothing,"[34] is repeated emulously. "We must shoulder our full share of responsibility within anthropology," says Binford in 1962. "We all want . . . to contribute to the knowledge of laws of human behavior," echo Fritz and Plog. The laws that we must and can formulate, Binford states in 1968, deal "with the dynamics of systemic functioning and the evolution of cultural systems."[35] Hill repeats it in 1972: "Whether we admit it or not, most archaeologists are trying to describe and explain various aspects of prehistoric human behavior." "Prehistory derives research problems . . . as a result of concern with the development of behaviour," says Glynn Isaac.[36] Schiffer's book is entitled *Behavioral Archeology*. One could pile up more quotations ad infinitum.[37]

Since these are laws, they have to be valid for all periods and all parts of the globe. Binford reproaches Braidwood for an explanation which is valid only for western Europe and not for the Near East.[38] "Laws are timeless and spaceless"; they are "atemporal, aspatial," repeats Schiffer in 1976.[39] "The basic tenets of the [archaeological] discipline," says Clarke, must have "a form as appropriate in Peru as Persia, Australia as Alaska, Sweden as Scotland, on material from the twentieth millennium B.C. to the second millennium A.D."[40] In short, they must be universal.

Fine. It's a grandiose objective, and the means of attaining it follow from the definition of laws. So just what are the laws of human behavior that are deemed indispensable to the scientific explanation of archaeological phenomena? What anthropological laws—be they universal or not, determinist or statistical, no matter how they are obtained—is the New Archeology setting before us so that we can at last explain archaeological data scientifically?

No Laws

In 1968, wishing to demonstrate that anthropology is a science and that its development is not "permanently arrested," Spaulding was declaring that refutation was possible "only by the discovery of more laws or empirical generalizations."[41] To support this view he cited—in addition to social anthropology—the articles of the 1965 Denver symposium. But this is flying in the face of the facts: if you apply to the New Archeology what he says about anthropology, the laws discovered are not very conspicuous, and their abundance is not their most obvious feature. This is not the miracle of Cana. As usual, and despite his insistence on the need for laws, Binford conspicuously fails to come up with any. What he says in 1972 about systemic models ("Thus far

... I have not offered systems-specific models," whereas he has just stressed their importance[42]) is even more applicable to laws: one cannot find any in his writings. Except for a reminder of the law of cultural dominance[43] (which is not his—it is an anthropological or sociological law, not an archaeological law), one looks in vain for examples (or even a single example) of a specifically archaeological law in *New Perspectives*. It's all very well for Fritz and Plog, two years later in 1970, to stress the implicit and undemonstrated nature of the laws that are used, consciously or not, by all archaeologists (they take the trouble to search for them and make them explicit), and to describe at length the method that must be applied: they do not apply it effectively themselves and do not offer any examples of a validated law.[44] The situation scarcely seems to have changed a year later, and it is in a quite crestfallen tone that the *Explanation in Archeology* trio—having, as usual, stressed the fundamental and essential nature of laws, which alone permit one to explain or "predict"—state, that "However, no such culture processual law has yet been confirmed."[45] In 1972, archaeological laws are no more numerous in *An Archaeological Perspective*; and the same year Renfrew, recalling Binford's aim of four years earlier, is forced to recognize that "Archaeology has . . . so far failed to formulate universal laws."[46] The following year, Charles G. Morgan concludes a harsh critique of the New Archeology with these words: "Nothing which could plausibly be construed as a cross-cultural law or law of cultural change has yet emerged"; "All this was true," Lev Klejn admits in reference to Morgan, although not agreeing with all his points.[47] One can look at the index of each of Clarke's three volumes—the word "law" doesn't appear in that of 1977 any more than it does in that of 1972 or 1968. There is a flagrant absence of these much vaunted laws.

Mickey Mouse Laws

And yet, the insistence with which the role of laws had been highlighted was such that the New Archeologists couldn't fail to discover a few and present them to the dazzled scientific community. Alas! They were tiresome truisms and have been called "Mickey Mouse laws."[48] "As the population of a site increases, the number of storage pits will go up," or "the size of a Bushman site is directly proportional to the number of houses on it"! "Undeniable truths", as Kent V. Flannery said with savage irony.[49] They are of the same order as the old adage "when you're going forward you're not going backward," or "just before his death he was still alive."

On a level which is a little higher, however, one could cite the contribution of Mark P. Leone[50] which touches on the eternal problem of the pueblos, already studied by William A. Longacre and by Hill. The law proposed by Leone can be formulated as follows: increasing dependence on agriculture (as opposed to hunting and gathering) increases the "social distance" (measured by the "variability" of ceramic styles) between the minimal economic units (the "families"). Indeed, one can postulate that pottery is made, and the traditions in this craft passed on, by women. And one observes that when women come from another village, the pottery is more variable than in an endogamous structure. It is therefore necessary to establish and demonstrate this still hypothetical law, to turn it eventually into a confirmed law. Leone applies the method: if dependence on agriculture increases effectively, then the result, he infers, must be a decreased variability in the toolkits. So he examines the types of grinders (*manos*), projectile points, and scrapers that can be found in a dozen sites including the one he is excavating; he quantifies his data, constructs graphs, and establishes that the types covary among themselves and with pottery. Subject to these quantifications being correct, the consequence deduced from the initial hypothesis is confirmed: these nearly simultaneous fluctuations show well that as agriculture develops, variability in pottery does too, and endogamy increases. "Thus . . . his . . . law is confirmed." There is no need at all to stress here the childish nature of the demonstration (variability in pottery can be explained in many other ways); this example is characteristic enough.[51] Who would dare rely, who has ever relied on a "law" like this?[52]

Consequently, the New Archeologists tried to do better. The cruel lack of laws—which were declared indispensable to true archaeological "explanation" but were recognized as being still extremely rare in 1971 by Watson, LeBlanc, and Redman—constituted a challenge that could hardly fail to be taken up at some point. Leaving aside a certain number of more or less sporadic and more or less comical attempts (the "Mickey Mouse laws" mentioned earlier), one of the most positive and most systematic procedures is that of Schiffer in his *Behavioral Archeology* of 1976.[53]

Schiffer's Laws

Indeed, what Schiffer presents us with here is not just some isolated law, but a whole series of laws, linked to each other and thus virtually capable of being systematized into a body of theory, and involving not minor problems but a certain number of questions essential to all archaeological research: for example, those which involve and inter-relate all remains of different types that were discarded or abandoned on the spot; all objects that were actually manufactured or used on a site; the frequency of their use or discard; their chronology; the number of "houses" occupied, and so forth. It is obvious that if any one of these terms could be learned from the others in a sufficiently exact way, it would be a great advantage. Well, Schiffer offers us mathematical, calculable relationships. So it seems to me that it is worth examining in detail the way in which he establishes his relationships or "laws" of cultural "transformations" (of material formerly in use that has now become archaeological), as he calls them: let's remember that this is a fundamental element of the New Archeology's epistemology and methodology. I think readers will be rewarded for their pains and for the minimum of attention that is necessary. Don't let the mathematical look of the equations impress you. They're as easy as can be.

Schiffer starts by defining a certain number of factors which, quite obviously, are involved in any argument of this type. The following initials are used:

T = total
D = discard (objects discarded)
t = time (duration of discard)
F = total frequency
f = frequency by "household"
c = number of "households"

M = manufacture
p = production
S = full total (of objects under consideration)
L = uselife of an object
U = use
b = number ± of uses
k = number of these objects in a "household"

(By "household," of course, he means the minimal subunit which, grouped, constitutes a community). Having set this out, Schiffer starts by a series of four "equations" which are nothing other than "definitions" expressing current notions in a mathematical form: thus, the total number of artifacts, T_p, through time t, is equal to the rate of manufacture, F_p, multiplied by t:

$$T_p = F_p t \tag{1}$$

and likewise the total number of discarded objects, T_D, is obviously the product of the frequency of discard, F_D, and the time during which this discard occurred, t. So one can set out:

$$T_D = F_D t. \tag{2}$$

In the same way one can see that total frequency of discard, F_D, is nothing other than the frequency of partial discards from each household multiplied by the number of these households:

$$F_D = f_D c, \tag{3}$$

This is patently obvious. So, then, returning to the total of discarded objects, T_D, one can combine the two previous expressions (2) and (3) and obtain the following "important expression":

$$T_D = f_D t c. \tag{4}$$

Schiffer illustrates this equation in a very clear way by means of the following example: if five households discard three manos per year for five years, then "a total of 75 manos will be discarded": one cannot argue with that.

Schiffer is now in a position to continue, and he is going to propose a "fundamental equation" which allows one to calculate T_D—a community's total discard during time t—in a different way, by means of two other factors which have not yet arisen: the total of objects, of the type under consideration, used on the site (S), and the "uselife" (L) of each of these objects. It is indeed clear that the longer an object lasts, the less often it will be thrown away: in other words, the frequency of discard and of uselife vary inversely, and this can be expressed by the equation: $T_D = f(1/L)$—that is, T_D is an inverse function of L. On the other hand, the greater the total number of objects of this type used on this site, the more the discard rate will increase; it will vary proportionally: $T_D = f(S)$. And of course, the longer the time during which this process takes place, the greater the total number of discards: another directly proportional variation: $T_D = f(t)$. Consequently, by combining these three different expressions of the same T_D, one obtains the following "law":

$$T_D = \frac{St}{L}. \tag{5}$$

The total of discarded objects equals the total of objects of this type present on the site divided by their uselife and multiplied by the time that has passed (these last two measurements being, of course, in the same units—days, months, years). It's not $e = mc^2$, but it's not far off. Here at last is an indisputable and fundamental law. The New Archeology has kept its promises—at least, to all appearances.

As a matter of fact, Schiffer immediately specifies that since S and L are not and cannot be "absolute" values but are statistical, this is a

statistical law, a fact which does not of course diminish its interest, or
its value. He also adds—and this is quite another problem—that the
law and the corollaries he is shortly going to derive from it presuppose
four conditions which he formulates very explicitly: the first is that
during the period of time under consideration the uselife of the object
be supposed constant; the second is that the general total of these objects also remain constant, of course; the third, that no reuse, gift,
theft, trade, and so forth should intervene; finally, that there should be
no import or export. If all of that is accepted, then the law is valid. If,
for example, in a prehistoric community there is a total of fifteen
scrapers ($E = 15$), each of which can be used for an average of six
months, then in four years 120 scrapers will be thrown away. One
couldn't put it better.

One can now move on. For example, by combining equations (2)
and (5), which both express T_D in different ways, or, if you prefer, by
replacing T_D in equation (5) by its definition in which time and the
total discard frequency appear, one immediately obtains: $F_D t = \dfrac{St}{L}$,
and, by "simplifying" the two terms of this equation, each of which
features t,

$$F_D = \frac{S}{L}. \tag{6}$$

A "useful" relationship, Schiffer tells us; and he gives us this example.
A total (S) of four objects of a given type, with an average uselife (L)
of two years each, will be thrown away at a rate of two per year on
average. So one can "predict" the rate of discard and, consequently,
knowing the number of discards, calculate either the total number of
objects of this type present on the site or their possible uselife. Isn't
that grand? Here's something that was way out of reach of "traditional" archaeology. This is what the New Archeology has brought us.

But Schiffer is not going to be satisfied with this—far from it. With
the aim now of bringing in the variables which condition the use of the
objects under consideration, such as the use frequency of the objects,
F_U (and no longer the frequency of discard, as previously), and the
average number of possible uses for each object (b), which are linked
by the expression $L = \dfrac{b}{F_U}$ (because it is obvious that an object's uselife
is all the greater the more times it can be used, and shorter the more
often one uses it), he is going to deduce no less than five fundamental
laws or relationships. Without henceforth going into too much detail,

I present them below: by replacing L in (5) by the expression that I have just given, one obtains $T_D = \dfrac{St}{b/F_U}$, that is, the following "law":

$$T_D = \frac{StF_U}{b}. \tag{8}$$

Example: if, in a prehistoric community, they use three axes 150 times per year in all, each ax capable of being used an average of twenty-five times in succession, then in five years they will throw away $\dfrac{3 \times 5 \times 150}{25} = 90$ axes. Q.E.D.

But since S can be replaced by the number of objects k present in a household, multiplied by the number of households c ($S = kc$), equation (5) becomes:

$$T_D = \frac{kct}{l}. \tag{10}$$

This new "law" is illustrated thus: if, in each of the five households of a village, they use two jars with an average uselife of one year, then in ten years they will get rid of $\dfrac{2 \times 5 \times 10}{1} = 100$ jars.

If you're interested more particularly in the *rate* of discard, then easy transpositions allow you to measure the different variables. Thus, by combining equations (2) and (8), you get $F_D t = (SF_U t)/b$, and if you simplify by eliminating factor t,

$$F_D = \frac{SF_U}{b}, \tag{11}$$

a "fundamental" equation giving the rate of discard as a function of the pattern of use of the object under consideration. If one now recalls that $S = kc$, then this equation (11) becomes

$$F_D = \frac{kcF_U}{b}, \tag{12}$$

which quite simply expresses the rate of discard as a function of the variables affecting the "social units," the "households" (their number, and the number of objects of this type that each of them contains). If, in each of the fifteen households of a village, they use one razor blade every day, and if it can be used fifteen times in succession, then they will throw away an average of one razor blade per day ($\frac{1 \times 15 \times 1}{15}$). This can be written in a simpler way, since, as we've seen above, F_U/b is equal to the reciprocal of $L(\,1/L)$,

$$F_D = \frac{kc}{L}. \tag{13}$$

Anyone who has had the patience to read and follow the demonstration this far must recognize that the result is impressive: in just a few minutes almost a dozen laws have been established that touch on fundamental archaeological processes. It makes you wonder how they weren't discovered earlier! At any rate, in the applications that the author promises will be given in the following part of his book, one can expect sensational results, of a rigor and a precision unequaled until now.

Critique

However, it is advisable to recall the restrictions that Schiffer himself placed on his theory: the laws have only a statistical value, and they assume that a certain number of conditions are fulfilled: but are these conditions the slightest bit "realistic"? Is it probable, on an archaeological site of the usual type—the sort that all archaeologists know— that the "uselife" of the objects remains constant, and, what is more, that their total number will not vary? And after all, on top of all that, is it conceivable that no internal exchange (reuse, "change of owner," etc.) or external exchange (import or export) will take place with regard to the type of object under consideration? And there is worse to come.

If you care to take a close look at Schiffer's procedure, you will see that it "mathematizes" a series of processes in which all terms are assumed to be known: he acts as if one knew the totals of manufactured objects, discards, households, the exact duration of the process (of occupation), the uselife of the objects (or the number of uses to which they can be put), and the rates of manufacture, of use, and of discard. But in the huge majority of cases these data are not known in any exact or even approximate way. No doubt one can determine the average number of objects of a given type in a household (k) which is involved in equation (10). But apart from this factor, how can one estimate the uselife, even as an average, of a utensil in the period under consideration? Present-day experimental reproduction has every chance of providing very misleading results.[54] How can one know with even a minimum of precision the duration of an occupation, other than in exceptional cases? In consequence, all the calculations of frequency or rate involving the time factor are impossible. Finally, is one ever sure of knowing the total number of "households" in a habitation? Can one ever be certain that one or several households a little apart from the others, or isolated, did not contribute to the refuse deposit? And, especially, by way of consequence, how can one imagine that one has gained possession of the full total of discarded objects? The only thing one can be sure of is the total of objects found; but—and Schiffer says this himself—that's not the same thing. The total of objects found is most certainly less than the total of objects that existed of old, and the proportion found is unknown. Schiffer's suggestion that you can "estimate" this proportion is an illusion—or a cop-out.[55]

Thus, even if Schiffer's equations are correct, they are not of much use. In order for them to be useful it would be necessary—since these are all first degree algebraic equations—to know the value of all the factors except one, which could then be calculated. What I have just said shows that this can (almost) never be the case. It is all theoretical, idealized. The examples provided are demonstrative only for the specific reason that all the data are quantified: their probative value seems clear, but it is only illusory. Of course, no concrete example is provided in support. It all amounts to this—and here one clearly recognizes the New Archeology: that if only one thing is unknown, then one can calculate it. And no doubt it quite often boils down to this: if nothing is unknown, then one knows everything. And vice versa.

Waste Products Law

The same criticism applies to the calculation of the amount of waste production, which follows on from the preceding equations. The demonstration of Schiffer's mistake is almost amusing. Certainly, if one could know, for example, the total production of a potter's kiln from the number of firing failures, it would be extremely interesting. But how does Schiffer proceed? One can hardly believe one's eyes. The frequency of waste production, he tells us, is nothing other than the global frequency of manufacture of the objects under consideration affected by a coefficient k_1 (equal to the relationship of the total waste production to the total production):

$$F_{Mw} = F_{Ma}k_1, \tag{14}$$

If one recalls the first equation ($T_p = F_p t$) and combines it with equation (14), thus expressing F_{Mw} as T_w/t, one obtains:

$$T_w = F_{Ma} k_1 t, \tag{15}$$

This equation provides the total that is being sought—the total waste production: it equals the frequency of manufacture multiplied both by the coefficient of waste in relation to this production and by time. Q.E.D.

There is just one little snag: even assuming that you know time t, that is, the duration of the operation, you don't know the waste/total coefficient: this is precisely what you're trying to find!

Imperturbable, Schiffer continues: since the frequency of manufacture, multiplied by time, gives this total production (it is the definition: $F_p t = T_p$), equation (15) becomes: $T_w = T_a k_1$. An "important relationship," he says with a straight face. Indeed, one can write it as: $k_1 = \dfrac{T_w}{T_a}$, which is nothing other than the definition of k_1 (see above) ! We're back at the starting point; we're wallowing in pure tautology; we're going round in circles.

Schiffer doesn't stop after such a good start, and he next lines up a dozen supplementary equations (17–28) on the duration of processes: this is indeed a problem, as I have pointed out. He proceeds in the same way, and I will spare the reader all the details. Suffice it to say that Schiffer—after having learned in passing that "no use or discard of an element can occur before manufacture" (which is perfectly correct and constitutes a principle that is universally used in chronology) or that "discard begins when an appreciable quantity of the element is no longer found suitable for use," which is equally undeniable—having repeated the same thing several times in barely different forms, and once more having assumed that all data (initial and final) are known, triumphantly reaches the conclusion that an object's manufacture span and discard span are of equal duration, whereas this object's total use span is, or can be, longer: in other words, you can go on using a tool after the end of its manufacture and until it is thrown away! Nobody has ever disputed this;[56] it's hard to believe anyone ever will.

When one has been promised "a respectable number of quantitative archeological laws,"[57] one has some cause for disappointment. The quantification, the mathematization of current concepts, is mere eyewash. It's a bluff. What we have been shown is amateur algebra, joke mathematics—the archaeological equivalent of a toy chemistry set. It's useless and can never be anything else; it teaches nothing.

South's Law

And yet Schiffer has had emulators, and his attempt is not an isolated case. Thus South, having shown with his Carolina artifact pattern (see above, pp. 43–44) the observed regularity of the percentages of different types of objects found on sites, points out that these regularities and this variability can be generalized in the form of a "law" which he formulates as follows: "The by-product [i.e., the remains found] of a specified activity has a consistent frequency relationship to that of all other activities in direct proportion to their organized integration."[58] In other words, it all goes together, and, insofar as the different activities are integrated, the discard frequency of one is linked to that of another. He gives an example and even an application: the quantity of nails, hinges, spikes, glass, and so forth found is proportional to the surface of the ancient structure. If the latter has completely disappeared, therefore, one can nevertheless calculate its surface. At Brunswick Town, for example, the "architectural" remains and the square footage of the houses are known, and the floor-space measurement represents about 16 percent (0.16) of the number of these remains. Reciprocally, in consequence, one simply needs to multiply the number of these remains by 0.16 to obtain the floor space. So the law is quantified and usable. But who would dare to calculate the floor space of a vanished structure in this way? The sources of error are obvious. And of course, in South's own opinion, even if the law, unquantified, is theoretically valid for other sites, its quantified form, the only one that can be used, is valid only for Brunswick, if that! So the law does not keep its promises in any way. Moreover, South's "law" had already been formulated in a different form by Schiffer the previous year: "The quantities of different elements produced are in constant proportion to one another."[59] But that assumes that the rate of activity (the frequency of manufacture) remains constant: it would seem that this needs to be demonstrated. And besides, Schiffer, who was under no illusions, concluded that these ratios were "not always so constant" since the discard rate also varies.[60] So it is yet another disappointment.

Finally, it seems clear that apart from the "laws"—implicit or, for that matter, sometimes explicit—of traditional archaeology, which it submits are not demonstrated, almost the only laws that the New Archeology can put forward are those it borrows, ready-made, from anthropology: like the law of cultural dominance, quoted by Binford in 1968 in connection with the origin of agriculture, or that of the "amplification of deviation," cited, for example, by Renfrew in connection with his "multiplier effect" and derived from the work of Magoroh Maruyama.[61] Others are borrowed from sociology, like those mentioned by Klejn: the law of minimum effort, or of minimum risk; and yet others borrowed from biology, like the law of natural selection, or the law of biotic potential,[62] laws which Klejn declares are "discouragingly trivial," adding that they are not respected by social factors.

The "law and order" archaeologists too, in their field, have striven to impose their order far more than they have actually succeeded in elaborating the laws which they declared at the start to be utterly indispensable. In 1972 Renfrew, realizing the New Archeology's failure on this point, was already adding that it "has . . . so far failed to formulate universal laws, and it seems unlikely that it will be able to do so."[63] In 1980, Robert C. Dunnell, in his review of the preceding year, scarcely mentions the problem of laws; he quotes Schiffer and stresses his contradictions, and, with regard to ethnoarchaeology, the New Archeology's latest incarnation, he does not hesitate to write, "the principal goals, . . . the establishment of behavioral correlates and the development of laws relating the interaction of behavior and material culture, have been rudimentarily realized at best. There may be serious doubt that they can be realized at all."[64]

The hypotheses are not validated, the laws are slow in coming: so what? In a very typical way the New Archeology, that new Proteus, is going to change its mind quite shamelessly. It seems we got it all wrong. It is not the laws that really counted. And besides, there was some mistake about their real nature. As a finale in the variations on the notion of law, South was already saying in 1977: "Understanding does not come until we ask why the law is seen to be applicable?"[65] The following year, Dwight W. Read and Steven A. LeBlanc, in an article to which I will return soon, criticize both the exaggeration of the role attributed to hypothesis testing as a criterion of scientific procedure *and* the search for laws for their own sake because laws, which are expected to confirm hypotheses, have to be confirmed themselves. And if this is done by hypothetico-deductive reasoning, then the argument is circular.[66] One could make the timid suggestion here that it might perhaps have been better to notice this before. But the same year Binford himself enters the lists, more definitive than ever—at any rate, as much as before when he was saying the opposite: in his critique of the above article he reveals (as had Clarke in 1972) that laws are not to be sought or "discovered" because they have to be "invented" (as Fritz and Plog had already said in 1970[67]) in a creative way; on the other hand, since each law has to be explained by a more general law, and so on right up to obvious axioms, a law must be a consequence logically deduced from a theory.[68] An almost Copernican U-turn. After the hypothetico-deductive method, after the so-called laws—OK, theories it is!

4 Theories

Theories

In 1962 Binford was already denouncing the "theoretical vacuum" of traditional archaeology.[1] But for his own part he immediately took up a position in the framework of anthropology, and he accepted and supported the application of systems theory to archaeology. The theory was not new; only its introduction into archaeological research was revolutionary.[2] On the other hand, Clarke, in 1968, in the first lines of *Analytical Archaeology,* denounces the lack of "a body of central theory capable of synthesizing the general regularities within its data. . . . Archaeologists do not agree upon central theory," and they are "lacking an explicit theory." What ought to be done is "to relate analytical archaeology to archaeological central theory."[3] Four years later the definition he gives of models is that they "relate observations to theoretical ideas."[4] Preoccupation with theory is no less strong with Renfrew who—though judging the ecological view to be ill-adapted after the subsistence economy stage—adopts and refines systems theory: "Surely," he says, "one feels there must be some central, core idea, some unifying concept to make our definition of civilisations something more than a polythetic bundle of apparently ill-assorted culture traits."[5] The same year, Hill stresses "the importance of theory," which, for him as for the authors of *Explanation in Archeology,* can only be systemic.[6] That is still, at this time, Binford's point of view—but though he harshly criticizes the theory underlying traditional procedure[7] he is still very far from according the construction of a specifically archaeological theory the importance that he is soon going to attach to it.

Central Theory, Middle-Range Theory

In effect, as I have said, since unvalidated empirical generalizations have never been laws, and since laws are no longer simple validated generalizations, theories are now, in a way, the source of laws: laws have to be logically deduced from theories—not discovered by empirical observation, but imagined, in the most creative sense of the word; and the only role of generalizations is to confirm laws.[8] In a more precise way, Dwight W. Read and Steven A. LeBlanc—also in 1978—repeat that theories are not "experimental" (or universal) laws, but "systematic connections between experimental laws about qualitatively disparate subject matters."[9] Theory, in a word, is a synthesis of different laws, and it is from theory that the latter derive their strength.

As they understand it, all theories are not situated at the same "level" of generality. There can be very specific theories, theories of a very high level, and intermediate theories: Binford especially, in 1977, made himself the advocate not just of "general" theory but of "middle-range theory," that is, "ideas and theories . . . regarding the formation processes of the archaeological record" (those "transformations," cultural or noncultural, in which Schiffer had already taken an interest). "Without the development of a body of theory treating the relationships between statics" (present) "and dynamics" (past) prevalent in the archaeological world, "no real progress will be forthcoming."[10] So we've been warned.

Now that this new line of approach has been defined in this way, we are, as usual, going to see what becomes of it in practice.

As a matter of fact, applications are a bit thin on the ground. As Binford himself states with some bitterness, leaving aside those people who are opposed to the principle itself and those who agree with it but who have not come up with any original theory, "thus far little progress has been made, although many persons have seen the challenge and accepted it."[11] As we shall see, he will therefore feel obliged to mount the battlements in person. However, Read provides a pretty characteristic example, on the very theme that had been the subject of ironic criticisms, which the New Archeologists clearly found hard to stomach: namely, the relationship between the size of a population and that of its habitation.

This application follows on from a theoretical article, which I have already cited, by Read and LeBlanc, and which seems to fit completely into the new approach I've mentioned, at least on the surface.[12] In this article the two authors advocate a new approach, that of "abstract theory" or "formal theory" founded not on universal laws, themselves confirmed by empirical data, but, first, on the definition of fundamental notions and of axioms; second, on a set of rules relating the "calculus" to the concrete observations; and, finally, on a model, or interpretation, which alone can confirm the theory's applicability to the real world. The example which follows is explicitly presented as an application of this formal theory of analytical organization.[13]

Read's Theory: Area of Habitation and Population

We had a good laugh at those Bushman sites whose surface area increased with the number of houses! This time, it is going to be nothing less than a *precise* relationship (meaning mathematical). The mockers are going to look silly. . . . And, as a matter of fact, the argumentation is worth following closely.

In accordance with the principles he has just expounded with Le-Blanc, Read starts by defining the theory's terms—as it happens, there are nine of them. One can summarize them as follows. The population of a habitation is the total of inhabitants in each residence location (house, hut). A *camp* (he's going to deal exclusively with this type of habitation) is a habitation in which the residence locations do not encroach on each other and are each occupied by a single "family"; what's more, it is neither a "village" nor a "city." (Just as an exercise, for the beauty of the thing, Read feels the need to give these very simple definitions in a mathematical form: for example, to say that residence areas don't overlap: $' r\cap r' = \emptyset$, for all distinct $(r, n_r) (r', n'_r)\in R '$, that is to say, for any residence r or r' containing n or n' inhabitants and constituting part of the whole of habitation R. As a matter of fact, one doesn't know if all this is done to make a favorable impression on readers, even at the risk of discouraging them, because these particular mathematical formulas don't crop up again afterward.) A village is not a city, and a city is neither a village nor a camp. Then Read decides to restrict himself to camps, for which he adds the following five secondary definitions. In a camp, two residence locations will be said to be "adjacent" if there is no other closer to them than they are to each other. (One has to admit this is obvious, like the preceding definitions.) Furthermore, a camp will be said to be "full" if all the residence locations touch, "uniform" if they all have the same surface area, "simple" if the residence locations form a circle around the center of the habitation, and "regular" if the three preceding conditions are fulfilled. I should make it clear that the habitation, no doubt based on the Bushman case, takes the form of a full circle, and the "residence locations" that of smaller circles inscribed in and tangential to the great habitation circle.

Next Read moves on to axioms: there are two, the first being that, in a habitation (and therefore in a camp), the spatial relationship of residence locations (concentric in this case) is independent of the population; the second, that the area of a residence location is proportional to the number of its inhabitants. Curiously, and in contradiction of the actual definition of the term, he points out at once that these axioms are not, perhaps, universally valid.

Then, from these axioms, and in accordance with the definitions he has put forward, he is going to deduce not, as a matter of fact, general propositions about habitation/population relationships, as one might expect, but properties specific to three possible models; he is going to consider these in succession, and compare them with data gathered by ethnographers. In the first model, for example, all residence locations touch, inside the circle that represents the habitation; in the second, on the other hand, the residence locations are separated by a constant distance, *l*. I shall not go into detail about the demonstration of these first two models: suffice it to say that the equation giving the surface area of the habitation from the population—an equation expressed by a "linear regression"—does not fit the ethnographic data, as plotted in a graph; or if the data fit (second model), the model nevertheless has to be rejected for certain reasons (in reality, camp areas decrease more rapidly than the model indicates). It is therefore necessary to produce a third model, and it is this one I am going to examine in a little more detail because it is the solution Read is going to retain. I would ask readers not to let themselves be impressed by the problem's mathematical formulation: in reality it is child's play, and the only two notions one needs to keep in mind are the circumference (2π multiplied by the radius; or, if you prefer, π multiplied by the diameter), and the area of the circle (π multiplied by the square of the radius)—these are elementary.

In this third model (fig. 2) the residence locations are once again spaced regularly within the habitation circle, but this time in such a way that the distance separating their points of tangency with the great circle is constant and equals *L*. It is assumed that there are *m* residence locations (six in the figure), each containing *n* inhabitants, so that the population $p = nm$. All that having been put forward, here is the demonstration: the great circle's circumference is equal to *L* multiplied by the number of residence locations (Lm), and so its radius can be expressed (since circumference equals $2\pi c$—*c* is the radius—therefore $c = \dfrac{Circ}{2\pi}$) by the equation:

$$c = Lm/2\pi, \tag{19}$$

or again (since population *p* is equal to *nm* [$p = nm$], then $m = \dfrac{p}{n}$) by

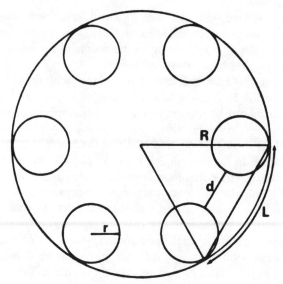

Fig. 2. Habitat and population: model of a Bushman camp. After D. W. Read, *Current Anthropology* 19 (1978): 316, figs. 3 and 5.

the equation: $c = Lp/2n\pi$, that is, if we turn $L/2n\pi$ into a single coefficient α,

$$C = \alpha p, \tag{20}$$

which gives the radius of the camp as a function of its total population.

But it is more interesting to express the camp's area (and no longer just its radius) as a function of population p. This is the goal of all this research. The camp area πc^2, Read tells us quite correctly, is: $a = L^2 p^2 / 4n^2\pi$, which, by grouping $L^2/4n^2\pi$ into a single coefficient β, becomes the following fundamental equation:

$$\alpha = \beta p^2, \tag{21}$$

which shows that, in the hypothesis of the distribution figuring in the third model, the dimensions of the habitation area increase in linear fashion like the square of the population. This is the equation of the theory. It fits the data of the ethnographer Polly Wiessner, and it is a confirmatory deterministic version of their intuitive conclusion, but for different reasons than Wiessner's. She had found a value of 0.5 for α, and 1.96 for β: now equation (21) enables one to predict an almost identical value of $\beta = 2$. In these conditions, $L = 10$ meters, which corresponds to what is observed: Bushman huts have a diameter of about four meters. The hypothesis that there was a constant relationship between camp area and size of population called for the determination of a fixed spatial relationship between residence locations: one sees that the simplest model did not fit the bill and that these camps were not "full" (adjoining residence locations); that the houses were not separated by a constant distance, but that the third model was the right one. These results were "not obvious": the equation was "not necessary." So it seems like a total success—even if the value of the results obtained for hunter-gatherer groups other than Bushmen still remains to be investigated. Therefore the conclusion is that axiomatic theories can indeed be constructed. One can only say, Bravo! Binford has not been crying in the wilderness.

Certainly, Read admits very honestly that his results do not contribute anything new and are limited by various restrictions: they assume, on the question of population figures, a certain demographic stability (but things are like this, *grosso modo*, he assures us); and the circular layout is a characteristic of hunter-gatherers, which is not always the case (but it is the case for the Bushmen). Certainly, he has also limited himself to dealing with camps, "but the results can easily be extended to villages and cities." [14]

Unfortunately, there is another problem.

Critique

The first thing that strikes one is this: the third model is presented to us as being fundamentally different from the second, which is rejected. But in reality they appear identical. What difference is there between a regular spacing of residence-location circles and a regular spacing of their points of tangency with the circumference enclosing them? It is absolutely the same thing (if the diameters don't change). This seems obvious, and the calculation gives l as a function of L, or vice versa. [15] So under these conditions, how is it that the third model doesn't arouse the same objections as the second?

This is not all; it is not even the most serious problem. If you care to examine the final equation (21) closely, and blow away the mathematical or pseudomathematical smokescreen, you find that it is only an identity! It says nothing other than: the surface area is the surface area. How is it obtained? With the classic formula of a circle's area, $a = \pi c^2$, but expressing c as a function of the population, that is $2\pi n$, which gives $a = \pi \dfrac{L^2 p^2}{4\pi^2 n^2}$, or, by simplifying the π, $a = \dfrac{L^2 p^2}{4n^2 \, \pi}$, which is what was set out for us.

But what does this mean? If you care to recall that population is equal to the product of the number of houses m by the number n of inhabitants ($p = mn$), the expression $a = \pi \dfrac{L^2 p^2}{4\pi^2 n^2}$ can be written $a = \pi \dfrac{L^2 m^2 n^2}{4\pi^2 n^2}$, or, by simplifying the n, $a = \pi \dfrac{Lm^2}{4\pi^2}$, which shows that the number of inhabitants of each house *is no longer involved*, that the only factors which appear in the reckoning are the number of houses m, and their distance apart L; that is, in fact, the circumference (which is Lm)!

It is no longer surprising, under these conditions, that the camp area increases like the square of the "population," because the circle's area quadruples when its radius and its circumference double.[16] In fact, population is not really represented; the average number of inhabitants in each house is not taken into account, only the number of houses. So the "law" doesn't concern the actual population (whether there is under- or over-population makes no difference) but only the area and the circumference.

In this way one can better understand why the calculation of β was a surprise (see above, p. 66).[17] But then we come back to the famous formula which provoked a smile and which was our starting point: the size of a Bushman site is directly proportional to the number of houses! Or, if you like: the more the circle grows, the more its area increases. The theoreticians of the New Archeology, who were already the champions at nontesting hypotheses, are—when it comes to laws or theories—very much the record holders in tautology of all kinds. The most curious thing is that apparently none of the nineteen authors of comments (which follow Read and LeBlanc's article and the appendix we've just studied), nor indeed Binford (who, contrary to what one might have thought, comments on and criticizes the two authors in a pretty harsh way) seems to have noticed this strict observance of the principle of identity, A is A. And yet there were some mathematicians among that lot.[18]

Binford and the Nunamiut Eskimo

The situation is grave; it is time to call out the guard and Binford himself. One year after his call for the construction of archaeological theories, in fact, he wanted to set an example and risk his own skin. Moreover, in the circumstances, this does not entail leaving the ever-present Bushmen, because the whole of Binford's article is written to counter the South African ethnology of John E. Yellen, who is guilty of all the sins and, in a word, is an "inductivist": the crime against the intellect.[19]

On the other hand, Binford once again returns to the type of problem he had already brought us in his article on the Lower Paleolithic (see above, p. 27): the meaning of variability of "assemblages." But he leads us very far off in space and time, since it is no longer a question of Western Europe or Africa but of Alaska, and no longer of prehistory but of the present day. In a way, this is, in fact, very significant; it is no longer a matter of actual archaeology but of "ethnoarchaeology," that is, "observations believed to be of interest to archaeologists but experienced in the context of an ongoing living system,"[20] a situation where shooting a rifle at empty beer cans plays an essential role.

The subject of the study is a temporary hunting stand, used for about three weeks every year by the Nunamiut Eskimo for the tracking of game. Prompted only by his courage, Binford spent no less than thirty-four hours there in two years (1971–72), including twenty-three hours in a single week the second year. One might wonder, as did Schiffer, whether, instead of freezing in the Arctic, Binford might not have done better to study an ordinary campsite on his home ground.[21] Be that as it may, it is from this site that he wanted to bring us back one of those archaeological theories whose lack is felt so cruelly. "This study," he tells us, "is an exercise in theory building."[22] It is his implementation of the wishes he formulated the previous year in the general introduction to *For Theory Building in Archaeology*, and he is going to apply the principles he advocated. That is to say, he is not going to indulge in empirical generalizations as Yellen did; he is not going to "seek" laws by trying to "discover" them; instead he is going to imagine a theory, create it, construct it, in a way, out of nothing. And the pride that he experiences through this exceeds all previous limits, apparently, in the realms of self-satisfaction. "The ideas are my inventions"; "my study has prompted by imagination [*sic*]"; and, what is more, "I have been able to imagine different patterns . . . that could be meaningfully interpreted if my imagined understanding . . . is correct." All of this is followed by the inevitable quotation from Hempel: "The transition from data to theory requires creative imagination; . . . theories are not derived from observed facts, but are invented in order to account for them."[23] So let's see how he proceeds.

His ethnographic account, it must be said, is very interesting. With regard to technological organization, for example, he observes that certain objects (coffee utensils, decks of cards, etc.) are left on site in a cache and are thus less numerous than if they had been brought for each stay. As for spatial organization, confined to three boulders between and around which the Nunamiut live, he noted five hearths, the choice of which depends, of course, on the wind; the men place themselves in a semicircle, backs to the wind, at 62 ± 6.8 cm from the hearth, and 33 ± 4 cm from each other (one can imagine Binford niggling over these measurements in the freezing cold): here they talk and eat their meals, but if necessary they can indulge in craft activity. On the other hand, other "activities" (including sleeping) occur in other places, without there being any exclusive specialization—at most, a statistical preference. As for getting rid of rubbish (what he calls the "disposal modes"), they can drop it, toss it over the shoulder, set it down, put it in a given place, or put it in a container that is then emptied elsewhere. Some of these hypotheses, moreover, can follow each other (a bone that has been sucked and thrown near the hearth can then be put in the rubbish container). To this one can add that they brush litter aside or move one object while looking for another. One can feel that nothing in all this is lacking in interest.

For Binford sees the three "dimensions" of behavior, which explain the site structure and the final disposition of remains. The first is that certain places are chosen to "optimize" a specific activity (e.g., observing game); the second is that technological organization is conditioned by the duration and intensity of the site's occupation (thus, the number of objects varies with the number of men); the third is that the size of the objects influences the choice of the disposal mode (one does not drop an empty beer bottle, one throws it). And just as the Three Musketeers are always a foursome, one final dimension is added to the other three—it seems that "the intensity of use was not evenly distributed among the recognized use areas. The various activities were not evenly distributed among the several areas."[24] Such are the "4 basic dimensions of potentially independent variability that interact."

But what does the theory Binford has created consist of? As a matter of fact, this is not brought out very clearly. It seems to consist of a series of propositions such as these: the more numerous the simultaneous activities, the more they will occur in separate places, because "it is impossible to imagine activities carried out simultaneously by different persons occurring in the identical space";[25] the proportion of craft activities decreases when the number of people present increases (to escape noise, one looks for a place away from it); activities interfere with each other, require more or less space, time, and participants, and produce more or less debris. Above all, if I understand Binford correctly, the variability observable in camp plans, in the sites' contents, is related to the different activities carried out there, and the latter are related to the seasons. As for the variability from one site to another, it is referable to differences of function; sites have a specific function: next to "residential" sites there are special-purpose sites.[26]

Against Yellen

These views are in complete opposition to those of Yellen, who thinks that identical tasks can, for the most part, be carried out in different places and, conversely, that the same place can be used for different tasks, the variation being explained by the social context (obviously, when there is no change in the "social context," the camp population remains the same). Yellen believes that "extractive" sites (i.e., where raw materials or energy are extracted, as opposed to "maintenance" sites where tools are made, etc.) leave no trace, unlike big camps; that there is no correlation with the seasons; that merely the number of occupants, or the duration of occupation, is the "cause" of a site's size! The "predictive" equations he offers are contradicted by the data, maintains Binford; if one used his equations, then among our Eskimo there should be a total of just under ten men: there are thirty-four; the occupation should last a little over a week: it lasts three weeks; there should be two families: there is not a single one! Finally, there should be a constant relation between the consumer demand and the debris left behind: however, the Nunamiut mainly consume dried meat, which leaves no trace, and the number of caribou killed has no relationship to the number of hunters and the duration of the hunt.[27] "How can 2 people," exclaims Binford, "reach such opposite conclusions" on such an identical theme? It is not at all because Eskimo are involved in the one case and Bushmen in the other: it is because, between Binford and Yellen, there are "extreme differences . . . in what we consider to be appropriate uses of empirical materials and the role of our thoughts versus our observations."[28] Yellen is just an "inductivist." His aim is to reach regularities, empirical generalizations: since the causes, in ethnography, are known from the start and the effects can be observed, as can the techniques that lead from the former to the latter, Yellen thinks he has the right to generalize, to infer a causal relation. But this is in no way an explanation: it is a simple description of the world, of appearances. Otherwise, why don't his "causes" work in the Eskimo case? He never isolated a cause!

Binford, on the other hand, has been "engaged in theory building": "We can build a theory of space use, and we can understand spatial patterning without recourse to vague notions of 'social context,'" and "only with understanding can we anticipate how observations will vary under changed conditions." He says it forcefully: "Progress can be made by seeking a processual understanding of the dynamics that produce different forms of archaeological patterning. It will not be achieved by trying to refine empirical generalizations, arguing that someone else is wrong because they have had different experiences, and fooling oneself into viewing empirical descriptions, no matter how complicated they may be, as explanations." [29]

Critique

As so often, when one reads the New Archeologists, one is left wondering whether one is seeing things. There is no point in Binford's cautioning the reader to "read what I have to say and to seek an appreciation," as he ought, "for what is attempted" so unforgettably, "rather than assuming," the poor wretch, "that he knows what I am doing and why" [30]; it is enough to leave one stupefied. For a start, who is saying that "someone else is wrong because they have had different experiences"? Yellen or Binford? But above all, Binford tirelessly reproaches Yellen for inferring inductive generalizations from his observations: yet what else is *he* doing? From one end of his article to the other he does exactly what he criticizes Yellen for.

Let's go back to what was said at the beginning. When Binford *observes* that the coffee set, the decks of cards and the anvils form part of the fixed furnishings, left or hidden on site, and he concludes from this that what he calls technological organization modifies remains where the activities might be the same; when he says—in his indescribable style—"we could expect that hunting stands which tended to vary in the modal group sizes would also vary in terms of the relative frequencies of activity-related archaeological debris," [31] what else is he doing but generalizing his observations? If words still have any meaning, he is the first to indulge in what he reproaches others for with so much acrimony: an empirical generalization. When he ascertains that sleeping and game watching always occur in two different places and that almost the same applies to rifle shooting or meals and conversations, whereas just less than 60 percent of card playing and craft activities occur in a distinct place, and when he then formulates the proposition that "spatial segregation of activities" defines the "patterns in the . . . remains," what is he doing except inferring a sort of general rule from observations, that is, generalizing his observations? One can take up all the points mentioned earlier, one by one, and the way he proceeds is always the same. And yet he loudly asserts the opposite—one would like to think he does so through blindness rather than dishonesty. But perhaps he might hammer home his point of view a little less violently if it were not problematic. Once again, no doubt, we'll be accused of misunderstanding him, of not having grasped the subtlety of his approach, of having missed the bus. And yet the reader can only take him at his word: read him and seek an appreciation.

In these circumstances, one can better understand the haziness of the theory and the contradictions in the argument: are certain places specifically reserved for a certain activity, or are they not? Yes and no. Binford says one thing and its opposite. Sleeping and game watching are allotted to two distinct places, but one of these two is also used for almost all the target shooting and more than half the craft activity: Binford concludes from this that activities are irregularly distributed among the different areas. But he also says that the segregation of activities is reflected in the patterning of the remains, that certain locations are chosen for a particular activity. All this is very confused, and his distinction between simultaneous and successive activities seems specious: while it is obvious that two activities cannot take place simultaneously on the same exact spot, they can take place in immediate proximity to each other. He is making false accusations against Yellen, whose conclusions are not so different (the same activity in different places, different activities in a single place), and when they diverge (presence of a nuclear family, search for daily and not seasonal means of subsistence, etc.) one might perhaps allow, despite what Binford has to say about it—that the difference in climate and general conditions between Africa and Alaska has some influence here.

Binford claims the merit of having "tried to move in (the) direction" of theory building; but although he assures us that he has not, in any way, summarized empirical experience [sic], or sought empirical generalizations, or used inductive arguments or arguments derived from ethnographic analogy (that beats everything!), in fact he has done nothing else. What is more, he does not derive any "laws" from this middle-range "theory": "I am not saying that all men will conduct the same activities in hunting camps" is an unexpected conclusion when one is aspiring to the deduction of laws from a theory.[32] And of course, true to his habits, Binford doesn't test any of his propositions, and he concludes with his usual briskness that all these are merely "hints, ideas to be explored in hopes of recognizing or inventing variables that could be used to explore causal relationships between activities and their organization in space"[33]—which, unless I am mistaken, was the initial aim of his research.

So, one year after having clamored loudly for theory building, this is what the pope of American and Americanist New Archeology offers us. We are entitled to feel disappointed.

And for all that, I have not wanted to raise the problem of the solidity of the epistemological principles that directed this theory about theory: more competent people have done so.[34] I only wanted to examine what the New Archeologists put into practice, even supposing their presuppositions are accepted. Whether it be Binford or Read, the conclusion is the same.

In reality then, twenty years after the beginning of the new religion, there has not been much progress. The theoretical "vacuum" of the New Archeology, deplored by Binford in 1977, has scarcely been filled: it has not even begun to be filled. The comments that follow the article by Read and LeBlanc are just a long dirge on the absence of archaeological theory.[35] In fact, Read and LeBlanc themselves said that there weren't *any* major theories in archaeology.[36] Robert C. Dunnell, in 1980, was able to write that theory was "still the scarcest of commodities" in archaeology.[37]

In reality, the only theories that the New Archeology can implement and that are worthy of the name are foreign to archaeology; and even if they are applicable to it, they come from elsewhere: they are set and group theory; systems theory, and notably its ecological form; perhaps structuralism; and Marxist materialism. But even supposing that archaeology really needs an actual body of theory, which is by no means everyone's opinion,[38] these are not specifically archaeological theories.

5   The Old Archaeology and the New: A Comparison of Results

An Epistemological Failure

Thus, in the specifically epistemological field that was essential—one might even say vital—in the eyes of the New Archeologists, I don't think it is an injustice to return a verdict on them of almost complete failure. Binford said in 1977 that "in the absence of progress toward usable theory, there is no new archaeology."[1] I'll gladly grant him the responsibility for this conclusion. We have already seen how far the elaboration of theories has gone; before that we found an absence of "laws" worthy of the name; and we started by showing that, where the validation of hypotheses is concerned, the New Archeologists generally preferred to leave that to other people and until later: when, by chance, they ventured as far as testing their propositions, they did not always meet with success. When one recalls that explanation lay at the end of this procedure, and with it the chance at last to attain a better understanding of the past, archaeology's ultimate goal, one cannot form a very high opinion of the New Archeology's contributions in the field it had marked out as its very own.

If there has been a contribution, it has not been in the epistemological sphere. Instead—and I will come back to this—it is both in the approach to problems (hypotheses, models) and in the field of methodology (statistics and computerization); this is quite different from the declared objectives. But what about content? One can apply to the New Archeology (and apply effectively, for once!) the method that it recommended so much to everyone else: if what we have just seen is not completely wrong, then the results—no longer epistemological, but in the scientific (historical, anthropological) sphere—ought not to have revolutionized our knowledge. This is an implicit principle that I am going to make explicit: a tree is judged by its fruits; I must apologize for doing it in a form that is immediately accessible to ordinary folk. So let's see.

The Essential Conclusions

On what points has the New Archeology helped science to progress? It is out of the question to present an overall survey, which would involve an immense amount of reading.[2] Instead, following the most orthodox procedure, I shall merely take a sample—which I would not dare to call "random" or even "haphazard." Having admitted that, if one then tries to reveal a few essential conclusions of the New Archeology, one could group together all those that center on the meaning of assemblage variability and that I have already had occasion to mention several times. For the New Archeology, this variability is explained, if I understand it correctly, by the variability of activities occurring in the sites: whether it be procuring raw materials (food, stone, etc.), or "residing" in a more or less stable fashion and putting the available materials to use; whether it be an activity that is constant all year round, or one that is seasonal (such as taking advantage of "aquatic" resources which are often, though not always, linked to a particular time of year: migratory birds and fish; or the resources of the hunt, available in the autumn rather than the spring)[3]; also whether it be the appearance of a new resource, vegetal, mineral, technological, or its undergoing a significant modification,[4] and its development in conjunction with one or several others. It is thought to be in this way—and not as traditional archaeology believed—that the composition of associated contexts varies; in this way, and not through the effect of movements of population (migrations, invasions, wars) or of ideas (diffusion of inventions, passing on of traditions, influences at a distance, etc.), or through an internal evolution of styles, with transitions from one stage to the other. Conversely, conservatism—for example, in ceramic styles—is thought to have its source and its explanation in the kinship system, in residential rules (matrilocal, matrilineal),[5] or in the way that communities which have become overpopulated spread out (a dispersion that is not "linear" but Brownian, of the "random walk" type).[6] I repeat that I am claiming not to summarize all the New Archeology's conclusions but simply to present a significant sample; and the reader will have recognized some of the key ideas of the Binfords, Renfrew, Longacre, Hill, and Clarke. I would now like to turn my attention to the nature, the type of these ideas.

Their Character

Of course, these ideas are not insignificant in any way. Traditional archaeology had undoubtedly exaggerated the importance of intertribal struggles or exodus of population; it had an indisputable tendency to give preference, in an anachronistic way, to the fascination that Mesopotamia is supposed to have had over the rest of the inhabited world ("Ex Oriente Lux")—whether it be the neolithization of the West or the "orientalizing" influences on the Aegean, for example. It had a propensity to forget what might have been happening in Africa or the Far East; and on the other hand it undoubtedly tried too often to find the explanation of ceramic changes in the pottery itself, without sufficiently taking into consideration the social context in which the pottery was produced.

Undoubtedly: but not always, and not uniformly. The minimization of the role of military operations or of the factual aspect of history is nothing new—nor is the recognition of the particular role of central or western Europe, nor the research in the Omo valley in Africa. As for pottery, it was long ago considered in relation to its social environment (even if only in its funerary context), and the production of hand-thrown pottery was attributed to women ages ago. The seasonal aspect—for example, of travel by sea, or fishing trips—was not overlooked either.[7]

The hypotheses the New Archeologists present are not as original as they believe or claim. As a matter of fact, many of them do not even maintain this—indeed, it's one of their leitmotivs. Whereas Binford—and this will come as no surprise—in all modesty assigns "enormous" importance to his suggestion that hand axes were not used for butchering of meat (in J. Desmond Clark's work, which he plunders, all signs already pointed to this), Hill, on the other hand, quite simply recognizes that "the . . . conclusions presented" in his article on Broken K Pueblo "are not, of course, wholly new; [previous] investigators have frequently been able to identify different kinds of rooms in prehistoric pueblo sites."[8] Clarke's inferences on Glastonbury certainly contribute something new in comparison with the conclusions of Bulleid and Gray: but where does this new contribution come from? From . . . Caesar![9] Where Plog assures us that he has extracted new information from Alfred Kidder's old data, Schiffer, for his part, candidly acknowledges that his conclusions "hardly qualify as revelations."[10] Read, as we have seen, admits that his final results are no different to those of his precursor, Polly Wiessner (see above, p. 66).[11] Besides, whether or not they have the honesty to admit it, the New Archeologists often leave the impression that they are not conspicuously original. In a general way, Clarke—after having reviewed the new "paradigms" from the point of view of their content as much as of their formal characteristics—confessed quite readily that, at a certain level, all the strands go back to the nineteenth century.[12]

If the New Archeologists' ideas are not brand-new, it is because not just their basis, but—and this may be even more important—also their nature, so to speak, are no different from that of traditional ideas. They are of the same type: they do not differ from those that any representative of traditional archaeology could have had. This is so true that, as I have said, certain of their hypotheses were first put forward in traditional archaeology. But even if that were not the case, the New Archeological positions are indistinguishable from conventional imaginings: the "idea" that different special activities modify the composition of remains in a prehistoric camp could very well have arisen (and perhaps or probably did so) in the mind of a traditionalist— whatever debility is ascribed to him—simply by chance or, quite naturally, through process of thought. The idea that men counted on exploiting "anadromous" fish could (or could have, or perhaps did) come to the mind of any archaeologist, even if he did not accord it as much importance as an old student of forestry and wildlife conservation like Binford did—even if he were inclined to reject it. Besides, how could it possibly be otherwise? Hypotheses arise in the same way in everyone's mind.

Their Solidity

But that is not the important point: whether a hypothesis is of the same order or not, whether it is original or not—no matter what it is like, what really matters is that it be demonstrated. Ten people may have had the same idea, but only the one who shows that it is well founded has any worth. If archaeology is and must be a science, its conclusions have to be as solid as those of the other real sciences—they have to be, if not definitive, then at least an indisputable and undisputed step forward toward an ever more detailed truth. If the New Archeology is to keep its promises, it must bring undisputed progress to science. This is the very least it could do, after all the reproaches it has heaped on its pitiful predecessors.

Alas, on this very point, we have seen that demonstration was not its forte, and neither was the validation of its hypotheses. The foreseeable consequence is that no unanimity—far from it!—has developed about the New Archeology's production, either among its opponents (that goes without saying) or the New Archeologists themselves (which is more surprising), or even in the actual thinking of particular New Archeologists.

As a matter of fact, one did not have to be a genius to see straightaway that while (for example) migrations, invasions, influences, diffusion, and so on did not explain everything, they had nevertheless played a role, at least in certain circumstances, and could not be excluded in a way that was as peremptory as it was absolute.[13] Examples abound, but it is more significant to cite Binford himself in support of this: when he puts forward his explanation of the origins of agriculture, he is the first to reintroduce the notions of emigration and invasion—wrapped in the folds of a formulation as complicated as it is abstruse—under the guise of "expansion of open donor systems" "at the expense" of the "adjacent environmental zone" and of "resident systems."[14] This is not the only contradiction we shall come across.

As for the explanation of assemblage variability through the different nature of activities carried out (functional or situational variability), a war-horse ridden by the Binfords whenever the occasion presented itself, simple common sense—a faculty that is spurned and, as a matter of fact, rarely put to use by the New Archeologists—would have indicated, here again, that while this concept of differential activity could perhaps, in certain specific and isolated cases, account for variations in material, it could in no way annul preceding explanations. It is not a traditionalist but Clarke who puts forward a random statistical interpretation (a so-called Monte Carlo model) of the phenomenon of "interdigitation" of layers, with which Binford is grappling.[15] But above all, far from being the least bit convinced by the Binfords in their analysis of Middle Paleolithic layers, the Bordes immediately challenged the hypothesis that seasonal differences, or different activities such as butchery or tool making, accounted for the interdigitation of layers. Because—and this small detail may have been overlooked by Binford, who had only recently arrived in the Old World—these layers are thick; so one would have to assume that for very many years Mousterians reserved certain caves exclusively for a particular activity and a particular season! In reality, and for many other theoretical and practical reasons, "since there are several ways of performing the same activities with different toolkits," shouldn't one go back to the starting point and acknowledge that the Mousterian types represent cultural differences?[16] Thomas Cook, one of Stuart Struever's pupils, states that the Binfords' theory has had little influence and that they have never done anything more than put forward an "alternative explanation" to that of the Bordes.[17] When you are aspiring to teach the world scientific procedure, this is disappointing.

And last, but by no means least, let's take the example of the articles by James Deetz, Longacre, and Hill on the "matrilocality" of women potters in ancient pueblos—the New Archeology's inexhaustible source of examples. Besides numerous criticisms concerning methodology, the very basis of their conclusions has been challenged, especially in the case of Longacre: spatial variability could well have a temporal aspect; and the two exclusive clusters, far from representing two units of matrilocal and matrilinear residence, could well represent stylistic variations through time.[18] As for Hill, who upholds an analogous thesis but brings in chronological differences, there is every likelihood that his clusters are artificial, like arbitrary electoral "wards"; and the replication of his factor analysis (the possibility of repeating an "experiment" is a typically scientific procedure)—insofar as one can identify the exact procedure he followed—did not produce comparable results except in a single case: it therefore follows that his clusters are essentially his own product.[19] I do not intend this to mean he was wrong, but it is by no means certain he was right: this gives some indication of how distant we are from a really "scientific" procedure and from conclusions that are above all suspicion. And yet Hill's article was "frequently cited as an example . . . of the hypothetico-deductive method," as Binford himself admits.[20]

I shall not bother to pile up more examples, though it would be easy to do so. Schiffer said the final word: processual archaeology has "simply . . . substituted one set of all-purpose causes—population pressure, environmental change and stress, various forms of intercultural contact, and assorted cybernetic processes—for an equally inadequate set of predecessor causes, such as innovation, diffusion, and migration."[21] It is not that these alternatives do not deserve equal consideration; but they are of the same type, and their demonstrative value is no greater.

Their Interest

Finally, one should add that a good many New Archeologists—among those who don't disdain fieldwork and aren't content simply to borrow their basic data from others—have made very welcome contributions: as examples, one could mention Hill and Plog, Flannery or Struever, Clarke, Renfrew, whose *Emergence of Civilisation* contains an excellent (traditional) study of the Cyclades, and many more besides. But this judgment is from the point of view of traditional archaeology and is quite independent of their significance in the eyes of the New Archeology. But perhaps the reader will agree (though this notion of "interest" is eminently subjective) that most of the New Archeology's propositions or conclusions are, on the whole, not exactly stimulating for the intellect.

Try as one may, it is difficult to get worked up about the processing of bones by prehistoric man, even if it is demonstrated to us that he brought back fewer of them to the camp as he killed more animals, and that he discarded a particular percentage of what he ate. Likewise, the idea that civilization developed in the Cyclades with the spread of the vine and of metallurgy combined, or that of wealth and the longship, will not strike one with amazement. One gets a similar feeling of being "underwhelmed" when one discovers that at Broken K there was an older cemetery to the north, corresponding to the pueblo's northern rooms, a more recent cemetery to the south, corresponding to the southern rooms: and, between the two, an ... intermediate cemetery, assigned to important personages. One might have expected as much. The idea that little pits on the Great Plains of America were used for hide smoking in the autumn, or pot smudging in all seasons, is not the stuff that dreams are made on. That chalcedony, less abundant and available at 2.5 kilometers from the Joint Site, was used more intensively because it was of slightly better quality than flint or quartzite does not provoke astonishment, any more than it does to see that ancient pueblos resemble modern pueblos, except in a few details which in any case are not certain. One often gets the impression—perhaps unjustifiably—that the New Archeologists, fired no doubt by emulation of the astronauts, are discovering the moon a little bit, and that they are making much ado about nothing—or at least about not very much.[22]

The Results of Conventional Archaeology

Especially as, during this time, ordinary archaeology did not cease activity. The New Archeologists had gleefully predicted its imminent disappearance. It is just one more point on which their predictions have proved to be wrong; one more mistake on their record. Certainly, just as it was out of the question to take full stock of the New Archeology's contributions, so this is not the place to paint a complete picture of the other archaeology's results: after all, such a picture would be very difficult to produce on a global scale. But in fact, while the New Archeologists were spending their time constructing theories and regulations which they were going to be the first to ignore, "classic" archaeology, conventional archaeology, and European prehistory were displaying behavior that was totally unexpected, incomprehensible, inadmissible: far from getting excited, far from even paying attention to the important events then occurring in Denver or Chicago, they were continuing to trundle along quietly, in the most complete ignorance or obliviousness, exactly as if nothing had happened. And not only did all the nations concerned continue to send their missions out into the world, but their archaeological journals never stopped appearing (indeed, they were enlarged with supplements), series of volumes were completed, monographs piled up, congresses were held, and even international conferences or symposia, all devoted, of course, to their little publications of material that was endlessly the same, to their rectifications of detail, and to rectifications of rectifications—in short, to their usual shortsighted, intricate, and laborious work, with no opening onto large-scale problems, the vast perspectives that alone would be worth opening up. Sometimes they even happened to bring up discoveries they were immodest and ridiculous enough to try to present as sensational, or even spectacular, but always in connection with the discovery of treasure, of course, with no other implication of scientific value. Besides, how could it have been otherwise? This was the period when—to take a few examples at random—discoveries were made at Omo (Lucy) and Olduvai, at Pincevent (a seasonal camp, after all), at Mureybet and its preagricultural fixed installations. It was the time when Tell Mardikh was identified with Ebla, with the inevitable treasures of golden jewelry in support; when we became aware that the Sea Peoples had built at Ras Ibn Hani, and the Phoenicians at Kition. It was during this period that Lefkandi in Euboea was dug, that the "limestone temple" was dug at Delphi (one more temple), that the tomb of Philip of Macedon was discovered, as were a Hellenistic town at Ai Khanoum in Afghanistan, the first cemetery at Angkor, a Ming tomb. Alas, all this did not tell us very much about the laws of past human behavior.

The Example of Nichoria

There is something pathetic in a recent review of the American publication on Nichoria in Messenia—an exemplary excavation which tried to transpose the best of the new concepts onto the most classical terrain (Greece), despite exceptional difficulties and with merit that is all the more praiseworthy.[23] The remains are so meager that, without the application of the new methodology, results would have been nonexistent, in the opinion of the reviewer himself. And it is in this connection that he expresses the wish that the New Archeology should not be likened to a poor archaeology: poor in material (but not in financial means). In a rather poignant way, he cannot avoid comparisons with the sumptuous discoveries—not only from the point of view of the spectacular but also (and especially) from the scientific point of view—of Akrotiri on the island of Thera, where everything the New Archeology is seeking through such indirect and complicated procedures is, in a way, provided immediately and directly.[24]

It is no less pathetic to see Schiffer conclude his *Behavioral Archeology*—after many theoretical developments, after the "laws" that we have looked at, after a long application to his site, after the results of the type I have already described—with the following important, final recommendations: that matchbooks should be made bigger, that people who bring back beer-can pop-tops should get a refund, that the use of cellophane should be forbidden, and that coupons should be printed on cigarette packets and no longer just tucked inside.[25] It must be said that one is not gratuitously caricaturing the New Archeology when one underlines this aspect of it which is so often derisory.

I repeat: the New Archeologists, if not New Archeology, have displayed great merits, and I shall return to this at some length later on; but these have been *external* to the framework of their theories—specifically, in the areas of approach to problems, work in the field, and techniques. It only serves to make all the more perceptible the disproportion between the New Archeologists' results—whether, as we have just seen, in their content or in their epistemological value—and their objectives.

6 The Spirit and the Letter

The State of Mind

If one adds to this the ceaseless variations of doctrine, the contradictions, mental confusion, internal divergences and internal struggles—to which I shall have occasion to turn my attention—this ponderous assessment makes it even harder to endure what can only be described as the New Archeologists' mentality, and the forms in which they or their followers express themselves.

The conviction—very human, certainly, but not very scientific—that they had found the truth, or at least its definitive basics (a conviction which sparkles in all the New Archeologists' writings), a truth steeped in science (they do not make this "explicit" and do not feel the need to demonstrate it any more than usual), as if through a superior and almost divine predestination is displayed in a characteristic cliquishness.

The first trait of this spirit is a prophetic triumphalism, all the more unwelcome since their results (as we have just seen) do not measure up to their pretensions. Binford is aware of this criticism and defends himself against the accusation of "messianism."[1] But, once again, this is contrary to the evidence. In 1968 he ends the presentation of *New Perspectives in Archeology* with these words: "Many of the papers in this book are radical in the original sense of the word. If we are successful, many traditional archaeological problems will prove to be irrelevant, and we will see an expansion of the scope of our question-asking which today would make us giddy to contemplate."[2] Nothing less. Four years later, he concludes (it is often in the conclusions that this state of mind is most apparent) by applying to archaeology (another common procedure) the views of Karl Popper on the logic of scientific discovery: "In such times of crisis this conflict over the aims of science will become acute. We, and those who share our attitude, will hope to make new discoveries; and we shall hope to be helped in this by a newly erected scientific system. . . . We shall hail [the "falsifying" experiment] as a success, for it has opened up new vistas into a world of new experience . . . the newly rising structure, the boldness of which we admire," etc.[3] Hill, too, ends his article by repeating (on his own account) a phrase of Thomas Kuhn in *The Structure of Scientific Revolutions:* "The significance of crises is the indication they provide that an occasion for retooling has arrived."[4] It is the glad tidings of the Annunciation. This prophesying sometimes assumes almost frenzied forms: Binford, in 1972 again, literally prophesies at the end (and elsewhere) of his *Archaeological Perspective,* and like any self-respecting Pythia, he has no trouble doing it in obscure terms: "I look forward to," "I predict," "I anticipate," "I suspect" occur in succession in this text which, it is true, is meant to be "prospective"[5] But one finds the same thing in the articles that do not have this character—"I expect," "I am suggesting," "I have suggested" (twice)[6]—except that "projections" are distinguished from "predictions."[7] The disciples join the chorus: thus, Schiffer, for example, saying great things about the "powerful framework" that will enable us to consider the "effects of various formation processes on hypothetical behavioral systems"[8] (this notion of "power," even though scarcely ever put into effect, of the "potential" of the method, is obsessional[9]); or South, the new Nostradamus, announcing that "dramatic changes will be seen in the decades to come" (it is true that, for him, a greater percentage of pins in a shop reveals "dramatically" a specialization in this activity!), and that the study of coefficients of variation (the simple relation of the standard deviation to the mean) "will require a revolution in thinking within historical archeology."[10]

As soon as they are no longer dealing with the radiant future of the New Archeology, their predictions become apocalyptic. I have already mentioned the dramatic end that was foreseen for traditional archaeology. It is an inexhaustible theme. This time, let's quote Gene Sterud: "There can be no question of returning to the state of the discipline of the past, even the most recent past." We are heading for an "enforced obsolescence of much of traditional theory and method."[11] Or Clarke: "*Now* . . . research students will test their professors' dicta and not simply accept them"[12]—as everyone knows, this had never been done before. But there is no hope: "the traditionalists" (the "conventionalists") "will continue to defend the old 'secure' paradigm . . . [Popper's] prediction has almost a frightening accuracy"[13]

The fact is that natural modesty is not the New Archeologists' most striking characteristic: that's putting it mildly! While the almost pathological vanity of a Binford contrasts with Clarke's (or Renfrew's) solid awareness of his own worth, while the modesty and pleasant nature of Hill or of Fritz, Plog, or Schiffer or many others is perceptible, it is amusing to see Thomas G. Cook give his "model" the name of Mark 2, after the name he assigns—humorously, of course—to Binford's model (Mark 1), which is none other, in all simplicity, than the abbreviation of . . . the first computer.[14] Similarly, a European probably cannot grasp the precise nuance of the discreet name South gives his Pattern: "Carolina Pride"! On the other hand, what is hard to deny is their feeling, displayed so many times, of belonging to a species of superior intellect.

Sects

Another trait is parochialism, and—no surprise in the United States—sectarianism. It was said often enough, right from the start, that Binford and his team formed a Mafia with its old members, its new members, and finally its little beginners.[15] This almost religious atmosphere—it has even been called "liturgical"—was emphasized not only at the start but also quite recently: "From the beginning the new archaeology placed a large emphasis on methodological cleverness. This approach came to be realized as an almost liturgical insistence on quantification and proper form."[16] Kent V. Flannery, as always, poked fun at the New Archeologists who "believe that Carl Hempel rose from the dead on the third day and ascended to heaven—where he sits at the right hand of Binford."[17] In 1978 too, David H. Thomas rises up against the idea that sampling is a good thing in itself and is becoming an "archaeological ritual."[18] It is clear that on one side there are the chosen ones, on the other the reprobates. One should read what Mark P. Leone said about the New Archeology in the same year—that it is not essentially texts that have made it progress, but "papers read, shouting matches after them, gossip, bull sessions in hotel rooms, victory celebrations, and cutting glances which told you whether or not you were one of the boys"![19] These "cutting glances" are the delight of Lev Klejn. What an eminently scientific atmosphere.

Talk of sects conjures up the fumes of incense, and there is no lack of devotees. One should see the New Archeologists quoting Kuhn or Popper, their idols; quoting each other insistently, even quoting themselves in desperation,[20] talking about themselves in the third person; one should see them congratulating each other in a tide of adulation, or Binford, with a straight face, welcoming South "to the science of archaeology," or accepting and then refusing—or pretending to refuse—the expression *New Archeology* or "revolution."[21] One of the peaks (and one that is hard to beat) was reached by Renfrew in a situation which, it must be said in his defense, lent itself to this sort of thing: the centenary of the American Archaeological Institute. "It is right, therefore, that I should say to you," he proclaims without hesitation, "that I believe that Lewis Binford, with his associates, has made a greater contribution to archaeological thought than any other worker in this century, and that the ideas and problems he has presented are fundamental issues for the archaeology of the Ancient World as well as for the New"![22] Let's recall here the hide-smoking pits, the chronology of pipe stems, the Euphrates salmonids, and the Mousterian interdigitation, the Nunamiut shooting at beer cans; but best not evoke the testing of hypotheses, the laws and theories of archaeology. . . . It is true—and this perhaps makes up for these failings—that the New Archeologists have no equals when it comes to tearing each other apart, reciprocally. Excommunication also figures in the system: Binford criticizes Clarke, guilty of having integrated all his borrowings (the statistics of Robert R. Sokal and P. H. A. Sneath, Peter Haggett's locational approaches, the "metalanguage" of systems theory) into—shock, horror!—a traditionalist paradigm of "culture," in essence what Binford ("much" of whose work he nevertheless cited) is criticizing at this same moment. "What progress has been made?" adds Binford, still with regard to *Analytical Archaeology.* "Very little beyond the hope that as archaeologists did more analysis using statistical procedures, it might dawn on them that their paradigm was outmoded."[23] What could be more amiable? Clarke is less ponderous, but, as I have shown, he proposes an explanation of Mousterian interdigitation that is fundamentally different from Binford's (see above, p. 79). Binford criticizes Flannery, albeit with a few circumlocutory precautions[24]; we have already seen how Flannery responds. Renfrew goes as far as casting doubt on the virtues of prediction; Schiffer, besides his impertinence about campsites teaching us as much as the Nunamiut (see above, p. 69), shows harshness towards the New Archeology that preceded him and that was incapable (whether it be that of Binford or of Clarke) of integrating past science.[25] Absolutely no one finds favor in the eyes of Binford, who, in addition to disparaging the whole world, even goes as far as denigrating Hill, the disciple one would have thought beloved: "I have not been able to find a single hypothesis in his work" (on Broken K), writes Binford, though he immediately acknowledges that Hill did not use the term but instead "faithfully" used "proposition"; never mind, his thinking lacks "theoretical relevance."[26] Binford even finds Dwight W. Read and Steven A. LeBlanc's article "frustrating," though they might have hoped for more gratitude; and he finds "regrettable" certain essential aspects of Michael A. Jochim's work, even though his "model" conformed to seasonal interpretations based, among other things, on small game and fish![27] It's enough to drive one to despair.

Days of Contempt

But this is nothing compared with the bottomless contempt in which certain New Archeologists hold the old, traditional archaeology. They vent their spleen on it with an arrogance, a self-satisfaction, a domineering self-assurance, a way of being (or trying to be) very patronizing, a sort of intellectual racism that is all the more unjustified since we have seen the way they themselves work, not respecting the principles they preach to others without respite, not testing their hypotheses, not making explicit their presuppositions, incapable of formulating a single law that meets the standards they themselves settled on, powerless to produce a single "theory" in the sense that they themselves understand, and finally, having nothing to present but a derisory total of results that are as insipid as they are uncertain. Along the way I have already given numerous examples. Suffice it to recall the tone of the review of the Heizer and Graham manual,[28] Binford's attitude toward Robert Braidwood or even toward François Bordes, K. C. Chang, or so many others. "Traditionalist" is the equivalent of an insult. One could say as much of "inductivist."[29] The New Archeologists proceed by "labeling": they do not try to see if one of their precursors or contemporaries is right or wrong, what he has or has not not contributed (that they plunder without restraint): it is enough that he has no taste for their absurdities for them to classify him as if they were pressing a button, to place a mark of "infamy" on him.

Very characteristic in this respect is the relentlessness with which Binford—when he has a go at a colleague—exaggerates, accentuates in every way the positions he is fighting against. No doubt this is one of those procedures said (wrongly) to be "quite fair": inflate the differences of opinion, the better to deflate them. But it reaches the point where he achieves the opposite result and gives the impression that the position he is criticizing is not that of the opponent but an unreal one, fabricated by Binford, which no one has ever upheld. For example, in the case of the oasis theory, Binford generously credits Braidwood with "orthogenetic" and "vitalist" views which Braidwood never presented as such—never under those names—having restricted himself (and Binford even quotes this) to an "ever increasing cultural differentiation and specialization of [protohistoric] human communities" with "increased experimentation" and "increased receptiveness."[30] It would not be so bad if Braidwood, even unconsciously, had adopted these mistaken ideas (besides, one would have to demonstrate that they *are* mistaken—Binford, as usual, considers this unnecessary) and Binford were dissecting the hidden error. But one gets the distinct feeling that as an excuse for drowning Braidwood in his aquatic resources, Binford is accusing him of hydrophobia! After all, what Braidwood is saying is not so incompatible with what Binford is spouting (and the latter, let us recall, is far from being demonstrated): even if agriculture and stock rearing originated in regions dependent on fishing and aquatic birds, subject to the pressure of less fortunate neighbors, it does not explain *why* or *how* the changeover to agriculture and stock rearing took place: here Braidwood's suggestions retain their value.

Ten years later, one finds the same attitude with respect to John E. Yellen (see above, p. 71). Of course there are differences of opinion, but Binford stresses them, gratuitously makes them look blacker. He treats Yellen's "generalizing his observations" as a crime: but as I have just shown, he himself does exactly the same thing, to the extent that one can legitimately wonder whether he is being entirely honest and what he takes the reader for. He reproaches Yellen—with the superior tone, the airs of an examiner—with never having understood and explained the differences separating Eskimo and Bushmen. But does he do it himself? "The challenge is to build a sufficient body of theory to explain the differences," he preaches.[31] But does he proceed to practice what he preaches? The "suggestions" he puts forward do not constitute, in his own view, the body of theory required, but he acts as if they did, with all the nerve of a street hawker. This is dangerously close to charlatanism.

No less characteristic of Binford, when he comes up against an objection that has been made to him, even by himself, is his capacity to modify his point of view without appearing to do so, and, under the pretext of making his thinking more precise, to turn it inside out like a glove, while acting as if he had always been of this opinion. We saw this in connection with laws: after having repeated to anyone who cared to listen that a validated hypothesis is a law in being, he thinks he perceives that laws have to be made up, and so he immediately rounds on those who thought they were doing right to adopt his initial point of view, quite correctly quoting him in support. It seems they had misunderstood. Moreover, he himself declares that he is not sure he understands them, and to be more sure he rewrites their text, making them say what they never said, which of course makes his refutation easier: but he does not make it any clearer for all that, because in a very shifty way he slips from "covering laws" to "empirical laws," and then from the latter to the spurned "empirical generalizations," and that is that: the trick's done. All this leaves one with an impression of a self-seeking spreading of confusion, at the very limits of dishonesty, and not exactly of a luminous clarification.[32] He would have done better to acknowledge that he had reversed his position. But one understands that—to paraphrase a famous saying about Mussolini— the New Archeology is never anything other than what Binford is thinking at any moment.

It was only very gradually that the New Archeologists toned things down a little and moderated their criticisms of the other archaeology. One of the first, Clarke, conceded in 1972 that the old archaeology had a few merits, a few advantages beside its disadvantages, even a complementarity (Who would have thought it four years before?) with the New Archeology. The fact is, he realized that the latter "will become old" in its turn, and that the former is still "flourishing."[33] With time, these bows by the New Archeology to the old continued to multiply. Where that same year Binford took credit for acknowledging (though with what condescension!) that Braidwood had "made many contributions," Schiffer devoted himself to a real reintegration—one might even say recuperation—when he reproached the New Archeology for not having unified the archaeology that collects the data (this is what he reduces the old archaeology to, in passing) and the one that builds models on a conceptual basis (this is his definition of the new), and even for not having provided any role "for expertise or the subjective element"[34]: we have to pinch ourselves to check that we're not dreaming But Binford sticks to his positions. The old archaeology is still the enemy to be overthrown, and the New Archeology's only indisputable merit, perhaps the only one that will last, will have been that of trying to destroy it.[35]

The Motivations

The reasons for this state of mind can be sought in two directions. For the motivations of Binford himself, whose attitude has sometimes (but fortunately not always) rubbed off on his pupils or followers, the autobiographical introductions to different parts of *An Archaeological Perspective* are a partial but direct source. His disappointments, the humiliations suffered in his career, his divorce, his frustrations are narrated here by the man himself in a "disarming" way which eventually makes him look almost likable.[36] Without excusing his attitude, they help one understand it better. But where his "associates" are concerned, these reasons cannot hold, and different ones have been put forward: the legitimate (and certainly normal) human desire to make a name for oneself, and, especially, to obtain a position—in short, a university post.[37] Flannery has described these earliest supporters, the "members of the first archeological generation ever to walk on water—who, once they had achieved some degree of national prominence (or tenure), forgot they had ever espoused processual studies and hastened to join the old guard on the pretext of 'bridging the generation gap.'" Alas and alack, "they include some of the very people whose earlier studies are frequently cited as good examples of process archeology"![38] Be that as it may, this illumination in no way modifies the theoretical positions or the criticisms one can make of them, in both substance and form.

Form

Even if the New Archeologists' state of mind is, and up to a certain point must remain, their own business, the form in which the New Archeology swathes itself is, alas, our business, and we are obliged to adapt ourselves to it, to suffer it, whether it be the texts themselves or their graphic illustration.

Everything has been said about the New Archeology's "jargon," but the subject is inexhaustible, and this inconvenience to the reader is renewed with every line. It is true that the problem is complicated by the peculiarities of English and American and also by the fact that, in the United States especially, the authors have no grounding in literature. What is more—and this time in England too—they are, above all, anthropologists rather than archaeologists; besides, their borrowings from other disciplines bring with them their own terminology, but in a context which is no longer their own. However, the biggest sinner is certainly Binford: it is clear that he has no command of any foreign language, ancient or modern,[39] or even of English: his students' witticism, which he himself reports, suggesting that he translate his writing into English shows that it is not only Latins who have this impression.[40] One would not suspect Renfrew of being ill-disposed toward the New Archeology, but in his review of *Analytical Archaeology* he does not hesitate to use the word "pata-archaeology," as one says "pata-physics," after A. Jarry.[41] Robert C. Dunnell states gloomily that the borrowing of concepts and techniques, carried out on a large scale, "is the primary cause for the decreased readability of Americanist literature in the late 1960s and early 1970s."[42] One wonders why he does not include more recent material too.

The vocabulary and terminology, for a start, present some astonishing morphological peculiarities, bearing no great relation to what one believes to be the rules of composition. There was plenty of jeering (and he took it badly) about Binford's marvelous "technomic" (technonomic?),[43] but what can one say about the universal "taxonomy" (for taxinomy?), the unutterable "taxon, -a," "societial," the inevitable "processual"—which isn't even in Webster's, a book which is pretty accommodating—or "uniformitarianism," derived from geology, and which *is* in Webster's, that word of lightness and elegance? There is no end to the examples one could quote. Certainly nobody is obliged to know Latin, Greek, or Hebrew, and no one is safe from mistakes in neologisms, but there are none keener to fabricate new compounds from old languages than those who do not know the first thing about them; none more eager to use terms whose origin or proper meaning they do not know. I have quoted Binford's "empirical experience" (see above, p. 73): Why "le" ratio? Why "data *is*"? Why "*a* necessary criteria"?[44] Why "quod erat demonstrando [*sic*]," when there's Q.E.D.? Even when the word exists, it is often used incorrectly: "paradigm" is a fine example of a wrong meaning, even though it has finally passed into common usage; primary and secondary "discards" are no less "de facto" than the material abandoned on the spot, which is decked out in this expression[45]; "militaristic" is used for "military" (this has nothing to do with militarism or antimilitarism), "systematic" for "systemic," and these are not necessarily misprints.

One can also mention the abuse of the expression "in terms of," specifically outside any terminological context, or of the alternative conjunction "and/or," which is simply a refusal to be precise.

Nothing in all this is very serious; but it becomes more serious when this quite comical vocabulary is put to use in gibberish that is not funny at all. Here Binford is no longer the only one concerned; he and Clarke are two of a kind. Abusing the English language's possibilities for putting several epithets in front of the noun, each of these authors, to an equal extent, lines up interminable sentences as far as the eye can see. In these the essentials are drowned in almost ritual adjectives, stacked up with no precise relationship, which they could have dispensed with in view of the context; the adjectives themselves are complicated by one or several adverbs and are often followed by a cascade of complementary names! Examples have been picked out before (notably by Renfrew[46]), but this is the very substance of many New Archeological texts. Let's open Clarke's introductory article in *Models in Archaeology* at random; here is what he writes in connection with a case of experimental archaeology, and consequently with something very down-to-earth: "This model then allows two different aspects to be simultaneously investigated, first of all providing an estimate of the labour time and methods required to build a massive bank and ditch with replicas of prehistoric artefacts, second to record the complex micro-geomorphological post-depositional processes of decay and collapse by sampling the earthwork, at appropriately estimated intervals of time, by excavation." Phew! A few pages further on, in connection with Binford's pipe stems, this iconic model "may be crudely but adequately expressed in a mathematical deterministic model derived from the straight line regression formula for the scatter of values," and so forth. On a more abstract subject, in connection with locational theory: "Thus Zipf's principle that the volume of activity over distance declines as a function of the distance from the reference site provides a frame for archaeological catchment area analysis and the Chinese Box territorial models." [47] It is not an oratorical exaggeration to say that there are a thousand examples like this. The first paper Binford submitted to Albert Spaulding was denounced as "practically unreadable," [48] and Binford acknowledges that "English was a mystery to me." [49] It seems to have remained as much fifteen years later: "Is stylistic or production variability independent of vessel function . . . ? If not, why are there differences in the relationships between design characteristics reflecting stylistic, symbolic, or simple informational aspects of production?" [50] This is certainly something to ponder. Or again, in 1978: "It should be pointed out," he says about Nunamiut technological organization, "that organizational properties may vary *within* a system situationally and thereby contribute appreciably to intersite variability within a system." [51] That's crystal clear. And the reader should not imagine that knowing the context out of which any quotation is lifted would be very illuminating or that these are isolated examples, chosen from spite: it is not worth the bother; this is the daily bread.

And yet there are occasions when Binford shows a sense of humor, [52] and the autobiographical sections (i.e., the nontheoretical sections!) of *An Archaeological Perspective* read almost like a novel. It is true that on occasion Clarke displays a poetic side, when he compares models to a "fountain" of hypotheses for testing, or a humorous side when he notes that a "flow chart" all too often succeeds only in modeling the satisfaction of its operator. [53] But these moods never last long.

Whereas certain of the recent New Archeologists—Schiffer, for example—would almost be more than a match for their masters in this, it is no less true that the texts by Longacre, Hill, Plog, and even South sometimes, show that it is possible for the New Archeology to be clear, or at the very least readable. And of course there's Flannery, who always stands apart, on this point as on so many others.

This jargon is not used unconsciously: Clarke especially makes it one of the characteristics (which no one will dispute) of the New Archeology, and takes up its defense: while admitting that it is "ugly and deplorable from the point of view of prose," he says that "aesthetics are not the prime criteria of communication within specialized disciplines"; and in any case, he adds, in the tone of someone quick to make promises, "Yesterday's jargon is tomorrow's prose."[54] It sends shivers down your spine. Renfrew has the same view of things eight years later, although he reads far more agreeably: "Good prose style is not the most rigorous criterion for real meaning." And reproaching the traditionalists for assuming "that any educated man has an easy familiarity with Greek and Latin (and probably a smattering of some Semitic language also)" or that he understands "an abbreviated reference to *IG* or *CIG* or Pseudo-Xenophon," he alleges that it is "often difficult to find exactly the right words to express new ideas."[55] This may be a somewhat unflattering definition of the New Archeology, but of course nothing is easy: this is why the slightest effort toward clarity would be appreciated all the more. Poor Boileau, who believed that what is well thought out is expressed with clarity.

This wooden language, "jargon-laden and wooly," is in large measure responsible for the discouraging character of the New Archeology and for the truly unfathomable boredom it produces so liberally. It contributed to the New Archeology's isolation from the rest of the archaeological world[56]—something which may have given it some pleasure, and which it may even have desired. Never was phraseology so spaghetti-like.

It is all the more shocking because the New Archeologists' texts are always very carefully composed. Even Binford manages to separate his paragraphs carefully (but not the major divisions of his "Postpleistocene Adaptations"), and as a general rule he uses the classical norms of a paper: he sets out his plan, follows it, summarizes each part, and then the whole, in a very clear way. In this, as in the rest, he is followed by his disciples—which shows well that in things that seem important to them, such as the succession of ideas, the New Archeologists are capable of making an effort in the format.

References and Illustration

On the other hand—but this is an American trait which is not peculiar to the New Archeology—their system of references is the one we know only too well. Books and articles are cited by date (and not by the title or its abbreviation), preceded, if it is not mentioned in the text, by the author's name, but not always by his Christian name(s),[57] which can cause mix-ups, and followed, in general though not always, by the page number.[58] This system has but one advantage—for the author and not the reader who, unless he has the memory of an elephant, has to go through an extra intermediary to obtain the reference he wants—a date, often common to several authors, and less eloquent than a title which is generally recognizable.[59] One striking characteristic of the New Archeology's references is that they direct you to texts which give very imperfect support to the position being upheld.[60] Notes, usually footnotes, are rare; they are replaced by parentheses in the text: it is true that they are most often confined to the references mentioned above. While articles in collective volumes are often preceded by a summary and followed by their own bibliographies, a bibliography for the whole work is often lacking, though there is usually an index. Where references to figures, or rather, the numbering of figures is concerned, a complex system—peculiar to each article or each chapter of the volume, that is, two or three digits, usually not accompanied by the relevant page number—comes under the same reproach as the references: it is convenient only for the author when he is writing, not for the reader.[61]

Moreover, the illustration, and especially photographic illustration, is meager for a number of reasons,[62] and the slightly more abundant graphic illustration is rather curious. It seems to oscillate between very complicated diagrams and infantile sketches. Into the latter category one can put certain "models"—the type that comprise a circle or square with a single arrow coming out of it—the necessity for which is not obvious[63]; or more sophisticated drawings, like the calligrams of Apollinaire, in the form of a halberd or a snail,[64] full of indications written in by hand as if by a child and, indeed, perhaps intended for that category of readers, if by chance the book hasn't already fallen from their hands; or finally, drawings which waver between Rupert Bear and comic strips with speech "bubbles." [65] This kind of "Peanuts" imagery is pretty astounding and very revealing (fig. 3). On the other hand, at the opposite extreme, we are faced with models, diagrams, and flow charts that are often highly complex, stuffed with cartouches joined by wavy lines or arrows,[66] sometimes dotted or interrupted by question marks. All of this, of course, is intended to "visualize" (as is said so elegantly) an extremely complex "process," whose presentation in the text is difficult to read. But the figure is itself so incomprehensible that it is necessary to put under it a caption that is often inter-

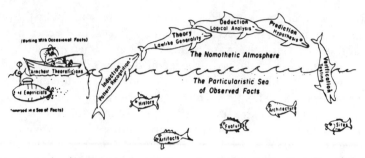

Fig. 3. Example of New Archeological illustration. Stanley South, *Method and Theory in Historical Archaeology* (New York: Academic Press, 1977), p. 15, fig. 2 (after J. G. Kemeny).

minable and, in its turn, obscure.[67] It used to be said that "one picture is worth a thousand words." The use the New Archeology makes of illustration gives you the feeling that a brief, clear text would perhaps be more worthwhile than a labyrinth one gets lost in (fig. 4).

A Cloud of Smoke

These particularities of form in the New Archeology are more important than they appear. Because if "the medium is the message" (Marshall McLuhan)—whether it be writing or drawing—then, consciously or not, these particularities of form are not anodyne or, as they say, "innocent": they have the effect not of securing communication (as Clarke and Renfrew asserted in perfect harmony) but of distorting it. By hiding behind this phraseological smokescreen, the New Archeologists are acting as if they want to conceal the inconsistency of their thinking and to have it taken for what it is not. At the start, and probably in the huge majority of cases, apart from a few careerists at the very most, this concealment is neither voluntary nor even conscious. The New Archeologists are sincerely convinced that they have found a panacea, a winning formula—in short, *the* solution. But if they feel the need to adopt this "intolerably arrogant" tone,[68] to gather together in a jealous, exclusive sect, if they prefer to use an obscure means of expression, if they are aggressive toward traditional archaeologists, it may not simply be because they are aware of possessing the truth but, on the contrary, because they are perhaps not so sure about it—with good reason—and do not want to show this in broad daylight. If they attack, it is to defend themselves; if they are so patroniz-

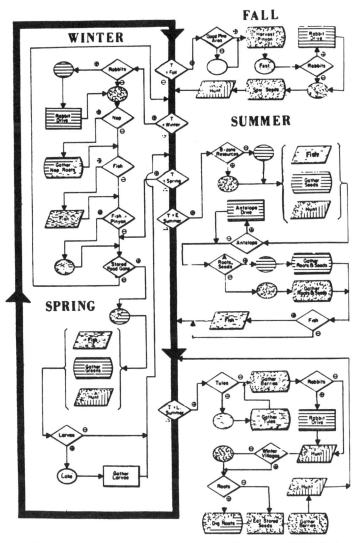

Fig. 4. Model of the Shoshone economic cycle. D. H. Thomas, in *Models in Archaeology*, ed. David L. Clarke (London: Methuen, 1972), 679, fig. 17.3.

ing, it is to give themselves courage. They want to assume the airs of philosophical, mathematical, logical, and scientific rigor even if, as we have seen, this is cruelly denied by what they put into practice and by their results: all the more so, in fact. Humanly, all too humanly, they practice to deceive. And they have sometimes succeeded.[69]

7 The Conned

The "Conned" and Followers

As a matter of fact, not only did the huge majority of active archaeologists (almost all the international teams working around the world; around the Mediterranean, for example, or in the Near and Middle East) decline to take the trouble to refute the New Archeologists' point of view, they practically ignored them, met them with silence, and continued their usual work with splendid indifference ("the dogs bark, the caravan passes"), with a steadfastness which first seemed ridiculous to the New Archeologists (an admission of helplessness) but which eventually worried them—indeed, worried them more and more, as we have seen. The same did not occur with certain enthusiastic souls, in love with innovation, less strong perhaps and no doubt less experienced, who were clearly seduced into raptures of admiration: for want of a better term, I'll call them the "conned."

I am in no way using this term to refer to the real followers of the New Archeology outside the English-speaking countries, those who are its "supporters" for one reason or another, even if in a fleeting way; their distinguishing feature can be seen in the fact that they practice the discipline effectively and publish their results. In general, these people have shown themselves to have a more critical mind. Though Carl-Axel Moberg, for example, and Bohumil Soudský (a New Archeologist before his time) welcomed the New Archeology with open arms, they did not do so without maintaining personal points of view or without important reservations on essential points.[1] In France, J.-C. Gardin's route has been exemplary. After having been very deeply impressed by the new views, and even strongly convinced of their soundness and their promise, he then returned—quite quickly really—to far more mixed feelings. One can illustrate this evolution by comparing, for example, the two reviews he published, four years apart, of

Clarke's two books—or, rather, by comparing their conclusions. In the review of *Analytical Archaeology*, published in 1970, Gardin mentioned three possible reactions to the New Archeology: the first was agreement with the objectives and faith in the possibility of achieving them; the second was partial agreement on some of these objectives and doubts about the possibility of achieving them; the third was rejection both of the principles of theoretical synthesis and of prediction in the archaeological sphere. It seemed clear that his personal preferences were for the first attitude, or at least the second.[2] In the review of *Models in Archaeology*, which appeared in the same journal in 1974, he sees things in a completely different light: the hypothetico-deductive method is merely one half of the traditional method and thus has nothing original about it; nor has "modelization": "Is this really the first time that archaeology is trying to link the study of material remains to wider frameworks and objectives than those of historical typology?" It would be a glaring "untruth" to uphold such a view. There is neither a revolution nor a crisis, "or else there have been several of the sort in the last hundred years." Gardin ends by appealing for an "impending," "intelligent" archaeology, one illustration of which is his *Archéologie théorique*, published in 1979 (an English version, *Archaeological Constructs*, was published in 1980).[3]

Such intellectual courage and lucidity are not the strong point of the conned, perhaps because their distinguishing feature seems to be split from the world of effective, active research carried out in person and, by way of consequence, from what is generally meant by publications that are specifically archaeological (I shall define what I mean by this), rather than theoretical or, at another level, journalistic. Fortunately, this split can be merely temporary, and the conned can become real archaeologists, new or not; on the other hand, any archaeologist may remain a little bit conned. By his very nature, the archetypal conned archaeologist who, no doubt through Kantianism, does not get his hands dirty (or at least does so very little), contributes nothing original as far as either theory or material is concerned. He is content simply to embrace the faith, but he does so with the greatest eagerness; and his critical faculty, inasmuch as he has one, is pretty broadly selective and attacks (with certain exceptions) only the targets that have already been picked out; attacks on the new principles are far rarer. He is the worthy emulator of the American students who deserted Braidwood for Binford: a move which, with the benefit of hindsight, may not have been such a good idea.[4]

Critical Faculty

In France, a feeble example of this attitude can be found in a collective article written by four young and, moreover, very likable authors—none of whom, unless I am mistaken or missing something, had yet left any notable traces in archaeological bibliography, when, in 1971, they could not wait any longer to give us their point of view on the first manifesto of the New Archeology (*New Perspectives in Archeology*).[5]

As one might expect, "traditional" archaeology has a rough time of it. "Refuge of the old humanist dream," "ethnocentric and colonialist," "science of artifacts," requiring "flair above all," "exhuming" these objects by excavation, a simple "collection of groping manual techniques, whose degree of precision is in general not given over to any particular objective of study," following this with "interminable sorting and reclassifying operations [just try and draw up a list of the archaeological works that are a lot more than that]," "almost exclusively orientated . . . toward producing catalogs and the clarification of details," caught "between the accumulation of data and the poverty of its concepts," moreover, "unsuited to abstraction," perpetually "compressing" new artifacts "into preexisting knowledge," "not knowing what a discovery means," formulating hypotheses that are as "legitimate" as they are "untestable," even its "most admissible and most fruitful works" are worthy only of being recommended "in order to have their reasoning formalized and their inconsistencies corrected; to have the knowledge that remained implicit separated out and made explicit"; contemporary archaeology (this is in 1971–78) can scarcely yield anything other than "self-satisfaction" to the specialist, "master of his own knowledge," and to the historian, characterized by his "literary skill"! One can recognize here, and with no great originality, it must be said, the New Archeology's criticisms of its precursor.

Nor is it surprising to find our quartet particularly keen (except for a few reservations) on the inevitable hypothetico-deductive method, "the real change"; on computing and processing data (the examples of this provided by *New Perspectives* are judged "very attractive"); on "the establishing of new models"; on data banks which "would shorten by several years the time necessary . . . to amass one's documentation . . . without the possession of a private card index permitting someone to monopolize [this] documentation"; on "resorting to mathematics and computers" (as if they were exclusive to the New Archeology); and, finally, on building "proper archaeological theory"—(they quote two attempts at this which are "very rich in results"). However, the formulation of the "laws of cultural dynamics," advocated by Binford, gives rise to no comment on their part. One finds here nearly all the banalities that the New Archeology is always harping on.

Perhaps the most distressing feature is the timidity of the criticisms they venture to make here and there, criticisms that are, moreover, more or less adapted and noncommittal—in connection with the validation of hypotheses or, again, concerning Hill's article on Broken K, which we know so well. One cannot see what they mean by their remark (about the female potters) that "it would have been much more interesting to pursue the reasoning without looking for a hasty interpretation outside the chain of reasoning," and as a remark it is scarcely incriminating.[6] Similarly, their allusion to a representation of evolution that is less simplistic than the Gaussian curve is extremely elliptical.[7] It was subsequently shown that many other criticisms could be leveled at Hill's article (see pp. 40, 87, 127), whereas they find it "remarkable." On the other hand, the critical reactions they quote concerning the Binfords' manifesto—that is, essentially that of Donn T. Bayard—are treated with great condescension: indeed, all of Bayard's assertions are given in the conditional mood. And yet, here again, subsequent events showed that he might have deserved better.[8] In reality, it's clear that our "gang of four" was deeply impressed, not to say "conned," by *New Perspectives*. Yet the silence of the majority—of what is actually called the "silent majority"—was pretty indicative, even if you consider only the massive German silence, since everything Latin has no interest.[9]

This attitude was understandable in the beginning, but to a large extent it has persisted until today. At more or less regular intervals one sees the same caricature of traditional archaeology being presented— always as being "humanist," "imperialist," "a peaceful business of excavation"[10]; the same unsubtle admiration for the hypothetico-deductive method appears, and in examples that are sometimes particularly ill-chosen[11]; and there is the same lack of any critical faculty wherever the New Archeologists are concerned.[12] It is with no surprise that one notes the barely diminished echo of the triumphalism I denounced among our American cousins: "Here is a New Archeology moving forward"[13]; the same peremptory tone: "One would wish these choices to be conscious choices," or "This practice . . . is rarely made explicit; it would gain by being made so,"[14] which recalls some of our quartet's best moments ("scientific procedure . . . one of the simplest formulations of which is: to know what one is doing," or "what makes archaeological discourse boring is the poetic impotence through logical inconsistency"),[15] and it sometimes reaches real heights: traditional archaeology "does not enable one to understand a culture in term [*sic*] of process,"[16] or, "in short, history would have a meaning."[17] But which one? This detail isn't provided.

Variability

On the other hand, one trait which is peculiar to the conned, and which one does not find (and with good reason) in the American original, is an extreme sensitivity to "share fluctuations." The conned archaeologist—an imitator and camp follower, always tossed between the desire not to miss the last train to the future and the fear of not abandoning ship in time—is perpetually testing the wind, on the lookout for its slightest shifts. Just as he exaggerated strict observance in the beginning, one can expect him to turn his coat immediately, in accordance with events at successive conferences, as soon as he perceives a change in fashion. After having cried with the pack against humanism, now here he is evoking it with a certain fondness: one shouldn't "lose all affinity" with it.[18] And what of the new methodology, the "theoretical renewal" that was being praised to the heavens not long before? With hilarious casualness, he now tells us that "these problems of method, reasoning, and validation having now either been resolved or fallen into disuse" (it would have been interesting to have the breakdown into the two categories made clear), "the problem of a theory . . . continues to present itself no less strongly."[19] Yes, the review of *New Perspectives* "was a little too favorable."[20] What about computers? It is not so long ago that, in France, for the first time, people were singing us the praises of the storage of information in computers, and its processing, from excavation onward, by means of a terminal located nearby.[21] Alas! The results do not seem to have been more rapid or all that conclusive, and "a diminution" of this type of research is revealed: "an inevitable reflux," they conclude in a profound way, as if anyone apart from them had ever expected the opposite.[22] In short, "after the years of methodological euphoria" one notes "a certain disenchantment concerning the omnipotence—mixed up until now—of computer studies and of a methodology that was often inspired by philosophy of science."[23] Is this a return to the obvious? Not yet; the next U-turn is not long in coming. Binford having been, meanwhile, the object of an "edifying" ovation at the Forty-fifth Congress of the Society for American Archaeology, they set off again quite merrily: "The *New Archeology* has definitively won the match," although "nowhere" did one "hear praise for the merits of hypothetico-deductive reasoning which made it famous for a while." Moreover, "its jargon is adopted. . . . It is edifying" (yes, this too!) "to read the summaries"—and the same goes for its plan of exposition, "even if," the reporters add disarmingly, "it's most often a trick of presentation"![24] Without any great risk of being wrong, one can foresee other U-turns, and they will not be the last pirouettes.

The Motivations

The reasons for such an infatuation are not exactly the ones you might envisage for the New Archeologists across the Atlantic; no doubt many people genuinely feel admiration and enthusiasm for a doctrine which attracts them, but this scarcely does credit to their critical ability, and especially for that reason, I think it a pity. Then again, there is probably a desire (itself traditional) to break free from tradition, to find a role in opposing (the "generation gap"), before the next generation does the same to them; perhaps, too, a perfectly legitimate need—leaving aside particular cases of sheer careerism—to make a name for themselves, to stand out from the crowd at all costs. But above all there is a trait that, by definition, cannot be borrowed: fascination in the face of supposed power, a feeling of inferiority (not to say an inferiority complex) in a field where, paradoxically, this inferiority is by no means obvious. The reality of archaeological work (let's not go into archaeological publication just yet) cannot but plunge them into confusion.

8 An Attempt at an Assessment

An Acknowledgment of Failure

The New Archeology claimed to reveal to us what archaeology was and what it should be. It has failed to do so, to a very great extent and on essential points. With the objective of at last making archaeology a real science, it advocated a method of scientific explanation, based on hypothetico-deductive reasoning and aimed at the validation of hypotheses; we have seen it was foremost in not validating its own hypotheses (with certain exceptions) which were, moreover, not very convincing. In this, with a characteristic mental confusion, it was doing exactly what it reproached traditional archaeology with—and the latter was not always guilty. What great progress. . . . Next, it claimed it would produce laws of past human behavior: apart from ridiculous truisms, it has put forward only "laws" that are unusable (which took as known things that were not known) or tautological (which described the problem without solving it). Finally, it wanted both to derive its laws from theories and to organize them into a body: it fell back into tautology or the unvalidated hypothesis. It came full circle. In consequence, the concrete results it has been able to offer have been very meager and not at all the indisputable kind one would have expected, even if temporarily, of "scientific" results. It is the archaeology of sterility—as is shown by the frequent repetition of identical articles, repeated pure and simple from one compilation to another.[1] The attempt to conceal this vacuum under an arrogant jargon succeeded only among the converted. In short, the "takeover bid," one might call it, that was made for traditional archaeology (which was not impressed) has failed.

For what reasons? It would be too easy for the New Archeology, after having fallen into step without thinking, now to try to turn the page—to move on, with the same thoughtlessness, to other chimeras of the same ilk. It would be too easy for it, after having tried to make everyone join in this passing fancy, to then want to force others into the same contortions. The least one can do is try to learn a lesson about what has happened. The reader will note that, until now, I have not called into question the philosophical, logical, and theoretical presuppositions of the New Archeologists: I have accepted their assumptions, explicit or not, and have passed judgment only on the way they put the principles into practice and on the results they produced. That was a preliminary.

Logical Reasons

And yet numerous objections of an invalidating nature were made—from the beginning and as things progressed—about the logical foundations of the reasoning that was presented as indisputable. In 1969 Donn T. Bayard recalled the existence of other forms of validation of hypotheses, the role of induction, and noted the "alchemic" character of the new theory.[2] In 1973, Charles G. Morgan presented a critique, as radical as it was destructive, of the "model" of explanation by a covering law, a model that "is at best controversial and of limited applicability,"[3] and he showed particular harshness toward the authors of *Explanation in Archeology*. And yet the model was an article of faith. As a supreme insult, two New Archeologists, Dwight W. Read and Steven A. LeBlanc, go as far as casting doubt on the virtues of the hypothetico-deductive method—which they judge to be too formal, and which does not sufficiently take into account the content of the demonstration—and of explanation by inclusion under a covering law![4] It's curtains for Hempel. Donald E. Dumond had set the tone in 1977[5]; Paul A. Larson continues in 1979: "Many have considered Hempelian methodology an important approach for archaeology, but this point of view is currently in some disfavor," with all due respect to the ever faithful Plog.[6] In 1979 the Salmons sound the death knell: this "would have been heresy but a few years ago," comments Robert C. Dunnell.[7] In retrospect, the "historic" New Archeologists who had swallowed cut and dried the slightest word by Hempel and Oppenheim look a bit naive, like overly credulous simpletons.

As for the "nature of the theory," Bayard had already cast doubt on its role in 1969[8]; and D. J. Meltzer, in 1979, concluded that there was stagnation in this area: the metaphysical position has not changed.[9] Meanwhile, Binford had taken upon himself both the defense of the theory and its refutation.

Philosophical Reasons

Such a generalized and structured failure can only have a fundamental cause, and what seems to be the root of the evil has been identified and denounced for a long time now, on all sides, without the least effect on the New Archeologists. Put very roughly, it is the fact that the concept they have of science wrongly assimilates man, his behavior, and his history to the subject of the exact sciences, of physics, biology, natural sciences, geography, or linguistics.

Indeed, if the notions of law, nomothetics, and nomology occupy such a central place in the New Archeology, between theory on the one hand and "explanation" on the other, it is obviously because the New Archeologists suppose that there are laws governing the fate of humanity. Their ultimate goal, as I have said, is the formulation of these laws. No doubt their materialist philosophy is not—in the majority of cases, except perhaps at the start—a "vulgar mechanical materialism" or "technological determinism" of the type that was first attributed to Marxism[10]. But materialist philosophy, the positivism referred to by Leslie White, Spaulding, Binford, and even more recently Schiffer, is indeed mechanical and determinist, a very prescriptive determinism.[11] Still more recently, South's reminder about evolutionist positions refers to Darwinism, a victim between 1900 and 1950, he says, of a reaction against it, as was scientific functionalism.[12] Systems theory is, in a sense, "mechanical," with its positive and negative feedback, its inputs and outputs[13]; behaviorism searches for the laws of human behavior[14]; part of ethnology is based on a determinist materialism.[15] For the New Archeology, to explain a phenomenon is to be capable of predicting it, and this means that it is predictable.[16]

This determinism, whether declared or latent, can only have been strengthened by certain recent theories, no longer from physics only but from biology. As Stuart Struever says, "In recent years, there have been major advancements in the physical and biological sciences. Aspects of these advancements have enormous potential significance for increasing the archaeologist's capacity for interpreting the prehistoric record of culture, environment and human biology." [17] Now, for "sociobiology" there is no freedom for man: he has only an illusory feeling of liberty.[18] The American behaviorist B. F. Skinner has the hero of his novel, *Walden Two,* say: "I deny absolutely that freedom exists." According to R. Lewontin, for sociobiology, "What makes the individual, what presides over his development, from birth to death, results from social organization . . . and, in this sense, social organization, ontologically, precedes individual history." [19] For his part, the biologist

Henri Laborit maintains that there is no freedom: all kinds of determinisms are at work.[20]

But these points of view have raised objections. For Lewontin, sociobiology is merely a "vulgar Darwinism," "of the nineteenth century," and its optimization by natural selection of the best adaptation sounds, all things considered, like Voltaire's Pangloss: yet one can acknowledge that all is not for the best in the best of all possible worlds.[21] For Jacques Ruffié, Edward O. Wilson—the father of sociobiology—is a neo-Darwinist, but the "new synthesis" of evolution which proposes a standardizing process (all individuals in identical conditions are identical) is contradicted by the establishment of genetic polymorphism, which reflects the instability of the environment. It is chance which first chose between the alternatives; natural selection came into force only after that; the increasing complexity of the combinations set out new alternatives; this growing complexity is an "inexorable march toward freedom."[22] Freedom, determinism: one finds these two notions in Jacques Monod's book, the title of which— *Le hasard et la nécessité*—is derived from Democritus. While there exist huge patches of determinism, "pure chance, chance alone . . . is at the very root of the prodigious edifice of evolution."[23]

Besides, the New Archeologists very quickly replaced the concept of a mechanical, automatic determinism with a more flexible relationship which would take probabilities into account more than necessity, and which would be more adapted to archaeological phenomena. In 1972, Renfrew, with his usual subtlety, takes great care to point out that "the systems approach . . . need not imply any rigorous or prescriptive determinism."[24] The same year, Clarke (who in 1968 had already mentioned statistical and stochastic models) used, in connection with the expansion of Neolithic Danubian populations, a random walk model inspired by the physics of gases, by Brownian motion, in which, like molecules, settlements are "constantly in motion, constantly colliding in fresh random associations with a constant interchange of inhabitants and artefacts."[25] The reference to physics, even that of fluids, is significant. And yet, in 1969, Bayard had brought up the fantastic quantitative disproportion between physical or astrophysical phenomena and cultural (and particularly archaeological) phenomena, of which the number is "much too small to be described by such rigorous statistical laws."[26]

Be it dynamic determinism or probabilistic determinism, it is still well and truly determinism. How could it be otherwise for the "law and order" archeologists? It is not by chance that Wilfred Shawcross tries to apply the two laws of thermodynamics to prehistory.[27] And, as

Lev Klejn says, if "it is true that the question arises of how we are to reconstruct" a past "in which chance plays a part" by basing ourselves on laws, if it is true that the choices of history are "frequently accidental and unpredictable," once the choices are made "the laws of one of the alternatives come into force." [28] After chance, "implacable" necessity, as François Jacob would say. But "in this system," Ruffié would echo in reply, "very little room is left for freedom."

This is certainly the fundamental alternative. Between instants of pure chance, are there only entire stretches of determinism, or also moments of free choice? It is not a new problem, and it is going to be around for a long time.

But it is not an archaeological alternative: it is philosophical. And so it is not for archaeology to decide. Not that archaeologists do not have the right to have (or do not in fact have) their own philosophy, conscious or not, explicit or not. But they do not all have the same one. Is it obligatory to adhere to a particular philosophy in order to do proper archaeology? That might perhaps be the opinion of a certain number of archaeologists. But it is an attitude that is not very "scientific," it seems to me. What would we say if, from the Far East, for example, we learned that one cannot practice archaeology in those regions (or, why not, in the entire world) without embracing the Buddhist cosmology, or the Taoist, or Zen? At that rate there would be as many archaeologies as philosophies, and we would be certain to have left the domain of science. Mathematics are not Christian; biology isn't Marxist.

The New Archeologists are not under suspicion of spiritualism, one can allow them that. Their quest for a body of theory, systematizing explanatory laws, can only be conceived in a materialism that is determinist (statistical or stochastic) and evolutionist, be it neo-Darwinist or, better still, behaviorist, even if their behaviorism has to be updated. I am in no way saying that they are wrong, and I have just suggested that an archaeology worthy of the name should not take into account personal convictions in this area. But then, in these conditions, why their failure?

Because their failure is not in doubt, even by their own admission. Let's quote Binford himself: "In the absence of progress toward visible theory, there is no new archaeology," he said in 1977.[29] We have seen what can be thought of his 1978 attempt with the Nunamiut. One can always hope (he doesn't deny himself this; he's a specialist in hope). Such is not Renfrew's opinion, which I have quoted: "Archaeology has . . . so far failed to formulate universal laws, and it seems unlikely that it will be able to do so." [30] Nor that of Paul A. Larson in 1979: "I strongly disagree . . . that substantial new theoretical contributions are in order. . . . The theory building of the New Archaeology has become obsolete." [31] No theory, no laws, no possible validation of hypotheses, and so, consequently, no "explanation." The findings are clear—even if they are harsh after twenty years of New Archeology.

Why this fiasco? The only possible explanation—if one can still use the word—seems to be that there must be a truly radical error somewhere in the New Archeological concept: that is to say, an error concerning not a particular episode of logical procedure, nor the actual definition of objectives, but the very nature of archaeology as such. Isn't it possible that the New Archeologists, despite their self-assurance, their arrogance, their intellectual terrorism, were simply mistaken about what archaeology, the object of all their attentions, is in reality?

So, when it comes down to it, just what *is* archaeology?

9 What Is Archaeology?

I said at the start of this book—and I repeat it here—that there is no question of proposing a terminological definition of archaeology. There are already quite enough of them, and it would serve no purpose to add another. There is no question of wanting to characterize archaeology afresh by its most general objective, especially as everyone (even including the New Archeologists) is in agreement on this, precisely because it is so general that it is not useful ("improved knowledge," "better understanding of man's past"). Neither can one characterize it by its "midterm" objectives because, conversely, agreement on this point would be difficult (the "laws" of archaeology, for example); or by its "subject matter," its sources, its "material," the "remains of the past," in whatever state they have reached us; or by its time span (everything that precedes the present moment, up to yesterday—only the present, perhaps, and the future are excluded). Even less can it be characterized by the different methods it can use in the most varied domains. Finally, it is out of the question to "reduce" archaeology to another discipline, history or anthropology (Gordon R. Willey and Phillip Phillips's formula "Archaeology is anthropology or it is nothing" is opposed by Kent V. Flannery's "[evolutionist] anthropology is archaeology or it is nothing"; and it has repeatedly been said in certain European milieux that archaeology, all things considered, is history, just as prehistory too is the history of periods without writing—which is a point one could discuss at length): nor should one reduce archaeology to the "paleo-" category of everything: paleoecology, paleoethology, paleogeography, paleoethnology, and so forth.

Nor, for that matter, shall I adopt the various formulas that identify archaeology with archaeological praxis and which the New Archeologist Charles L. Redman cites as if they were self-evident and of no great interest: "Archaeology is, of course, what archaeologists do" (in consideration of which he plunges in with his own definition of archaeology—methodological, objective and teleological).[1] Archaeologists do, and can do, all sorts of things, and everyone is far from being in agreement about them; and the real problem is to know what one must or must not do: by definition, just because you can do something does not mean it is right.

No, the problem seems to me not so much defining archaeology in itself (by its content, its aims, its means) as identifying what distinguishes it most clearly from other disciplines, by proceeding (as in semiology or structural linguistics) with a search for what distinguishes it from other closely related disciplines and thus defines its specific nature. For this, I am going to reintroduce the notion of praxis—but in a different way, not the sort I have just set aside in its current form.

What Archaeology Alone Can Do

Despite the presumptuousness of this subheading of which I am sadly aware, I propose to consider not what archaeologists do or can do, but what they are capable of doing better than any other investigator—one can go so far as to say what *they alone* are capable of doing, to the exclusion of any other specialist in a related discipline.

Not, of course, that they can lay claim to a sort of private hunting ground, or a monopoly, an exclusiveness. There is nothing to prevent anyone from competing with them, and people have not failed to do so. Everyone can do everything, but with differing degrees of correctness. The archaeologist too, God knows, can do other things besides archaeology: But can he do them as well as the specialist of the speciality in question? The whole problem lies there. . . . What seems distinctive to me about archaeology is the thing the archaeologist can do better than anyone else: the thing that, whether they like it or not, people are almost forced to leave to him if they want to go any further; the thing that induces people, at least temporarily (and naturally subject to verification), to trust him, whether they want to or not, whether they acknowledge this or not.

Now, if one considers things from this point of view, then the thing which is "up the archaeologist's street," so to speak, is—and one hesitates to put it forward after the tide of contempt and horror unleashed on this point by the New Archeologists—what one has to call the production, the *establishment* or reestablishment of "facts." The establishment of facts! Can you imagine? Now there's a novelty! First of all, there are no "facts." Of course, of course. All the same, like everyone, the New Archeologists, their supporters, and even the conned (in those cases where they might spring into action) are forced to start out from them (in any case, we know they never go far). This is the basis of everything: it is the root, and one always has to return to one's roots—or at any rate not go too far away from them, as popular wisdom and intolerable common sense tell us.

The Establishment of Facts

Whatever the reasons, the interest, the necessity that may have brought an archaeologist to collect particular types of facts (it may be the site itself or, in the site, its chronology, its cultural affiliation, or its topography, its urbanism, its architecture—public or private—its craft activity, its pottery, its coins, its metallurgy, or its cemeteries, its art, together with its agriculture, its imports or exports, its relationships with the region, etc.), in short, whatever his approach to the problem, whatever the perspective from which he views his work, be it historical, anthropological, sociological, ethnological, the true archaeological activity, the one in which the archaeologist finds his identity and is aware that no one can take his place to advantage, is certainly the "establishment" of facts. In the most general and characteristic case, that of an excavation, it is when he notes a mass of rubble, locates one wall, then the others, and sees a plan forming; it is when he uncovers a beaten-earth floor, or a pit in this floor; it is when he examines the material abandoned on this floor, its various components; it is when he isolates this material from what he then finds underneath, which is thus, as a rule, older; it is when he recognizes the bones of a particular animal, the seeds or stones of a particular plant, puts to one side for later examination a particular fish bone or a particular sample of earth likely to be rich in pollen; it is when he differentiates between discarded bones and a grave, between a simple hearth and a localized or generalized blaze; it is when he does this that he is accomplishing work that no one else is better able to do, that no one else can ever do again—especially not the armchair archaeologists, the very people who will use his observations. He knows that, if he makes a mistake, sees things wrongly, misunderstands, his conclusions will then be irremediably falsified and cannot but lead to other errors among those who use them.

It is when, having left the site for the lab or museum, he examines his "finds" more or less summarily and makes the first observations, separating what is already known and thus recognizable from that which is unexpected, unknown, surprising—even if he is temporarily incapable of identifying a shard's fabric, an object's function, and does not understand what a particular peculiarity of structure corresponds to; it is then that he is doing his true archaeological work, and he could not be replaced by an incompetent amateur, a historian, or an anthropologist, and especially not by a theoretician. When he dates a fragment of pottery, when he determines a clay, a provenance (and in many cases he has to suspend judgment), when he restores an entire object from a fragment by basing himself on complete comparative specimens that he knows of, or which he seeks out and knows where to seek them out, he is doing what a specialist in another discipline could not do.

The best part is that certain New Archeologists carry out and know this work perfectly well, even if some of them judge it to be "relatively uninteresting," "natural history in the nineteenth-century sense,"[2] even if "competence" seems to them, with certain exceptions, as absurd as chronology, typology, or "parallels" and other "type fossils."[3] Yet, among the New Archeologists, those in the field, at least, are forced to go through all this, even if they are ashamed of it. And they *should* go through all this if they are really looking for new facts to validate hypotheses.

Finally, it is when the archaeologist uncovers from these fundamental data the regular associations or dissociations, their contemporaneity (and their possible covariance) or their sequence; when he draws the graphics, the diagrams, cumulative or not, the histograms, triangles, "matrices"; when, with or without a computer, he separates out the essential factors, calculates the chance whether an anomaly has any significance, whether a percentage of a sample is representative, in short, when he processes his data and produces a pattern or model which expresses how they interact: it is then that the archaeologist finishes his own work, because he is the best person to appreciate the possible significance of his material, his "catch" of reality, and to test, invalidate, or confirm his initial opinions.[4]

Facts and Approaches to Problems

The New Archeologists, breaking down open doors as usual, objected that in the preceding archaeology there were no "raw," "neutral," "objective" facts, no "basic data," no "unstructured" data collections,[5] no data that "would speak for themselves." (Did anyone ever believe they would?) Facts appear only in a "frame of reference," in the framework of an approach that has been explicitly set out beforehand: as Glynn L. Isaac (like many others) says, "It is now recognized that 'facts' are never reported without some frame of reference, some notion of how things work."[6] The "now" is delectable and quite typical, because once again the New Archeology is discovering the moon in a pompous way. Everyone always has, and has always had, a "frame of reference": whether it was explicit or not, conscious or not, is another matter. But you cannot function in any other way. Their argument rebounds on them—How is it that they do not see this? If one cannot observe or perceive anything without a minimal "theory," then, since observations were made, there was at least an elementary frame of reference; it could not have happened without one. It probably wasn't the New Archeology's frame of reference, but that is a different problem: it is not that the traditional archaeologists had no approaches to problems, it is just that their approaches were different. Their crime is thus lessened, if one assumes that the superiority of the new approaches is proved—and generally, this is left unproved. "Data" are not given as they stand to anyone waiting for them, in some mysterious way: they are perceived, "extracted" from the whole of reality, even by the traditional archaeologist.

This is so true that the New Archeologists, without noticing it, tumble into one of their most astonishing contradictions. What is it? From the start they have been complaining to their readers about these data collections which cannot be constituted per se, these simple accumulations of data with no defined goal, these facts which "don't speak for themselves."[7] This is nothing new: Lucien Febvre, for example, long ago said that "facts" were not cubes of mosaic or tesserae, constituted once and for all, and manipulable as they stand.[8] But it is with some amazement that one sees New Archeologists treating them precisely as such: at least, those who borrow their data. (And here the word regains all its etymological meaning!) Because in fact they are obliged to borrow them from others. They vie with each other in using excavation reports, with, needless to say, an unspeakable contempt for the poor wretches who first extracted the data from the ground, wrote them up, and published them—without of course understanding anything about what they had found. We have already seen Clarke's case, in connection with Bulleid and Gray at Glastonbury (see above, p. 30). Binford, it is true, excavated a few square meters at the site of Pomranky, more at Hatchery West, and indeed spent thirty-four hours on the Nunamiut "Mask" site, in conditions that were certainly very harsh: but as a general rule he dips into the bibliography of V. Gordon Childe, Robert Braidwood, and so forth, whether it is to explain the origin of agriculture or to obtain his "sample" of the African Paleolithic, after having made great use of the work of all his predecessors: Henri Breuil, François Bordes, the Leakeys, J. Desmond Clark (I'll come back to the way he treats Clark), Maxine Kleindienst, and so forth.[9] Likewise Sally Binford, although she has excavated at Shubbabiq in Israel, uses the reports by Alfred Rust on Jabrud, in Syria, and by Dorothy Garrod on Ouadi Amoud.[10] Longacre, Hill, Flannery, Plog, Struever, and, of course, Renfrew, to mention only a few, exploit their own discoveries but also use other works—and likewise Schiffer or South. Obviously they have the right to do so. But in doing this it seems they are oblivious to their own contradiction: on the one hand they maintain that pertinent facts can be collected only in the framework of very specific approaches to problems, and on the other hand they use facts that have been gathered within an approach quite different from theirs. What could be better proof that they are wrong?[11] If they bring in facts gathered by other people in a different perspective, then it means they can do so; and if they can do it, then it was perhaps not as indispensable as they said to subordinate the choice of observed facts to the approach to the problem.

If truth be told, they often complain that the necessary facts have not been gathered. Hill cites the example of those who tried to use other people's reports: "Most reports . . . do not even provide information suitable for describing activity areas within sites, much less for describing aspects of prehistoric social organization, warfare, seasonality, storage techniques, and so on—not to mention data for solving complex explanatory problems."[12] Of course; even though many of the points mentioned above seem to form part of the everyday content of many reports. Isaac regrets the inadequacies of his corpus; Binford deplores the very poor quality of the data used by Michael A. Jochim.[13] South finds himself confronting the distressing situation that nails (important vestiges of, and evidence for, vanished wooden architecture) were not counted in Newfoundland; he deeply regrets that a pattern similar to that in Carolina has not been established for Virginia, Maryland, or Pennsylvania: this would have permitted a better evaluation of his own pattern.[14] But hasn't it always been more or less like this? One never has all the useful data at one's disposal. Didn't Hill himself, by his own admission, omit to note the traces of burning on certain pottery vessels?[15]

On the other hand, all the exercises in "rewriting" to which I have already alluded assume—whether they say so or not—that the basic facts are, if not correct, at least usable for their ends, even if they are not the facts one would have wished for. Clarke takes the data established by Bulleid and Gray as "given."[16] David H. Thomas, for his part, starts out from the "initial facts" of Julian H. Steward and declares that he accepts them all as "unimpeachable." [17] This constitutes a recognition that facts exist outside any particular approach to problems. Clarke himself refers incidentally to an "archaeological reality," others to a bibliographic or museographic "documentation" that must be "amassed." [18]

The point is that the frame of reference—if it is not only useful but inevitable—must not be conceived as a unique, exclusive, narrow point of view, limited to the single problem that is preoccupying someone. The approach to problems must be broad, flexible, and even changeable, adaptable. If it is specific and rigid, it can indeed enable one to sort out only the facts which relate to the problem being studied, the "pertinent" facts. It is an ideal situation. In the first place, the pertinent facts are not, by definition, the only ones: What does one do with the others? One solution is to destroy them, or to ignore them, which comes to the same thing. But that represents a dead loss for other approaches to problems, for other research. This is what the worst early archaeology did: whatever seemed to hold no interest used to be destroyed. The pottery of Delphi, during the great excavation, ended up in the spoil heap for the most part, and this happened even more recently on other sites. The recent levels—medieval, Byzantine— were destroyed because people were not interested in them. And yet this is what Hill is coldly envisaging: "There are even occasions . . . when one must make a choice between one kind of data and another, since the collection of one destroys the other," whether one is working on a large scale or in great detail. [19] Binford observes this in connection with inductive archaeology: "Destruction of this record in search of facts relevant to a single context precludes the possibility of subsequent search for facts relevant in a different context," [20] but exactly the same is equally true for "processual" research. Besides, the pertinent facts that are sought may not be those that were expected, but contrary facts which do not conform to the hypothesis. This is what Binford— though the situation occurred long before, and very often—calls "little" or "big surprises," [21] depending on whether certain characteristics alone are not present, or whether the conflict is even greater. In this case, at least, one is staying within the framework of the hypothesis, even if one has to discard it. But one must then feel embarrassment setting in with regard to nonpertinent facts which have been pushed aside and which could have been or could now be important. Then again, something else can happen: relevant facts may be completely lacking. One knows examples of sites that were opened up with the intention of finding Egyptian material in Cyrene, Cretan exports at Al

Mina, elsewhere pottery of the Geometric period, somewhere else again some conclusive inscriptions—and where there is nothing Egyptian to be found, almost nothing from Crete (but from the Cyclades and a different period), no Geometric material, or innumerable acts of emancipation of slaves. In this case the problem, one might say, is solved by being removed; the combat ceases for lack of combatants. But what is to be done with the material which has, in a way, taken the place of what was sought, and which has no connection with the initial approach to the problem? Should one ignore it? Or change one's opinions and enter a direction of research totally different from the one desired?

Finally, and very frequently, the situation is more complex: one certainly finds the type of facts one was looking for; one also finds what one was not looking for but was expecting; however, in addition one finds other facts that one was not expecting at all. These may be already known or completely unknown, "mysterious," and it is not enough simply to say that they are not in keeping with one's initial approach to the problem. One such case was a Thracian site where the excavator reckoned on finding associations of local material and Trojan material; what he also encountered was not, for example, an unexpected stratification (the "big surprise"), but some unknown material from central Europe.[22] In these circumstances, to uphold at all costs the initial approach to the problem no longer has any point. Obviously the approach has to be changed, and one has to start again from a new basis. Contrary to all the rules and directives, one has not got the answer, whatever it might be, to the problem that was set out; one has answers to a question that has not even been asked yet.

Toward an Open Approach to Problems

The idea that a strictly defined approach to problems must precede all research—an idea that is generally accepted today—is all the stranger because in our time we have seen a proliferation all over the world of very important and richly financed archaeological operations which do not follow any approach that has been defined beforehand, at least in a precise way. Here again, it is the answer that suggests the question. These are *rescue* operations. Any discovery is truly fortuitous (even if one might have expected it by virtue of a certain number of considerations), and it is the unforeseen find that suggests the hypotheses and the subsequent research.[23] How can one reconcile this situation with the demand that theories, problems, and other a priori ideas determine the choice of data to be collected? The exact opposite is what occurs here—even, of course, if the fortuitous discovery is merely considered interesting and its exploitation is directed only by virtue of a set of ideas that were conceived beforehand.

In reality, experience shows that an initial approach to a problem is, as a general rule, joined or even replaced by successive approaches. Leonard Woolley was looking for contacts between Minoan Crete and the Near East: his excavation at Al Mina threw remarkable light on contacts with the Aegean in the ninth and eighth centuries B.C., an almost perfect counterexample of the thesis that an approach to a problem precedes research and does not follow it—and one could give many other examples. Therefore an approach to a problem must not be exclusive or limited to a single question. Or at least it should be placed within a much wider framework, with less well-defined outlines—one that is more flexible, hazier, with variable multiple components, with several stages, with subsidiary approaches in reserve, replacement approaches that are potential but likely to be converted into reality—in short, a general approach "of variable geometry," contrary to what the New Archeologists assert. Naturally, this general approach to problems cannot but reflect a philosophy, at least a partial consensus, from which it follows and which it expresses; naturally, too, it is by no means forbidden to have a very specific question in view that one would like to answer. But this would be suicidal if one did not also keep in mind, if not other possible explanations or solutions of the problem under consideration, at least the possibility of other approaches that could equally well be considered or substituted. The situation will then improve.

This is so true that the New Archeologists are forced to admit it, as if it were not in contradiction with the principles they set out the moment before. Hill, for example, after having declared—in an extremely orthodox way, and very forcefully—that "since we are faced with a potentially infinite amount of data, we are *forced* to make choices as to what to collect," admits (in response to the objection that one is thus "imposing" on reality a preconceived view that is not necessarily adapted to it) that "hypotheses can be altered, should be altered, and nearly always *are* altered in the face of data," that "most investigators have . . . more than one set of hypotheses in mind when carrying out their research."[24] My sentiments exactly. But if the hypotheses change, then quite obviously one must choose other data: "This leads to further data observation," and so on and so forth. But previously these data were not observed, whereas they could have been—indeed, very probably would have been—by a traditional archaeologist, free of the

New Archeological blinkers. The example already cited in connection with Hill himself—"Unfortunately, the pottery in the special rooms was not examined for evidence of exterior burning"[25]—is typical: this sort of observation forms part of the everyday routine of the traditional pottery expert. But it did not form part of the hypothesis, and so it was left out; and meanwhile Hill did not judge it necessary to (or could not) reexamine the artifacts, something anyone else would have done. Likewise, he specifies that the deductive method does not imply that one "will either ignore or fail to see obvious things in the field that [one] is not preprogrammed to see [sic]"; or again, "I am not aware that hypothesis testing has prevented any investigator from gathering traditionally important categories of data."[26] I quite agree; but if this is so, if one has to add all other data (or at least all the data that were "traditionally" kept) to the many categories of relevant data—and Hill has just said that there is no rule about this among the traditionalists, who aspire to recording "everything"—then one really must record "everything," even if that is just a manner of speaking, of course. He does not appear to be aware of the contradiction.[27] It is true that this is merely one more contradiction in New Archeology, that monument raised to the glory of the contradiction.

If there is a general approach to problems in the sense that I have tried to delimit, there are also facts that are "general." And this is certainly acknowledged by the New Archeologists, albeit furtively, on occasion, in passing, in diametrical opposition to their sacrosanct principles. Binford bases himself on the "data" gathered by others; when he brings into his argument the result of observations—"We observe . . ."[28]—he is referring to facts collected outside his approach to problems; likewise when he advocates the revelation of all the patterns of organization, and not just those one is interested in.[29] Hill refers to data "that lie ready at hand—they are more or less obvious things to collect."[30] Renfrew talks of "raw data," of "basic material," Ezra Zubrow of "base data." Clarke speaks in passing of an "archaeological reality," South cites "readily obvious . . . data."[31] Basically, although this is not really correct, it might be simpler to admit (merely from the practical point of view) that facts exist independent of any precise approach to problems. This is the opposite of what is proclaimed by the New Archeology.[32] But maybe one just has to get used to it.

Against the Manipulation of Facts

Besides, the New Archeologists returned pretty quickly to the establishment of facts, relevant or not. Certainly in the beginning and, again, quite recently, they showed an astonishing casualness about facts, ignoring them or, on the contrary, fabricating them, often "manipulating" them for the needs of the cause. Thus, in a very significant way, Binford completely invents the presence of "discoid" tools at Kalambo, which the excavator does not mention at all; for this he takes the average of the percentages at other sites; in this way one would hope he is not too surprised by their concordance! Afterward he regrets this falsification—there were no discoids—but, for all that, he does not rectify it.[33] As he has the nerve to say, data do not limit our knowledge.[34] Quite! Plog and South renounce the search for missing data.[35] Similarly, Renfrew extrapolates the demography of the Cycladic early Bronze Age to all of Greece and all periods.[36] Schiffer, "in the absence of the relevant data," declares quite plainly that he has "simply . . . made a reasonable guess" (*sic*).[37] Clearly, it is not necessary to rack one's brains. South is a virtuoso in this area. I have already mentioned the absence of nails in Newfoundland: in reality they were there; they had been conserved but not counted and thus did not figure in the reports. Any traditional archaeologist would have tried to count these nails or have them counted: but South extrapolates the figure from his beloved Carolina: in this way confirmation is assured.[38] If the percentage of certain objects is too high, never mind—you simply have to remove them and replace them by their pro rata in three other sites.[39] Binford praises South's "formula" (which enables one to calculate the "average" date of ceramics). "Why [does it] work so well?" he asks, not without admiration. It is quite simple: apart from the fact that it is based on the dates of the start and end of manufacture, which are known . . . from texts, when the formula gives a date that is contradicted by the facts, by the known dates of an occupation, South purely and simply substitutes his date for those. Isn't this easier?[40] Another way of manipulating facts consists of "simplifying" them when, for example, one site's chronology is more detailed than that of others, to make comparison possible. This is what Jochim does when he ignores the information at his disposal on the occupation of the Jagerhaus cave in order to make his data more homogeneous with those on sites where the material is not differentiated in this way.[41] One could cite other examples.[42] Finally, simulation procedures—which in other circumstances certainly have some interest—can, in other cases, boil down to a pure and simple fabrication of facts.[43]

But the very excesses of these distortions of reality once again bring out the importance of submission to the facts. For example, it is striking to note Read and LeBlanc, in the article studied earlier, insisting finally on "careful archaeological research in the more traditional sense," and to see one of the commentators on that article supporting the same view: "Progress . . . will have to come chiefly from the good judgement and care with which, day after day, 'empirical' archaeology is carried out."[44] No one is forcing them to say this.

"Hold it right there!" the New Archeologists and their supporters will cry in unison—and the conned will echo them in a higher key. To reduce archaeology to this conception that is so "old-fashioned," hackneyed, empirical, particularizing, inductive, prescientific, and so forth is, in short, to go back twenty years. It is reactionary. It means sweeping aside at a stroke all the progress made toward a higher, fuller conception of archaeology. It means holding on to the idea of an auxiliary science. It means forgetting that archaeology has a vocation to become a full science and that, far from immersing itself "in a sea of facts,"[45] it must "raise itself" to the explanation—in the full sense of the word—of man's past, bring out the laws of his past (and present and future) behavior, and finally, offer us a theory worthy of Einstein that will give some shape to the dust of events and enable us to predict them in the past and even—Why not?—the future. It means ignoring cultural dynamics, processes, hypothetico-deductive reasoning, validation of hypotheses, the absolute necessity of a well-set-out approach to problems. In short, it is untenable, indefensible. And above all— above all—it is unworthy of us. It means we want to limit ourselves to the role of drudges of science, the technical assistants of research[46]— we, who are or want to be authentic scholars, scientific scholars of the twentieth and even the twenty-first centuries. One cannot stand in the way of progress. This retrograde point of view is condemned in advance (by the . . . facts), and, besides, the New Archeology has "definitively won." And the future will prove this soon enough. In a word, ridiculous.

First of all, should I dare recall the bitter experience of these blusterings? I hope I said enough in the first part of this book about the distance there is between the pretensions and the results of our braggarts—their practice contrary to their talk, their self-evident laws, their inconsistent theory, the remarkable meagerness and uncertainty of the conclusions—in short, as was said by one critic who is particularly malicious and may be suspected of bias against the New Archeology, about this "anarchy of uncertainty, optimism, and products of extremely variable quality."[47]

Next, I might perhaps be permitted to recall that, whatever the legitimate prejudice in favor of any novelty ("New!" say American advertisements), and taking as read that a true novelty must be greeted with a priori benevolence (even if things are not yet completely in shape) because the progress and future of research are based on endeavors of this type, when all is said and done, it is not the antiquity or the novelty of a point of view which gives it value: it is its content. A new concept is neither better nor suspect because it is new, an old concept is neither inferior nor superior because it is older: it is good or not so good regardless of its date of birth. An identity card does not allow one to judge a thesis or its author: the question is whether the thesis itself is correct. And here things are not so simple, to say nothing of the false novelties, the new labels on old bottles of an archaeology which (as certain English archaeologists still say) "is new only for those who don't know any."

The Difficulties of Identification

Finally, I can reassure those who might think it humbling to devote oneself to the establishment of archaeological facts. This is not as unworthy of their immense talents as it might seem. If truth be told, it is not easy; it is an enterprise that is at least as difficult as, and perhaps more so than, the invention and demonstration of a law (or a would-be law) or the building of a theory, be it "middle-range" or general—always supposing that it is not, as we have seen, a crack-brained notion. "Facts" are at the base of any later construction; one erroneous "fact" compromises a whole thesis, and you need a lot of talents—for observation, knowledge, competence, intellectual capacity, conscientiousness, and care—to establish a single fact solidly. You probably need more talents than you do to produce an interpretation that is as hazardous as it is pretentious. As Jacques Julliard said, in connection with facts in history, rather than archaeology, "Far from starting out from facts, historians are already very happy when they can establish some." "One has to be very scholarly to grasp a fact," he added, quoting Alain.[48]

The extreme difficulty of establishing facts—and this is where the proper work of the archaeologist is concentrated—is found at many levels of research, from the most general to the most elementary, and it involves very different types of facts, from the most "material" to the most elusive, from the known to the unknown. Since literally everything in archaeology boils down to that, the subject is infinite; I shall give only a few examples and endeavor to classify them.

A first distinction arises between "known" facts, which consequently are recognized at once, and "unknown" or at least uncertain facts that cause difficulty for one or several reasons. One gets the impression that the New Archeology most often deals with the former:

stone tools are of such and such types—this is admitted without discussion—and the interesting stuff comes next. However, it was necessary for someone to establish the typology of the Mousterian and for
others to fine-tune it.[49] Obviously, things are very different in cases
where the facts discovered are not identifiable. This is not the same
thing as a "surprise" (because the surprise can come from the unexpected presence of a particular object in a particular context, but the
object itself poses no problem); it is something more than surprise, or
it is a surprise that bears on the determination, the identification of the
fact itself. As is well known, this happens frequently in archaeological
research and can arise at the most general level (for example, the
Nazca "lines" in Peru) or at the most modest level: the "structure" in
a site, the "object" in the structure.

Faced with an unknown object that he has just found or "exhumed,"
with which he is in direct contact, the archaeologist's precise role is to
try to identify it. It is only afterward, long afterward, that the historian
or the anthropologist can take it over and use it. One of the first steps
(often neglected or unrecognized) is establishing its "state of preserva-
tion": Is the object complete, as it seems, or incomplete? Is it broken
or not? This does not seem much, but it is a first point which it would
be difficult to establish without the competence of an archaeologist.
To take one example, how many architectural "monsters" have been
taken very seriously by commentators who were unable to perceive
that an original structure had been modified by a late alteration?[50]
Next, there is the material: stone, marble from a nearby source or
from far away, nonlocal clay, bone, or ivory, faience. It is the archaeologist, and no one else, who is capable of appreciating this type of
data or of concluding that he needs to call in a specialist and send an
object or a sample to a specialized laboratory: it is not the historian,
who perhaps will never see anything other than a photograph or a
mention in a report and who—if he is standing in front of a fragment
of pottery with no comprehensible decoration—will not be able to
identify it as Cycladic or Euboean, Siceliot or Greek. It is none other
than the archaeologist, poring over the object, who will be able to
identify the technique used (such as the pads used on Magdalenian
cave walls which alone explain the identical configuration of neighboring spots of color) or the repetition of resemblances and differences of
drawings on the fourth-millennium pottery of Susa, which implies the
use of a multiple brush. Then the form has to be defined, especially if
it is incomplete, through comparison with, or memory of, complete
examples: Who, other than the archaeologist, can reconstruct from a
tiny but characteristic fragment the total form from which it comes

(and its provenance and its date), as the paleontologist can reconstruct a dinosaur from a phalanx? As for the decoration, or in any case its technique if not its composition and its motifs (which may start to lead us into the field of art history or iconology), once again it is the archaeologist who will have to specify them: whether or not there is a slip, whether there is a preliminary sketch, or alterations, or a particular superimposition of traits or of colors. It is also the archaeologist who can "see" a fragment of decoration that is incomprehensible at first sight because he will know he should place it vertically, in accordance with the inner surface of the shard, and here again restore what is missing. Finally, it is he who will have to determine the function of an unusual form, of a particular plan, a decoration that is out of the ordinary—and who, lacking inscribed or written indications, and without recourse to scientific dating methods, will propose an "archaeological date" based on "parallels" that are dated (whether approximately, relatively, or "absolutely") thanks to historical texts.[51] The theoretician, the historian, the anthropologist would have a very hard job to take the archaeologist's place for all this. They can only leave it to him; this work is incumbent on him.

There is one final piece of expertise which summarizes all those already mentioned: it is, of course, up to the archaeologist—and apart from him, there is not really anyone else except the professional antique dealer who can take on this task—to identify fakes. This is a formidable trap into which the nonspecialist (and, moreover, often the specialist himself—some pretty illustrious examples are known) has every chance of falling.

Turning now from the scale of the individual structure or the particular object to that of a site in its entirety, it is for the archaeologist to determine the general topography, to disentangle complex plans that have been altered by later modifications, the much later "intrusions," and to avoid confusing them with previous or successive states. This work is often extremely delicate, and all subsequent calculations depend on its results: Who, on sites spanning centuries, hasn't found himself confronted with this brainteaser? Its difficulties tend to be underestimated by the excavators of relatively "simple" sites of only one or a few phases. It is the field archaeologist who must determine (and he alone can) the broad lines of the plan, with all the spatial organization, the access roads, the gates and defenses, the streets, lanes, and alleys, the doors (often omitted), the external and internal circulation, the possible existence of upper stories, unroofed courtyards, systems of water supply or drainage, the wells, the squares, the "sectorization" of an agglomeration into quarters of different character (residential, craft, commercial, political, religious, etc.). It is a tangle that is rarely easy to unravel.

It is also the archaeologist's role to establish the site's chronology, to identify the successive phases of construction, of repair, of destruction (and he must not take a simple fire, a very localized blaze, for a general conflagration), of reconstruction, and of temporary or definitive abandonment. It is perfectly ridiculous to jeer at chronological research, as the New Archeologists do—they could not do anything without it, and they do not fail to exploit a chronology once other people have taken the trouble to propose one. Who else but the archaeologist can be certain of the "closed" nature of a deposit and thus of the at least approximate contemporaneity of its content, of the adjustment of one construction onto another and thus of both its relative posteriority and its partial contemporaneity? Or on the other hand, the superimposition of a particular architectural layer and thus its posteriority, the covering of a particular stratum by a successive stratum and thus—subject to certain rules that he knows—the sequence of materials they contain?

If we next look at the "macroscopic" level, no longer the scale of the agglomeration and its territory but that of the region, and then that of the "country" grouping these regions, it is the archaeologist—or, more exactly, the community of archaeologists working simultaneously in this framework—that one needs to ask for information about agrarian archaeology, the identification and dating of parcels of land, of cadastral divisions, of irrigation canals (Cambodia and now Afghanistan have been the subject of studies of this type), about clearances, the draining of marshes, earth embankments and dikes, bridges, and other methods of adaptation to the environment or of modification of surroundings. It is also the archaeologist who has to date the displacement of rivers, or the marine encroachments of recent periods.[52] It is he who has to identify and date the observations made from aerial photographs, or photographs taken by satellites, the interpretation of which would risk error without controls and dating on the ground. It is again the archaeologist who designates foreign populations present outside their proper zones, migrations and immigrations, and movements of population on the basis of their material (and in liaison with physical anthropologists). On the "international" level, one might say, it is he who traces the long-distance "commercial" movements (amber, tin, obsidian, spices, perfumes, etc.), "colonizations," and even—yes, indeed—"invasions." All of this is part of the work of the archaeologist as such; these are all details of the innumerable facets of the establishment of facts.

And it is not only these facts of a "material" order that are in his province. The archaeologist also must try to specify, through the tangible or visible remains that may survive, phenomena of mental types such as, for example, certain forms of technical behavior (the very prolonged persistence of certain pottery types, like the medieval "pégau" in the French Midi, compared with the rapid development in other periods and other places) or funerary customs (ideas about the beyond, respect or lack of it for previous graves, state of mind of the survivors, sexual or social differentiation between men, women, and children, rich and poor, slaves and free men), or again—whatever the New Archeologists might think about it—the accepted or undergone or refused influences from the East or from central Europe. Where can one find a trace of these "intangible" things—as the New Archeologists rather touchingly call them—if not in the archaeological "material," and who can interpret this material correctly at the most "literal," the most "factual" level if not the archaeologist first and foremost? This is what he can do better than anyone; this is what he must give top priority. It's his job.

Archaeological Demonstration

Certainly this work brings into play various methodologies that, as we shall see shortly, are rational, rationalizable, or rationalized. But it also involves (and with good reason) a few of the procedures that are most abhorrent to the New Archeology: I have mentioned competence, "flair," intuition, all of which must keep their rightful place. No doubt "competence" (which is not exactly the same thing as "authority," even less "argument by authority") can be analyzed, or "dismantled" explicitly, but by its very nature it manifests itself in an immediate way—which is not to say instantaneous—without providing its arguments. It assumes a great deal of knowledge and experience: this is no doubt why it is looked on so unfavorably by the fanatics of explicitness.[53]

What is there left to say about the urgent necessity to be explicit? Transparency, a glass house. And of course, if you look at it from a didactic point of view, it can only make things easier for the layman, the beginner. But must a researcher saddle himself with this nonsense? Because there is implicit and then there is implicit: a scholar can make his arguments, his assumptions perfectly explicit to himself and may not think it a good idea to pass them on to the public—after all, if the public thinks it indispensable to make everything explicit, all it has to do is carry out this procedure itself. John Beazley did not give us all the reasons that made him group together particular black- or red-figure representations under the name of a particular painter, workshop, or hand in that workshop. He reckoned that the concerned reader would be capable of discovering his reasons if need be, and no doubt he thought it tedious to repeat the operation in each of the thousands of cases he studied. He presented his conclusions. And even if some of them are open to discussion (especially where poorly defined secondary people are concerned, such as the helpers or the drudges of the workshop), who could deny that he has left us one of the monuments of traditional archaeology, which, in addition, lends itself to quantitative archaeology?[54]

On the other hand, what unimaginable dullness one often finds in the work of the explicit archeologists! It is all very well to be somewhat discursive, but there comes a moment when one plunges into pedantry pure and simple. Unless he is addressing himself to beginning students, it is hard to see why Clarke should set out in detail the nine successive "intellectual" operations of "disciplined procedure,"[55] or why Binford should line up six stages of reasoning: observations, then proposition, deduction, prediction, bridging arguments, ending with the final hypothesis. It might perhaps have been possible to jump more quickly from one to the next,[56] especially since one is never explicit enough: things can always be made more explicit than one would think. After explicit, there's explicit and a half! It must be difficult for Hill—a supporter of explicitness if ever there was one[57]—to see himself preached at on this very point by Schiffer (after others): for indeed, at Broken K, Hill slyly concealed from us the "stipulation" that "the social unit of pottery manufacture is the same as . . . the social unit of pottery use" (by which he must mean, in clearer terms, that pottery is used where it is made). What's more, he hid another assumption from us: "that at least some pottery was discarded . . . at the location of pottery use"![58] I would never have guessed. Yet it is obvious that if the (female) potters don't break any pottery in their workshop, one can scarcely get any idea of their production. By way of contrast, what a lesson the Bordes give us about the role of flair, intuition, and competence! "In a test trench, after seeing about ten or twenty tools, or even sometimes flakes, one can tell if a Mousterian assemblage belongs to the Quina or M.T.A. facies, even if no Quina scraper or handaxe has yet been found. . . . But as yet this is a subjective matter of 'experience,' and the difficult, if not impossible task of defining these subtle differences, felt but rarely explainable, is yet to be done."[59]

When all is said and done, there is something rather pathetic about this demand for explicitness; it recalls the claim that scholars' personal card indexes should be placed at the disposal of everyone—and especially of those who have not taken the trouble or the time to build one up (as if access to a card index enabled you to use it in anything other than a very crude way, to gather a few examples or references you didn't know; as if having a data bank at your disposal might permit you to know everything at the wave of a magic wand—or rather at the push of a button; and as if scientific research were not something very different from a simplistic bibliographical documentation). What ignorance of intellectual procedure, which is often based far more on what is left unsaid than on what is said, far more on the implied than the expressed.

Moreover, the New Archeologists, contradicting themselves yet again without hesitation, reintroduce, if not "flair" (still impugned, at least in principle if not in fact, in favor of sampling), competence[60] (which, in any case, had done without their authorization) and, especially, intuition.

Induction

First of all, without saying it (and therefore implicitly!), the New Archeologists certainly use intuition when they put forward a hypothesis: since the latter has to be demonstrated by deductive reasoning, it is by definition an *intuitive* inference (or generalization).[61] Similarly, when they suggest "tests" allowing them to validate their hypotheses, there is no point in their saying that these tests are deduced logically from the proposition: Doesn't the very choice of a particular test over another involve intuition? This is especially the case as they do not proceed to carry out the test. When Carl Hempel, quoted by Binford, evokes "accepted" theories (in which, if they want to count as a law, universal propositions must be implied), for example, the laws of Galileo or Kepler, accepted before receiving theoretical grounding,[62] doesn't this acceptance involve intuition? But resorting to intuition in time becomes completely explicit and conscious: as we have seen, Binford reaches the stage of maintaining stubbornly that laws must not be discovered but "invented," and this invention involves "creativity," a capacity of imagination—and thus intuition.[63] The term appears in Read and LeBlanc's article in their concept of "an intuitively satisfactory explanation"; and though they still impugn the use of intuition in verification or confirmation (their position on this point is, they say, "crystal clear"[64]), on the other hand, faced with certain scholars' feeling of "dissatisfaction" with a particular deductive explanation, they ask the question, "Whence stems that sense of unsatisfactoriness, if not from the intuition of the scientist?"[65] We have come a long way from the initial anathema.

The fact is that archaeological demonstration is not (or not exactly) deductive reasoning, contrary to what the New Archeologists claimed with an insistence so tireless that it finally became suspect. Deductive, let it be clearly understood, and not inductive.

Unfortunately, the opposition between induction and deduction is one of the problems on which the New Archeology has diversified and piled up contradictions and confusions to the greatest extent—one can even say it has talked nonsense! At the start, one recalls the unceasing attacks against the "narrowly inductivist" approach—for example, by Hill or by Binford with regard to Jeremy A. Sabloff and Willey.[66] Indeed, for Binford the term "inductivist" will continue to be almost an insult.[67] Again, in 1980, Renfrew spotlights this point among the things one must make one's students understand.[68] And yet Binford himself is fully aware of the contradiction inherent in pleading for the deductive method and at the same time advocating "an essentially inductive data collection procedure";[69] but he gets out of it with one of his usual pirouettes. Hill too (though without saying so explicitly) is, in reality, advocating induction, when he points out that "working hypotheses are provoked by data"; to get out of it, he uses the word "abductive."[70] This word is used again by Fritz and Plog in 1970 and by R. J. Mason in 1972.[71] The same year, induction makes an appearance in Thomas's model of archaeological reasoning.[72] With time, induction was salvaged more and more regularly: for example, in 1976 by Thomas G. Cook, who reproached Willey for not being inductive (whereas Binford reproached him with the opposite)[73]; or the following year by South, who cites the "hypothetico-deductive-inductive cycle [sic]" already outlined by John G. Kemeny in 1959[74]; and by Read and LeBlanc, who specify its role in relation to hypothetico-deductive reasoning, in 1978.[75] J.-C. Gardin, in 1974, quite rightly condemned the "fallacious nature" of the opposition between deduction and induction, and the four reviewers of *New Perspectives* had, from the outset, stressed the danger of "neglecting the inductive part of reasoning"; one of them, in 1980, even goes so far as to mingle—a sacrilege!—the epithets of "inductive *or* deductive" in connection with positivism.[76] In short, on this point as so often, the New Archeology has said everything and its opposite.

In reality, and in a way that is very characteristic of the New Archeology, it is a typically false problem. If the structure of logical reasoning can only be what it is—if a demonstration can consist only of extracting or "deriving" one proposition from another—then things generally do not happen as the New Archeologists claim. In fact, to take an example, when one observes that wall A is "cut" by wall B (or, if you like, that wall B has cut into wall A) and that it is necessary to determine their relative chronology, one does not use deductive reasoning, strictly speaking. To do so would produce the following: (1) any wall interrupted by another is the older of the two (or something of this ilk: any wall cutting into another wall is more recent than the one it cuts into); (2) wall A is cut by B (or B cuts into A); (3) A is thus older than B (or B more recent than A). What archaeologist would bother to waste his time in reasoning like this? One passes, one "leaps" immediately from the observation to the conclusion: wall A, cut by B, is older; or wall A is older because it is cut by B. One does not feel any need to go looking for a covering "law"; one does without it. There is not a conditional proposition, a covering law, a deduction of a consequence, then observation that this consequence is realized, and finally the conclusion (if two noncontemporary walls meet, the older will be cut or covered by the more recent. . . . A is cut by B, etc.). The "archaeological demonstration" comes down to the same thing, but it "includes" the hypothesis and thus renders it useless as such. It contracts or "telescopes" deductive reasoning. The counterproof is easy to administer. Hill—the whole of whose article, devoted to the "methodological debate," seems finally to be a tissue of sophisms—gives a typical example in connection with Broken K: "1) The premise is stated that certain [ancient] rooms look like living rooms [of present-day pueblos] because they contain firepits and mealing bins. 2) Ethnographic data indicate that present day pueblo living rooms also contain these features. 3) It is then proposed that since the prehistoric rooms have these features they must in fact be functionally the same as the historically recorded living rooms."[77] In reality it seems clear that the conclusion is known from the start as is shown by the repetitions between (1), (2) and (3): it would be shorter to say "comparable rooms must have the same function." The premises are formulated for the needs of the cause.[78] The validation stage merely repeats this technique: the implications are deduced from hypotheses only because their confirmation or invalidation is already known. The whole thing is—yet again—tautological. The archaeologist knows the answer before he asks the question—or before he pretends to ask it, for the reader's benefit. If it is done for a didactic purpose or for popularization, then fine. It can help someone who is a bit slow-witted to understand things. But the two types of reasoning have equal value,[79] and the other one is shorter and quicker. The deductive form is just one way of presenting things, in a form that is perhaps easier to grasp but not more correct. Dare I evoke the spirit of geometry, the spirit of finesse, and Pascal? If "Socrates is mortal" implies "man is mortal, Socrates is a man, and therefore mortal," then the converse is equally true: "Socrates is mortal" represents, in a way, the syllogism—it replaces it, translates it. It only has the appearance of an affirmation.

A Return to the Facts

Whatever method of reasoning and of demonstration is chosen, there is no assurance (contrary to what the New Archeology seems to suppose) that the conclusion is valid and definitive. In most cases the very opposite occurs. A result is never more than provisional, even if it seems to present every guarantee, even if all possible precautions have been taken. A "fact" is never established "for always." It is always liable to be modified, adjusted, made more precise, at times even torn apart and overhauled. In the field of establishing facts, the "truth" is merely the "latest and best hypothesis; it is never more than temporary." It can be improved. Traditional archaeology abounds in rectifications, corrections, in wool pulled over eyes, in crude dating errors, in errors of provenance, in fakes taken as the real McCoy—and the New Archeology is not exempt from them (remember the smudge pits, the Kalambo discoids, the seasonal interdigitation of the Mousterian, etc.). The progress of our knowledge and understanding of the past moves forward through this hesitant development, these tentative efforts, these constant small alterations, which, little by little, make things more precise. If nothing is definitive, then nothing is completely lost either; even the worst mistakes play a useful role: "If the . . . Pattern [proves incorrect] this will be exciting news, for . . . the . . . Pattern will have served . . . archaeology well." Who said that? A New Archeologist about New Archeology.[80] "This is the beauty of the method," as Hill would say.[81]

In the case of a refutation (through criticism or through new or unknown facts), in the case of doubts, the only procedure is to return to the "facts" one started from, to reexamine them in the light of the new objections. There is an infinite number of ways to consider them; the subject is inexhaustible,[82] and so is archaeological "reality." This is what traditional archaeology has always done; and this is what the New Archeology is finding in its turn, as if it were a new discovery, when it puts forward other hypotheses, other observations, other verifications, and so on:[83] except that generally it does not do so.

No, the establishment of facts is not an easy task unworthy of anybody. It does not reduce anyone to a subordinate role: the most ambitious constructions, which aim the highest but fail to get there (or even to get near it), closely depend on it. To see the heart of archaeology in this is not to lower the subject to "simply a technique," as Albert C. Spaulding said,[84] because it brings into play all the archaeologist's knowledge, all his intelligence, all his imagination. And that is the key to everything that may follow.

If one is willing to accept that the establishment of facts is the archaeologist's proper role and mission, the thing that distinguishes him from all the "para-archaeologists" because he is capable of doing this work, and is the only one capable of doing it correctly—to the extent that if a historian or an ethnologist ventures to try it he is transformed into an archaeologist (though of what caliber remains to be seen), and on the other hand, that if the archaeologist extends his research into history or anthropology he ceases to act as an archaeologist proper and becomes, with greater or lesser success, a historian or an anthropologist—if one is willing to see this proposition not as a pure and simple return to the views of traditional archaeology (and thus, for that reason alone, destined for the dustbin of history) or as a pure and simple rejection of the New Archeology (and consequently a heresy doomed to the stake of the schismatics), then a whole group of questions that are all tangled together link up, and the different aspects of archaeology, like their extensions, fall into place: whether it be approaches to problems, excavation, "scientific" expertise, the statistical processing and computerization of data, the transition to history or anthropology, or, finally, archaeological theory.

10 The Territory of Archaeology

New Fields and New Problems

One of the least debatable merits of the archaeology of the past twenty years has been the extension of its "domain" and the subsequent enrichment of its approaches to problems.

The new "fields" of action—the new "territories," as Emmanuel Le Roy Ladurie says in connection with the historian—concern time (from man's most remote origins to the Middle Ages, rather neglected until then in archaeology, and especially to the modern and contemporary periods, with the recent developments of "industrial" archaeology) as much as geographical space (from northern Europe to Australia and Oceania, from the Arctic to South America). They include also the points of view, the conceptual aspect (from "spatial" archaeology to ecology, from "bioarchaeology" and "geoarchaeology" to "ethnoarchaeology," human ethology, etc.).[1]

In actual fact, quite often this extension and this renewal are essentially the product of a "nominalism," if not a simple verbalism, which is limited to sticking a relatively new word (or applying a banal word, but in an unusual way) onto realities that have already seen long service. Such, for example, would be the case of "urban" archaeology, one of the most typical pseudodiscoveries of the past decade (it is supposed to be the archaeology "of" the town, as opposed to archaeology done "in" the town, as if anyone ever excavated in a town without having the town as a whole in mind—for example, excavated the Agora of Athens while forgetting the existence of the Acropolis, the Kerameikos, the Olympieion, or the Ilissos). Similarly, the new nautical archaeology cannot help but recall a few memories and a few wrecks, models of boats, and so forth, whether discovered in the water or out of it; "underwater" archaeology, whatever its recent progress and results may have been, is above all a handy term by which to group together the former marine archaeology and lacustrine or riverine archaeology. The Anglo-Saxon rural archaeology, "of the landscape," seems to combine archaeology (farms, *villae,* hamlets, villages, etc.), agrarian archaeology (parcels of land, cadastral divisions, the study of which is by no means a recent phenomenon), paleobotany and palynology, and so forth, and it appears to involve as much paleogeography as archaeology, rather than to constitute a field (if you will forgive the pun) that is really specific.

It is nevertheless the case that these areas have been the scene of intensified research, and that a new word (for want of a veritable new concept) generally has the beneficial effect of systematizing the investigation: ethnoarchaeology, for example, has always been practiced in a small way; its constitution as a subdiscipline developed it and made it more precise—always assuming that it involves archaeology rather than ethnology. One could say as much of the archaeology that, with wonderful clumsiness, is called "postdepositional": the phenomena studied here have always been subject to piecemeal observations, but their classification under the term "transformations" will probably make their study more methodical. This is a positive move.

This widening of "perspectives," to take up a word that is dear to Binford, subdivided itself into a whole series of more precise approaches to problems. One has to give the New Archeology its due in that it contributed a few directions of research that were little known, or unknown. But if one takes the case of Binford, for example, what does it boil down to? A marked insistence on fauna and flora, on the role of rivers, fish, and migratory birds; the subsequent taking into consideration of purely seasonal activities as opposed to permanent occupation of base camps; the transference of research to present-day situations that are judged comparable to those of the past. I am not claiming to be exhaustive: but nothing in all this is really completely new, and it does not add up to very much. After all, the renewed approaches to problems are just the normal result of all thought; any traditional archaeologist could have had these ideas (and may actually have had them). But that does not take anything away from the New Archeologists' merits in this sphere.

Apart from the content of the approaches to problems, the way of tackling things seems to have turned aside (at least to a certain degree) from the traditional minute details and myopia, toward what one might call a macroarchaeology, or a macroscopic dimension of archaeology: surveys at a regional (J.-C. Gardin in Afghanistan, for example) or a continental level (with photographs taken by satellites), the consideration of very long chronological periods of several centuries, the introduction into archaeology of the "long term,"[2] or again, drastic simplifications concerning the study of certain materials such as pottery (classed as "red" or "nonred"), or architecture, seen "in bulk" in a synthetic and no longer ultradetailed way.[3] However, the question arises whether this always constitutes progress.

It will have been noticed that the renewed approaches to problems are, by their nature, situated outside and ahead of the methodological debate. It is not that approaches to problems do not form an integral part of archaeological procedure, but what they contribute are questions, the answers to which have to be tested; they do not contribute their verification. It is an irony of fate that one of the New Archeology's rare contributions is, in a way, situated outside its theories.

Excavation

If the distinctive feature of archaeology is, as I believe—once the initial approaches to problems have been set out—the establishment of the facts that are relevant to them, not to mention those that may not be relevant but that nevertheless turn up, then one understands the preeminent place accorded to excavation. Certainly, one may not have recourse to actual excavation in every circumstance: notably in the field of survey (especially on a large scale), or of ethnoarchaeology, obviously. One can content oneself (or be in a situation where one must content oneself) with "surface" collections, and the New Archeology (though not only the new) has often had recourse to this procedure. It has tried to rationalize it by developing "sampling" techniques a great deal. It would be a bit much to claim that the instructions concerning sampling are a real success. Quite apart from the eternal and invalidating objection—which the theoreticians have never managed to escape from, whatever they may say about it[4]—that a sample has its full meaning only if one knows the total "universe" the population is supposed to represent, whereas one only ever knows the material that has been discovered, and that there is no use in comparing it, in desperation, to the total material that existed formerly, the practical conclusions are pretty absurd. (J. W. Mueller, after extremely complex calculations, boldly reaches the conclusion that the best sampling rates are 90 percent, which is quite close to 100 percent, i.e., to nonsampling, or 40 percent, and that the latter is more economical than the former!)[5] Above all, the practice, as usual, falls short of the theory: the New Archeologists practice either "random" sampling,[6] or else 100 percent sampling[7]—that is to say, very often and not counting all the inevitable distortions, they abandon the idea of sampling "rationally." An "awful truth," as David H. Thomas joked.[8]

An excellent illustration of the defects of sampling is provided, as it happens, by its application to excavation. The laudable desire to escape from a "personal equation," from the arbitrary which falsifies everything, has led certain New Archeologists to choose at random— if need be, with the help of random numbers selected by a gadget[9]— the test-pits that have to be dug: with remarkable regularity, the choice obtained in this way has to be completed by additional test-pits, determined not at random but (fortunately) by more intelligent considerations.[10] Even Hill had to do it all those years ago! (fig. 5).[11]

As for proper excavation, the New Archeologists (during the entire initial period, and of course they were imitated by their usual followers) pretended to attach only very minor importance to it: perhaps because they felt vaguely that this is where the crunch came, and the emergence of a reality that was so fundamental and so different from their theories made them ill at ease. At the very most, they pointed out in passing that of course a good excavation was more worthwhile than a bad one.[12] But they did not make a song and dance about it: statistics or computers would take its place. One night of Paris would replace the dead of Austerlitz. Then, in a second phase, they could no longer avoid feeling the usefulness of quality work in the field; they began to deplore the "poverty" of other people's data,[13] especially from the point of view of stratigraphy and chronology—Who would ever have believed it?[14]—and they started explicitly to desire, in certain cases, an "exceptionally fine excavation control"[15] to identify, for example, "individual . . . episodes" of "secondary" refuse, in a single area, of the remains of multiple activities. A retraction like this was inevitable and predictable, as soon as it was no longer a question of theory but of work in the field and concrete problems. Besides—and fortunately—by virtue of the great New Archeological principle, which consists of doing in practice the opposite of what is upheld in theory, the New Archeologists in the field had not, in fact, applied too scrupulously the directives from Hill (i.e., to destroy, in certain cases, whatever is not relevant to the problem under consideration). And while Binford gets himself scolded by Donn T. Bayard because "most of his articles contain no maps, no sections, nor even photographs of the features under discussion"[16] (it is true that Binford insists on telling us that J. L. Coe taught him in a few weekends "all I was to ever learn in formal training sessions about practical fieldwork":[17] this will hardly be appreciated by those who believe that, in this area, one has never finished learning), and while, to take a more recent example, Schiffer's technique seems rather strange (he excavates "in arbitrary levels ranging in thickness from 10 to 20 cm," and his chronology

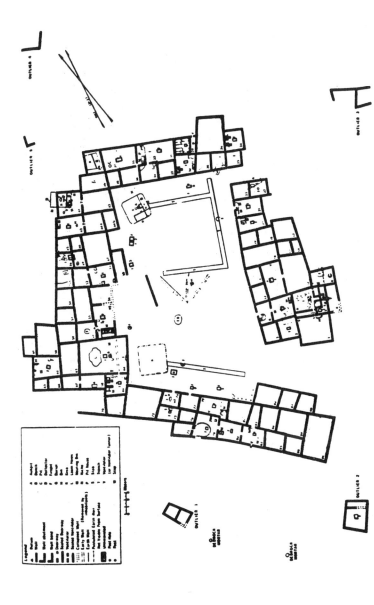

Fig. 5. The Broken K Pueblo, Arizona. J. N. Hill, in *New Perspectives in Archeology*, ed. Sally R. Binford and Lewis R. Binford (Chicago: Aldine, 1968), 105, fig. 1.

seems to rest almost exclusively on "bond-abutment relationships" [18]), the excavations of Stuart Struever and his pupils, for example, seem meticulous; one could say the same of the model excavation at Nichoria, in Messenia, and of many others. Fortunately Renfrew, as I have said, is fully aware of the problems posed by sites with multiple layers, as compared with sites of a single period. [19]

With a touching parallelism, the zealots who in 1971 were assuring us that "the possibly bad quality of the excavations of certain New Archeologists took nothing away [*sic*], in [their] eyes, from the value of the theoretical arguments" (one wonders what value these theoretical arguments would have attained "in their eyes" had they been combined with impeccable application in practice) or who ascribed to Mortimer Wheeler the view that "even the best stratigraphy does not guarantee the quality of the interpretation" [20] (all the same, one would hope that it does not endanger it), and for whom "excavating less, but better, has sometimes been an alibi for understanding less" (*sic*), who regretted, while they were at it, that "present-day missions excavate, with a more numerous personnel, surfaces that are far more limited than their predecessors' excavations of the last century" [21] (one suspected this explicit reference to the nineteenth century was coming!), these same zealots, therefore, immediately turned coats and fell into step. Excavation techniques have returned to favor—though the results have not always been very successful. Thanks to Wheeler, stratigraphic excavation had made decisive progress from 1954 onward: but in less than a decade French excavators had returned enthusiastically to the vast, continuous clearances they seem decidedly unable to do without. [22] Fortunately, once again, there still remained a sufficient smattering of the stratigraphic method to limit the damage; and even more fortunately, at least among some of them, the practice remained remote from the theory. While it is true that we have seen excavation by long parallel trenches presented as a remarkable novelty (it is an old technique, not of excavation but of prospection, and was applied, for example, at Tiryns in 1907), [23] and while the generalized use of the bulldozer to strip certain sites will leave endless doubt about the existence of at least a few bits of living-floors which have always been found elsewhere but by other methods, certain sites (for example, in the Arab Emirates) show that nothing has been forgotten. Moreover, one can foresee a return of the pendulum, with analogous causes producing analogous errors. In Greece, the German Institute, which for a long time was an advocate of continuous clearance, has recently adopted the Wheeler method. [24]

Be that as it may, and although for some people the main thing seems to be avoiding (or deferring?) that painful "moment of truth" that excavation represents in favor of survey or detection, and the preference for statistics at the expense of care and minute detail in archaeological excavation, it seems pretty indisputable that the latter remains not only the principal (if not exclusive) source of "facts," but also one of the best opportunities to "establish" them correctly. And this, as I have already said, is what I think is the specific role of archaeology. A closed deposit (a tomb, an intact pit, an isolated stratum, etc.) will always to me represent the best "assemblage" and the place where "clusters" are best interpretable, providing the material is recorded intelligently.[25]

Experimental Archaeology

In comparison with excavation, the different forms of "experimental" archaeology (which is not a recent phenomenon) constitute the check, the test, and represent the synthesis after analysis, and by virtue of this fact, they are important. Moreover, such archaeology assembles the most concrete forms, from the reconstitution of past conditions (for example, by accelerating the "weathering" of time, water, and wind) to the restoration of vanished structures (models, in the vulgar sense of the word: the Daphnephorion of Eretria or, full size, a house of the Aisne valley), and the reconstitution of the way of life, in fully "dynamic" form—stock rearing and agriculture—such as the Butser farm in southern England.[26]

In a sense, ethnoarchaeology can be added to experimental archaeology. However, it will be noted that the famous "garbage project" teaches us more about the behavior of the present-day inhabitants of Tucson, Arizona, in a "consumer" society than about prehistoric Indians.[27] One could say as much of acculturated Eskimo: here one finds oneself back at the eternal problem of the ethnographic analogy: the persistent imprecision, whatever may be said, of the relationship between past and present, between the remote and the very close.[28]

The different types of "models" (in the cybernetic sense of the word, this time), very well described and classified by Clarke,[29] can be considered more sophisticated forms of experimental archaeology. They are hypotheses that are likely to be tested. One could say the same of (or one would rank among them) the various attempts at "simulation" which have arisen more or less recently.[30] But these procedures must be handled with caution: the ease with which one can "control" the experiment (by freezing one or several variables as constants and observing the behavior of the variables left "free") is offset by the numerous more-or-less arbitrary assumptions that have to be accepted. In his study of the "transformations" (no longer quantitative but "spatial") that affect postdepositional processes, Schiffer tried to test his models by simulating not only their mechanism but the data themselves—the composition of the material supposed to be in place in the various "refuse areas" (e.g., rubbish pits). The results of his factor analysis "provide a complete confirmation of the model." Thus everything would be for the best in the best of all possible worlds, if one didn't have the perverse curiosity to examine things a little more closely.[31]

In effect, Schiffer represents the site by a grid of $6 \times 6 = 36$ squares (each represents a refuse area) and in its four corners are located four activities (nos. 1–4). Then he calculates the theoretical percentage of remains of each activity (using different types of tools), that is to say, the theoretical percentage of tools in each square. And it is here, obviously, that the difficulties begin. He puts forward no fewer than seven presuppositions: since the case he has chosen is that of multiple secondary deposits, for multiple nonoverlapping activities, he supposes that each activity involves ten types of tools, that the rate of activity is the same everywhere, that there is no sharing of activity or of tools among the four activity areas (thus, in all, there are $4 \times 10 = 40$ types of objects), and that the duration of activity is constant; then he adds that the refuse is discarded at the same rate, in constant proportions, and finally, and above all, that the quantity of discarded objects is smaller when the place of discard is farther away (i.e., varies inversely with the distance of the deposits). What is more, no percentage is zero.

One simply has to line up all these presuppositions to see that, taken one by one, each of them is not always tested: that is the very least one can say! Activities can involve the same tools, lent by one craftsman to another, different activities can occur in the same place, all do not require the same number of tools, the rate of activity and of discard is very likely to be variable (And why not nil?), and the same applies to the duration of activity: Schiffer himself acknowledges that the refuse materials are not in constant proportions.[32] Finally, one can well imagine that a major removal of rubbish to a remote pit may take place.

To this one must add that Schiffer's calculations (even if one accepts his assumptions) are often incomprehensible: Why, for example, does refuse area 1 (top left of the grid) have a coefficient 10 of waste from activity area 2 and only a coefficient 5 for activity area 3, which is situated at the same distance (bottom left)? Similarly, why do the coefficients representing the percentages of tools from the four activity areas vary only from 20 to 60, and why does their total not exceed 78?

It's a fair bet that a few extra presuppositions are showing up here. And what connection does all this have with reality?

The conclusion of the factor analysis (four factors containing, as variables of maximum weight, the ten tools used in each of the four activity areas) is said to be "encouraging": but isn't it just what he had put forward at the start? Yet again.

I have gone into detail only to show the danger of simulations that concern the data: it is another form of contempt for the facts. Simulation must not turn into dissimulation. It seems a better idea to use it with observed data, so that it concerns the mechanism of the model itself rather than its content. The facts should be established rather than simulated more or less arbitrarily.

Archaeometry

For the establishment of facts, archaeology finds extremely precious help in all sorts of "scientific" techniques that have been perfected or developed in the past few decades with a success that made the New Archeologists and others dream. There are so many questions in archaeological research that are much debated that it is worth saluting this noteworthy exception: one can even say, broadly speaking, that all scientific techniques, whatever they may be, are beneficial a priori and must be adopted.

Indeed, whether it be large-scale survey or medium- and small-scale detection, with spatial or aerial photography, if need be in false colors or in thermography, with measurements by electricity, magnetism, or radio waves; whether it be dating techniques, and of course radiocarbon, duly calibrated by dendrochronology, or remanent magnetism, or thermoluminescence (of soil as much as of objects), or potassium-argon, and so forth; whether it be the numerous different methods of physicochemical analysis—X-ray spectrometry or whatever the concurrent (but in reality convergent) schools may be, neutron activation of trace elements, or mineralogy, for the provenance of clays or the composition of metals; be it paleozoology, paleoanthropology, paleobotany, palynology, . . . there is no need to go on. The information provided by these methods is incalculable and generally very positive.

Except, however, that everything must not be taken as gospel truth: even since the calibration of C-14 dates, certain results have to be accepted with prudence. For example, at the site of Nichoria—to which I've had occasion to refer several times, and where the use of modern techniques has been vaunted (notably flotation, ethnobotany)—a curious illustration of their lack of rigor is provided by the two C-14 dates, one of which is clearly wrong by about + 900 years, the other by about − 900.[33] One could say as much of the result of certain surveys by magnetism or electricity: while in certain cases they are completely reliable, others make you wonder.[34] And it is pretty clear that, as soon as sites with thick and complex superimposed layers are involved, one cannot expect these methods to yield the same precision achieved for sites with single or very simple occupations. For a start, remanent magnetism demands remains that are well dated by other methods; analyses of provenance pose all kinds of problems that are far from resolved. In short, all the very elaborate techniques that are at present grouped under the term "archaeometry" must remain under the control of the archaeologists who benefit from them: this applies first, of course, in the general approach to the problem, which cannot be left to the physicists, but it is also true in the choice, the localization, the "comparability"[35] of the samples, and the final (archaeological) interpretation of the results. On the pretext that archaeologists are not, by definition, physicists and cannot enter into the detail of the mysteries of physics, certain physicists (who at the start are totally ignorant of the problems referred to them) have believed in good faith that they were replacing the archaeologists from there on. Although their contribution is priceless—in every sense of the word—this would be a confusion of ends and means. Moreover, some of them have understood this perfectly and have quite rightly put greater demands on the archaeologists who refer their difficulties to them.

The Elaboration of Data

Once a problem or an open set of problems has been posed and a research strategy chosen accordingly (survey, excavation, museographic or ethnoarchaeological investigation, etc.), and once the "raw facts" relevant to these problems (and, in passing, also those which are not directly relevant to them but may be relevant to other possible problems or to no problem that has at present been put together) have been obtained, carefully determined, identified, controlled—in short, established, analyzed, and also dated by means of scientific techniques—they must still undergo further elaboration in order to be used with a view to the solution being sought. It is a matter of moving on from the stage where objects or structures present themselves, in a way, as they are, in disorder—that is, as is well known, in an order (fortuitous or not) that is not the one desired. It is a question of describing them, classifying them, and bringing out the various possible relationships between them and with other types of data at the same site and in other sites, in a given period and in other periods. If one thinks about all the structures of all types (buildings, various installations, tombs), about the volume of pottery, small finds, bones, samples of all kinds, about the variety of lithic material at a prehistoric site, these often considerable quantities cannot merely be identified, localized, dated, and delivered as an amorphous mass; they have to be elaborated in various ways and from different points of view if one wishes to exploit them for one purpose or another. The question I have been putting forward in this connection since the beginning of this book is how we can know what in this work is—or is no longer—the proper domain of archaeology.

Description

Description, which prolongs and specifies the determination of the facts—whether one is dealing with the level of the individual, the subgroup (site), or a larger whole (region, country, or even continental or intercontinental area)—is consequently dependent on the archaeologist (excavator, museographer) who digs the object(s) out of the ground or a museum. In this sphere, as in others, people have wanted to get away from the subjective nature of descriptions—from impressionism, which is always distorted by personal equations. Descriptive codes have been proposed, which make explicit and precise the observations that are transcribed, but this was a little naive, since choices—even though explicit—are still choices,[36] and every determination of features or attributes rests in any case on arbitrary postulates. One of the favorite themes of the "objectivity" that was sought and proclaimed has always been "quantification."[37] In actuality it was not a novelty: one need only recall the measurements of topography, of architecture (in great detail), the ratios or proportions used for pottery forms, for the weighing of coins, and so forth. But no one used to publish the tables or the curves which are, quite rightly, given today. Sometimes quantification is reduced to simple numeration: a number is ascribed to an object, a form, a type, a soil color (Munsell Code), and so forth—for example, in inventories; sometimes it is a matter of mathematization that is a little more advanced: that a coin can be lost—at a point of time t_2—only after having previously been struck in a workshop at a point in time t_1, can be expressed by the following inequality: $t_2 \geq t_1$.[38] This changes nothing and apparently does not permit any substantial progress, despite the mathematical form given to the chronological relationship. But above all, quantification concerns the determination of percentages (in comparison with a total) and, through the introduction of time, of frequencies. Quantification has found some vigorous defenders, to the point where it is presented as an indispensable panacea: thus Ian Hodder and Clive Orton insist on the usefulness of quantifying the terms of a hypothesis to be "compared directly with the data," and claim that "the relative importance of different hypotheses for the location of the towns could be judged."[39] To take another example, South pleads with conviction in favor of quantification: enumeration on its own, or simple counting, has no sense at all—what counts (so to speak) is the proportion, the percentage of the total of objects that one group represents in comparison with another[40]. One must struggle against "antiquantification bias" because it does not allow questions "that can be answered only through quantification" (one can recognize here the love of truisms). This seems to be simple common sense, although the problem of determining the total (in comparison with which the percentage is calculated) remains—since the total found is not the real total[41] and, likewise, the duration (in the calculation of frequencies) is not always known with as much precision as for Carolina's historical towns. The merits of quantification are, moreover, debated in certain disciplines like botany.[42] (As for sampling, see above, p. 135.)

Be that as it may, description finds its favorite haven in what have been called data "banks" or "bases," which imply a "formalization" of descriptions and a quantification of absolute dimensions and of ratios of measurements. These data banks—where it is not a question of "documentation" or "bibliographic" banks (and even here there are difficulties)—pose the problem of the adoption of a "universal" code, which is obviously utopian, or failing that, of the compatability of codes. What is more, they are a little dependent on the (widespread) illusion of "push-button" science, that form of intellectual laziness: some people are not far from the belief that to obtain instantaneously the date and the provenance of a brick or a water pipe whose measurements they provide, they simply need to ask the bank. This is pretty puerile. Finally, it will have been noticed that the very notion of a data bank illustrates once again the contradiction of the thesis according to which the "facts" cannot and must not be collected except in the perspective of a very precise approach to a problem, since by definition the data are stockpiled in the bank only with a view to other, ulterior approaches to the problem.

One example of the difficulties, if not failures, met with in "objectivized" (rather than objective) description would be the "automatic description" or the "recognition" of forms such as the amphorae of Republican Rome: a lot of time and effort has been devoted to this specific application. The results appear rather disappointing. The principles of the description (which seem to have been influenced too much by statistics and not enough by the real needs of archaeology) are debatable. And the conclusion that the descriptive model "will not contribute much to specialized archaeology, which doesn't need it to identify a Dressel 20 Amphora" but on the other hand will help the nonspecialist[43] measures, at the very least, the distance 'twixt cup and lip.

Classification

Classification, which gives order to descriptions, remains (at least in its primary stage) the prerogative of the archaeologist. The presuppositions of traditional classifications (essentially typological and chronological) are arbitrary in a sense, but no more so than those of the New Archeologists. After all when one is faced with poorly known material, it is perfectly legitimate to wish to bring in a bit of order, and to classify it, even if only for convenience, according to its material (the "fabric"), technique, form, decoration, function, or date. The New Archeologists and their followers, as we have seen, could not say enough against the "catalogs" which, to hear them talk, were made simply for the pleasure of cataloging. Yet catalogs had—still have— their uses: the proof is that the New Archeologists by no means scorned to use them. Clarke uses the most recent of the typologies of fibulae to improve the date of Glastonbury; Binford does not hold in contempt the typology of the Paleolithic specialists of western Europe or Africa—in fact, he takes it as his starting point.[44] One sometimes has the impression that, to them, catalogs (which, aptly, used to be called "descriptive") are simple lists, and this is sometimes the case, it is true, although a first list saves time.[45] Those who sneer at catalogs would probably have a hard time compiling one; yet this adventurous attempt would show them that things are not as simple as they imagine. It sometimes requires a lot of time, work, and ideas to classify an object—assuming it has been identified beforehand, which is another matter—as a type or a subtype. The result of these efforts is visible (to the uninitiated) only as a simple mention of that type or subtype, and they are naturally inclined to think that it was a matter of course.[46] I have already cited, with regard to this sort of idea, John Beazley's "lists": who else would have been capable of doing one-tenth of them? Who doesn't use them? The New Archeologists, who already lacked exactitude, are pretty ungrateful too.

Quantification

But the refusal of anything that might appear intuitive, the fear of impressionism, the obsession with nondemonstrable and nondemonstrated competence have, over a long period, developed a whole group of data-processing methods that are all more or less linked to quantification and expressed in a visual, graphic form[47] that facilitates both research ("heuristic") and, at the same time, demonstration (demonstrative value). Whether it be composition analysis (of a clay, an assemblage, etc.), represented by histograms (bars, blocks), diagrams (cumulative, circular, triangular), scalograms, dendrograms; spatial distribution, represented by cartography, refined by quantification or periodization; evolution through time, expressed by curves, graphics, graphs, lines of regression, clusters of points, "seriations," "matrices"; or a combination of these points of view, chronotypology (or typochronology) has, apparently, gained in rigor and objectivity. To the extent that all these methods (which can be combined) can be carried out without the help of a machine—that is, "manually"—they are within the province of archaeologists who introduced them into archaeology or sometimes even "invented" them themselves; and they alone can say what is the "meaning" of a seriation, the concrete significance of a "factor" of analysis.[48]

But between the often very great number of data to be processed and, on the other hand, the possibilities offered by electronic devices, these methods—since they have the potential to be automated—have been "computerized": from automatic cartography to the handling of scalograms by computer, from dendrograms to the points on a curve, it has been possible to obtain everything in this way. Who today would prefer a slide rule to the electronic calculator? To this has been added the invasion—a pleasant one—of statistics, set to work by computer studies.

Processing by Computer

In the beginning, statistics were not linked to the computer, of course, but they rapidly came to use it. It is statistics that characterize to a great extent the "analytical archaeology" advocated by Clarke, who (here, as from other disciplines—indeed more so) grabbed armfuls of all the resources of statistics: contingency and chi-square, variance and covariance, regression analysis, factor analysis. And he even "unloaded" unhesitatingly onto archaeological research (quite often even before they had been applied, even if only once, even before knowing whether and to what degree they were applicable) all the methods of statistics: descriptive (Markov chains, Monte Carlo chains), analytical, and inductive.[49] Intended to divulge in an objective and explicit way the relationships that have been tacitly and intuitively perceived among objects or their characteristics (variables),[50] these techniques have become subject to the computer. They have deeply captivated recent generations of archaeologists and have spread like wildfire. With what results?

Once again, not the results we were led to expect; not the results one might justifiably have reckoned on. Binford had the merit, which one must acknowledge, of setting out in detail his factor analysis of the final Acheulian of East Africa.[51] One can follow him a long way, up to the decisive moment where one loses the thread: that diminishes the power of this laborious demonstration to convince the reader, since it could not be more tortuous. Above all, as we have seen, the rigor of the factor analysis itself hangs on the manipulation of introduced data (see above, p. 120). It is as if the arbitrary portion was simply shifted, taken back to the start, to the "grasp" of data, the choice of "program." Everything gained in ease of manipulation, in precision, and in time is compromised or lost beforehand. Has this factor analysis ever convinced anyone? Not François Bordes, in any case. Often one has the impression that a power hammer is being used to crush a nut. Is the use of tests (Fisher, or chi-square, that "magic potion" that says whether a particular observation is likely to be due to chance) necessary in many cases? Did it require a statistical test to convince us, with "less than one chance in a thousand that the association is not significant," that the Broken K fire pits are linked to the large rooms, when twenty-two out of twenty-three were found there? It is window dressing, almost charlatanism.[52] Two covariant curves do not establish a relationship of cause and effect (sales of vacuum cleaners and suicides; IQ and shoe size, etc.). The analyses carried out with a computer by James Deetz, William A. Longacre (multiple regression), and Hill (factor analysis) have been severely criticized by Donald Dumond as regards both their principle and their execution.[53] I have already said what I think of the factor analysis confirming Schiffer's simulation. Another example, this one criticized by a statistician, gives one even more food for thought: in an article that claims to be explicitly methodological, Daniel Stiles, in an attempt to determine whether the bifaces of the Acheulian and of the Developed Oldowan represent two actual cultural traditions, uses univariate and multivariate statistical methods. Albertus Voorrips shows that Stiles committed all possible types of error: correct use of the wrong methods, and wrong use of a viable method. His conclusion is harsh: "Conclusions based on results that suffer from these errors are often worse than no conclusions at all."[54] And Stiles has the honesty to accept the criticisms, at least in part. Use of computers has more of a future than the New Archeology does, but it would be naive to expect too much from it.

These examples do not give the impression of being the exception.[55] In any case, they illustrate the dangers of these computerized statistical methods which, though intended to avoid placing blind confidence in the decrees of an authority, end up by reintroducing simple faith in the conclusions of the statistician and the computer operator! These risks are increased as a result of the incompetence (at least for the present) of most archaeologists in matters of statistics and computer studies. But after all, archaeologists are no more competent in the field of weak radioactivity or neutron activation, in mathematics or palynology, and they can turn to statisticians and computer experts in the same way that they turn to nuclear physicists or other specialists. So here again it is advisable for them not to have absolute confidence in the results provided; above all they must, insofar as they can, be cautious about the procedures followed by the computer expert. Besides, the situation will change for the better before long, as the teaching of computer studies becomes generalized and becomes as necessary as the grounding in mathematics or topography or the minimal knowledge of photography an archaeologist is expected to have.

That is not the main problem, because, as Clarke said at the start, "Relationships summarized and expressed by such statistics only provide a statistical description of the situation within the data, they do not necessarily express a simple or functional relationship and great care must be taken in their interpretation and deployment in further hypotheses."[56] This is the whole problem—that of interpreting the relationships, the "structures" that are thus spotlighted in the data. Up to this point, the archaeologist could consider that he was "hunting on his home ground"—whether in the definition of a specific approach to problems, the acquisition and the establishment of facts, their description, their classification, or their processing. This would be the case even if he did it with the interdisciplinary help of various scholars and statisticians/computer experts, because he is in the best position to establish the facts and, after that, to classify them and grasp the various relationships with full knowledge of the facts. So, from there on, once he has reached the point of interpreting these results, of answering the questions set out at the beginning, it seems to me that he leaves his own domain and enters that of history, or anthropology, or philosophy of history, or sociology—a whole range of subjects, whose very existence shows clearly that one is no longer dealing with archaeology as I have characterized it: what the archaeologist alone is capable of doing or can do best.

This in no way means that the archaeologist must stop there and pass the baton: one knows well that this is out of the question and that many archaeologists—cruelly disappointed, and with the impression of having worked for others, of having taken all that trouble for other people—would refuse to do so, and refuse very forcefully. What I mean is that, from that stage onward, the archaeologist leaves archaeology *sensu proprio* and enters—or returns to—a different sphere (which is, moreover, variable) in which what he does can be done (and indeed is done) by people other than himself. No more, no less.

II The Frontiers of Archaeology

Anthropology or History?

It has been said and repeated often enough that Europeans are interested above all in history and Americans above all in anthropology[1]; as a matter of fact, it is very surprising, at first sight, for traditional European archaeologists to see archaeology in the United States classed under anthropology and taught with anthropology. For their part, the New Archeologists display a marked contempt for history, when, that is, they are not trying to reintegrate it by force into anthropology, which would thus contain everything, including history: (in order to save it, in a way, and tear it away from its natural mediocrity). The position of a Spaulding in this connection is significant: "There are [not] two kinds of explanations . . . historical . . . and scientific," each with its appropriate data. "There is only one kind of serious explanation, the nomological or covering-law explanation." "There is no such thing as 'historical' explanation, only the explanation of historical events," he adds, quoting May Brodbeck.

Prehistory itself is "historical": it is "the historical branch of anthropology"; it is not the past that enables one to understand the present, it is the opposite: "the past can be understood only through the present."[2] But in reality, outside this perspective, Spaulding himself stresses the opposition between "scientific" anthropology and history: the "explanatory generalizations of history" are a matter of common knowledge, they are implicit, they are "primitive concepts," "particularizing": all points by which they differ from social anthropology.[3]

In fact, the historical perspective and the anthropological viewpoint clash in a way that would be hard to dispute. This is not so much for the reasons that have sometimes been given: because anthropology is supposed to deal with peoples, history with people, or even a single person[4]; for modern history takes an interest, beyond individuals, in social classes and in peoples. Or again, since anthropology has as its subject prehistoric societies, of which neither the name nor the composition nor the origin nor the fate is known (or ever will be known, probably),[5] and whose "actors . . . are not individually identifiable,"[6] it is difficult to be interested in their history, unlike what happens with the historical periods, endowed with texts on which anthropology has *also* concentrated.[7]

No, the essential difference seems to be that anthropology has as its goal the "covering laws" of "cultural dynamics," the laws of behavior—valid for all periods and all places, "atemporal, aspatial"[8]— whereas history aims not at what happens (or has to happen) in a general way, but at what actually happened, whether it corresponds to the alleged law or not, whether it is the rule or the exception to the rule; it even has a preference for the exception rather than the rule. It is not a question of whether general or particular events, prehistory or historical periods are concerned. What counts is the eventuality which actually occurred, out of all those that were possible. One can see very clearly the transition from one point of view to the other—for example, in Renfrew: it is accepted by all and sundry, anthropologists as well as historians, that the aim of archaeology is improved knowledge of the human past, a better understanding of the past,[9] "and hence," Renfrew adds, "of the very nature of man himself."[10] Stating that, like man himself (*Homo sapiens*), "farming . . . developed independently in several parts of the world," he concludes that it is caused not by the "qualities of any specific group of people" but by complex conditions (of the environment, the society in question, its interactions with other societies) and the general properties and capacities of man.[11] History certainly takes an interest in "human nature," but its aim is not to define it once and for all, and forever, in a form that eternity will not change: rather, it is to grasp in what form it has really emerged and expressed itself; not so much events as *the* event, even—and especially—if it is contrary to what one might have expected; even—and especially—if it is a break with the norm. Not so much regularities (which does not mean that it does not take them into account) as the unexpected, not so much the rational as the irrational, not structures but conjunctures, not history's "repetitions" but its "stutterings."

This difference brings out that in their philosophies. For anthropologists, history has its laws, even if they are less explicit, less well known.[12] The idea that there can be exceptions to the rule is illusory: it is simply that the precise rule is not (yet) known. History, or at least a certain conception of history,[13] leaves a role to freedom among all the conditions which are supposed to determine it. It is not that history does not study "processes," as the New Archeology has maintained incomprehensibly: it is preoccupied with them, all the more so because it believes them to be nondetermined to a certain extent. The statistical laws of sociology, as Pierre Bourdieu repeated, are only "broadly" true: it is perhaps the "detail" (which does not mean the anecdotal) that interests the historian. This fundamental philosophical option thus brings us back to the very general framework, the view of the whole, the "aim" that is at the start of all archaeological research and that forms the researcher's specific approach to problems, according to whether his "ultimate goal" is the formalization of disembodied laws or the knowledge of what has in fact occurred, what has actually happened: the *past*.

History and Liberty

It seems clear that what we have here is not an obligatory direction, in which one is forced to go for fear of falling outside science, but, on the contrary, an option, a choice, that is personal and, if you like, "free," and that could not be imposed on anyone by force. For the adherents of anthropology, even if they are not strictly "determinist," men are largely determined. As a parallel, in sociology, Michel Foucault cites these "minute devices that make us visible and foreseeable." In Bourdieu's opinion, we have no desires in our own right, on account of the weight of social habits: "Behavior is an unconscious apprenticeship, and what we believe to be personal has been inculcated into us." So it is the discovery of these mechanisms that interests them. Hence the almost paradoxical nature of the interest they have in the past: as Bruce Trigger has said, in a way that seems unanswerable, if it is a question above all of formulating the eternal laws of behavior, archaeological data are very inferior to those contemporary man would provide: "There are no generalizations . . . that could not be gained far more efficiently from studies of contemporary societies." [14] One recalls Schiffer's suggestion to Binford: study a modern campsite rather than the Nunamiut (see above, p. 69). This is particularly true since the New Archeologists are irresistibly attracted by ethnography, by ethnoarchaeology: let's remember the Tucson garbage project; Schiffer's "fourth strategy," which goes from modern material culture to modern human behavior, is entirely ethnographic and no longer involves anything archaeological.

The nature of researchers' personal preferences is so clear that it has been possible to speak of "grafts," of grafting an anthropological viewpoint onto the desire for a greater systematization and the systemic surge that expressed it. [15] Besides, the New Archeologists, on this topic, are reduced not to arguments but to value judgments that recall tastes and colors: for Spaulding in 1968, "Identification of individual circumstances connected with a social innovation are unimportant"[16]; Renfrew, in 1972, slips from understanding of the past to understanding of human nature without any demonstration;[17] Hill found chronological taxonomy "relatively uninteresting";[18] Binford, in 1977, declares particularistic approaches to be "trivial," "uninteresting," and "boring" (which is pretty rich, coming from him).[19] And they have a perfect right to do so. Everyone is free to take an interest in one aspect of things rather than another. It is a matter of individual preference.

On the contrary, for those who feel attracted by history, a margin of freedom exists. Sartre's definition of liberty is well known: "Man can always make something of what has been made of him." Even a Marxist theoretician like Pierre Fougeyrollas maintains that historical laws, such as the class struggle, do not imply any "fatalism," and "the determinism . . . of mechanistic ideology in no way takes account of the class struggle; no law determines mechanically anyone's participation in the building of a . . .[revolutionary] party."[20] Or again, as Marguerite Yourcenar says, where the past is concerned, we are presented with "systems that are too complete, series of causes and effects that are too exact and too clear to have ever been entirely true."[21] "History has a meaning, it is at least, to a certain extent, malleable," wrote Pierre Mendès-France quite recently.[22] Consequently, the historicist archaeologists, without falling into the "chronology of contingencies," that "residue of sociology" against which Lucien Febvre spoke out,[23] are interested in the very difference which separates the foreseeable from the event, in this "subtraction," this margin which is "what in fact happened." To quote one of the preceding authors once again: "But, what can I say, things didn't happen this way."[24] "I don't want people to explain to me," someone dared to say, in connection with African ethnography (it is enough to give you a fit), "I want them to tell me things."[25] There is no discussion of tastes or colors.

But if it were necessary not to impose but to propose a choice between anthropology and history, it is perhaps toward the latter that archaeology should lean. As I have indicated above, anthropology, whatever it says about this,[26] might find it advantageous to (and in any case could, if need be) do without the temporal dimension, the chronological depth that archaeology brings. But history could not. It would mean cutting off a vital part of its substance, whereas anthropology, which works outside of time and space, according to its own declared objectives, is less dependent on it. But, I repeat, both these paths are open and valid: it is a question of general perspective.

The Distribution of Roles

It is the definition of this view of the whole that determines the precise type of approach to problems; in its turn, this approach to problems defines the type of "facts" that will be sought as a matter of priority (though not exclusively, as I have said) and that it is archaeology's proper function to "establish." And it is these facts, duly established, that will verify or confirm the assumptions put forward, according to initial choice, in the framework of history or of anthropology.

But putting the facts, established by archaeology, to work is something that can be carried out by anthropologists or historians—and archaeologists have no priority here. Certainly, many archaeologists will not be able to resist putting forward historical interpretations and confirming them with the facts they have gathered (or can gather); some of them, less numerous in the Old World than in the New, will formulate behavioral laws, cultural laws.[27] But where they were, in a way, irreplaceable during the establishment of the facts, by this stage anthropologists or historians will be able—advantageously—to take their place. And this is indeed what happens: I have given enough examples of American anthropologists using "archaeological" facts for anthropological ends; and there is also no lack of examples of historians handling archaeological "data" to construct history.[28] And just as historians and anthropologists try to do without archaeologists to gather their archaeological documentation themselves, often with great success,[29] in the same way archaeologists can become historians, epigraphists, or anthropologists: but as happens every time one leaves one's speciality, the result will perhaps—or probably—not be as good as if the work were done by a historian or an anthropologist. It would no doubt be better to use a specialist. Otherwise specialization has no value, and absolutely anybody can do absolutely anything; every archaeologist can improvise as a historian or an anthropologist, and any anthropologist or historian or epigraphist can play at being an archaeologist: Yes, but how? I repeat, it is not a question of private hunting grounds. Certain anthropologists are certainly excellent archaeologists—just as certain nuclear physicists have given themselves some grounding in archaeology. But that is the point: they have taken the trouble to do so, and despite that, they will perhaps never be as good at archaeology as if they had chosen that speciality from the start, to the exclusion of their own. Similarly, historians can be remarkable archaeologists (perhaps more easily than can anthropologists). And perhaps some archaeologists will be eminent historians, or unrivaled anthropologists: But after all, would that be the opinion of the specialized anthropologists or the professional historians? The question almost answers itself. Just like the anthropologist transformed into an archaeologist, or the historian changed into an archaeologist, the archaeologist can—if he is of a mind to—play very well at being a historian or an anthropologist; he can even make a complete success of it. The important thing is that he be aware that, in doing this, he is acting not as an archaeologist but as an anthropologist or a historian. He is no longer doing "archaeology," but something else.

Conclusion

Faced with the heap of errors, contradictions, and false novelties that had been piled up with arrogance and great insistence on research's doorstep by the New Archeology, and despite a few very meager results that floated on the surface, I found it indispensable to attempt a review. Naturally, reviews are always outdated, if only because of printing delays. Production goes on, points of view change, repentance follows repentance: that is no reason for not having a try; and just because "coats have been turned" it does not mean one should forget the original pretensions, because they can be instructive about the future, not only about the past.

I refused to be satisfied with the good marks the New Archeologists awarded themselves (when they weren't tearing each other apart) like "waves of incense" wafted with grotesque eagerness. I have tried to see for myself, and to judge on actual evidence. The result did not fail to surpass all hopes, all premonitions or first impressions. No doubt the New Archeology is not entirely negative, but if you want to assess the positive contribution it has really made, you have to look very hard. Its aims, in principle, were highly laudable: to make a science out of archaeology. Who, as has been said, would not have subscribed to that?[1] The fact remains that the New Archeology has, to a certain degree—which is perfectly natural—contributed a few new themes to the approach to archaeological problems, as I have said (the hypothesis of seasonal activity, for example). The New Archeology, by its very insistence, has had the merit of systematizing certain themes of research—not that these were new, strictly speaking. But an embryonic point of view is one thing, its systematic exploitation is quite another: one could, for example, cite "postdepositional" phenomena, ethno-archaeology (insofar as it is more a matter of archaeology than of ethnography). One could add the emphasis placed on quantification, provided it is not seen as a panacea. But besides that, how many of the "innovations," greeted with a flourish of trumpets, were in fact nothing of the kind? Without returning to the subject of the ineffable "val-idation of hypotheses," what can one say about the "processual" as-pect, discovered like the moon, or the regional approach, ethnographic analogy, the geographical or ecological approach? Did we have to wait for the New Archeology to reveal all these? It is in vain that it takes all the credit or goes off to war against windmills which, for greater secu-rity, it has built itself (with that talent for exaggerating a difference that scarcely exists, or destroying it easily because it is almost imagi-nary). Binford felt keenly the reproach that he had contributed nothing new except jargon, and he defended himself against it for all he was worth: but he persuaded only the converted.[2] As in photography, everything in archaeology was invented in the nineteenth century. One could transpose to archaeology what Jacques Ruffié writes about so-ciobiology: "The real danger . . . is to present old concepts as a new theory."[3] As far as method is concerned, we have seen how improbably the New Archeology used the hypothetico-deductive path, generally putting off, until later and onto other people, the testing of its assump-tions; we have seen the illusory and tautological nature of the "laws" that were supposed to help in "explaining"; finally, we noted the ab-sence of any specifically archaeological theory. Now, all these were the "spearheads." The meagerness of the concrete results was the only possible consequence: none of them has changed the face of science in the slightest, though one might have expected them to, given the assur-ance and the radical nature of the initial pretensions. Believing it was discovering the equation of relativity in archaeology, the New Arche-ology set off, like a pseudoscience and a new alchemy, in pursuit of the philosopher's stone, rather than $e = mc^2$.

Taking a look back, after fifteen years of militant New Archeology, Binford, in 1977, saw only "an antitraditional archaeology at best," a "rebellion" (Dare one add "without a cause"?), and feared that it was "a failure, providing only social excitement in a relatively dull field."[4] One could not put it better, and the situation does not seem to have altered since then. The New Archeology has not even "destroyed" the old, which, contrary to the forecasts, is still in excellent health.

On the other hand, by directing tremendous efforts toward the theo-ries and applications it preached from on high, the New Archeology has misled many of its adepts. It has certainly cost a lot of time and money and energy which would no doubt have been better used on less pretentious tasks, with less elusive and uncertain results. If, fortu-nately, the New Archeologists in the field have not let themselves (far from it!) be diverted from their real task, this is due not to the theore-ticians of the New Archeology but to an incomprehensible persistence of common sense, and a sense of reality. It has if not led astray, then at least diverted a great deal of effort, notably among young archaeologists who were conned by its bluff and who have taken an appreciable amount of time to realize this—even now some haven't understood and will continue to heap praise on the New Archeology. We need have no fears about that! Every criticism aimed at their idol will be taken as sacrilegious, excessive, biased, incomplete, irrelevant, unjust, embittered, even peevish. So what? They have been mistaken from the start about almost everything. It is my hope that readers will judge for themselves and produce the one thing that the New Archeology does not forgive: their personal opinion.[5]

In reality, the real progress made in the past three decades has not been in theory, as the New Archeology would have us believe: it has been in *techniques,* whether it be the contributions of the "sciences" to archaeology or the help of statistics, and especially computer studies. These advances are very real. But they are completely independent of the New Archeology: it was NASA that launched satellites, not the New Archeology, whose "thinkers" are hardly equivalent to the space engineers. Naturally there has been a tendency—and one can foresee it continuing—to link computers and the New Archeology, to drape it in the merits of a technique that it has only borrowed in order to uphold the myth of its superiority. Who are they kidding?

For my part, I have tried, as far as I can, to disentangle a whole group of notions that have been deliberately mixed up; I have tried to link them to each other, to unravel the incredibly tangled web that the New Archeology has woven. Of course archaeological research, like any human enterprise, takes place in a frame of reference, in a set of philosophical presuppositions: freedom or determinism, history, or anthropology. . . . How could things be otherwise? But once that framework is set out, consciously or not, implicitly or not, a problem or a group of problems is formulated which obviously reflects this fundamental position, and a strategy for resolving it is deduced from it. The role of archaeology is, I think, one that the archaeologist alone can play under the most favorable conditions: the establishment of the "facts," relevant or not. That is the heart of archaeology. It is there that the archaeologist acts like one. Not that he is incapable of doing other things, of going "further." Not that others cannot try to take his place. But then they become archaeologists, or the archaeologist becomes something else: a historian, a sociologist, an anthropologist. It is by no means certain that this to-ing and fro-ing is of great profit to knowledge.

Consequently, archaeology is in no way an "auxiliary" science of history or anthropology. It is no more an auxiliary than are physics or physical anthropology when they lend their assistance. Any discipline is the auxiliary of all others, which means that none of them is an auxiliary: it is "interdisciplinarity," "transdisciplinarity."

Archaeology is not, as Taylor or Spaulding called it with masochism or condescension,[6] a "simple" technique at the service of history or anthropology. We have seen that its practice brings into play all the intellectual resources, all the competence and knowledge, all the creativity that the other disciplines display. The establishment of archaeological facts is not an "amusement," an elementary activity that lies within the capability of just anyone. It has often been repeated that facts don't speak for themselves, that solutions don't "flow" naturally out of facts: that is one way of looking at things. In reality, when a problem is set out and the facts relevant to this precise problem are clearly and solidly established, then the solution is not far, and one does not need to be a genius to draw the conclusion, quite often, whether one pretends to "imagine" a hypothesis and discover its confirmation, or infers from these facts the generalization in question.

That said, the global interpretations, whether historical or anthropological, should probably be left to the anthropologists and historians. On this point I would agree with Taylor when he said, "Archaeology is neither History nor Anthropology."[7] The archaeologist is perhaps not the person best qualified to decide whether the class struggle is the motor of history, or if man's behavior is conditioned like that of a mouse in an electrified cage. In any case, others can replace him in this task to advantage.

I am not claiming this position is "new." That, above all, is what it claims *not* to be. Or rather, its only novelty these days is precisely a denial of being the "latest fashion": as such, it is astoundingly original! Saturation mounts in the face of these theses, which all, one after the other—and before the next ones come along—claim to be determining the latest fashion. But I hope that my position is also not a simple retreat, a regression toward points of view that are out of date, outmoded, outflanked to the left and the right: I hope for a renewed awareness of what constitutes the very essence of archaeology, the nature of archaeological work—not as it is practiced by the New Archeologists, alas, but as it should be practiced.

With all the swindling of a charlatan, the New Archeology has waged a campaign of "disinformation." Simpleminded and Molièresque, like a terrorist, it has caricatured the parallel archaeology, seeing no difference between what was being done a hundred, fifty, and twenty years ago. It is not Binford who had it right: it was Bayard, and

Morgan, and Dumond. They were treated with contempt, but the future will show which check bounced.

This is because archaeology, unlike the exact sciences, scarcely seems able—by its very nature—to be the scene of "revolutions," at least in the sense they thought in 1960. One might extrapolate to archaeology what an ethnologist, not known for the narrowness of his views, said of the social sciences in general, which "straight off tackle subjects that are too complicated": "It is more worthwhile to discreetly carry on with one's craft, to try to solve not the big problems of human destiny or the future of societies, but small difficulties, often devoid of current interest."[8] These words, it seems to me, suit archaeology perfectly today.

Abbreviations

The following abbreviations are used throughout the notes.

AJA	*American Journal of Archaeology*
Am Ant	*American Antiquity*
An A	David L. Clarke, *Analytical Archaeology* (London: Methuen, 1968)
AP	Lewis R. Binford, *An Archaeological Perspective* (New York: Seminar Press, 1972)
Arch Auj	Alain Schnapp, ed., *L'archéologie aujourd'hui* (Paris: Hachette, 1980)
BA	Michael B. Schiffer, *Behavioral Archeology* (New York: Academic Press, 1976)
CA	*Current Anthropology*
Em	Colin Renfrew, *The Emergence of Civilisation: The Cyclades and the Aegean in the Third Millennium B.C.* (London: Methuen, 1972)
Expl	Patty J. Watson, Steven A. LeBlanc, and Charles L. Redman, *Explanation in Archeology: An Explicitly Scientific Approach* (New York: Columbia University Press, 1971)
Mod	David L. Clarke, ed., *Models in Archaeology* (London: Methuen, 1972)
MT	Stanley South, *Method and Theory in Historical Archeology* (New York: Academic Press, 1977)
NP	Sally R. Binford and Lewis R. Binford, eds., *New Perspectives in Archeology* (Chicago: Aldine, 1968)
RT	Charles L. Redman, ed., *Research and Theory in Current Archeology* (New York: Wiley, 1973)

Notes

Translator's Preface

1. Terry Arthur, *Ninety-five Percent Is Crap: A Plain Man's Guide to British Politics* (Tampa, Fla.: Libertarian Books, 1976).
2. See P. G. Bahn, *Antiquity* 56 (1982): 148–49.
3. G. Watson, "The Charm of Being Useless," *Times Literary Supplement,* 10 December 1982.
4. See Stephen Jay Gould, *The Mismeasure of Man* (New York: Norton, 1981): 265.
5. Ibid., 262.
6. See Bahn, *Antiquity* 56 (1982): 148, for a classic sentence of this type.
7. L. Klejn, *CA* 18 (1977): 24.
8. Glynn L. Isaac, "Squeezing Blood from Stones," in *Stone Tools as Cultural Markers: Change, Evolution, and Complexity,* ed. R. V. S. Wright (Atlantic Highlands, N.J.: Humanities Press, 1977), 5–12; for the quotation, see 9.
9. R. A. Gould, *Science* 204 (1979): 739.
10. Gould, *Mismeasure of Man,* 158.
11. Lewis R. Binford, *Bones: Ancient Men and Modern Myths* (New York: Academic Press, 1981): 25.
12. See Lewis R. Binford, *In Pursuit of the Past: Decoding the Archaeological Record* (New York: Thames and Hudson, 1983): 106–8.
13. Edward Pyddoke, *What Is Archaeology?* (New York: Roy, 1965).
14. David Caute, *Sixty-eight: The Year of the Barricades* (London: Hamish Hamilton, 1988).
15. I would like to thank the late Glyn Daniel for helping to bring this project to fruition; Pat Winker and Chris Scarre for help in securing photocopies of some of the original texts quoted in the book; and above all, Professor Courbin himself for his invaluable help in the course of the translation.

Introduction

1. See C. Renfrew, *Antiquity* 43 (1969): 243.
2. See L. R. Binford, *AP,* 120.
3. On the meaning of the word *new* in New Archeology, see D. L. Clarke, *Mod,* 55.

165

4. See G. Gjessing, *CA* 19 (1978): 632, in connection with L. Klejn, *CA* 18 (1977): 1–42.

5. See K. V. Flannery, in *RT,* 47.

Chapter 1

1. See W. W. Taylor, *A Study of Archaeology,* Memoir 69 (Washington, D.C.: American Anthropological Association, 1948).

2. L. R. Binford, "Archaeology as Anthropology," *Am Ant* 28 (1962): 217–25; and D. L. Clarke, "Matrix Analysis and Archaeology, with Particular Reference to British Beaker Pottery," *Proceedings of the Prehistoric Society,* n.s. 28 (1962): 371–83. Born in 1930, Binford did undergraduate studies in forestry and wildlife conservation; he obtained his Ph.D., not without difficulty, in 1964.

3. D. T. Bayard and S. I. Kennedy, *Antiquity* 45 (1971): 3ff., 85–87 (Dr. Lewis D. L. Binclarke, *New Analytical Archaeological Perspectives,* University of Phu Wiang, Thailand).

4. C. Renfrew, *Antiquity* 43 (1969): 243.

5. See Binford, *AP,* 10, 13; L. Klejn, *CA* 18 (1977): 16.

6. Binford, preface to S. South, *MT,* xi.

7. See G. Gjessing, *CA* 19 (1978): 632.

8. Or Thailand. See R. C. Dunnell, *AJA* 84 (1980): 472.

9. Amazonia has been studied by the Meggers, and the !Kung Bushmen by Richard Lee. Tasmania has also been studied; see ibid., 476.

10. R. C. Dunnell, *AJA* 83 (1979): 437–49. R. W. Chapman recently drew up a review of the last five years in England.

11. Or "old," "former," or "current," this last term also being used for the "new" archaeology; besides, the latter, as the years pass, is no longer new, while the "old" archaeology still remains current. Similarly, archaeology today is already that of yesterday: in reality it would be better to give dates, if one accepts that all vintages are not of equal worth.

12. Binford, *AP,* 182–84.

13. See J. M. Fritz and F. T. Plog, *Am Ant* 35 (1970): 409ff.

14. J. N. Hill, in *Mod,* 64–68.

15. Clarke, *An A,* 11, 27.

16. Clarke, *Mod,* 53–54.

17. M. B. Schiffer, *BA,* 3.

18. See S. South, *MT,* 5–10, 14–16, 23. My emphasis.

19. Colin Renfrew, in *Geoarchaeology: Earth Science of the Past,* ed. Donald A. Davidson and Myra L. Shackley (Boulder, Colo.: Westview, 1977), p. 4.

20. Renfrew, *AJA* 84 (1980): 293, 295.

21. See Binford, in *Mod,* 113–15 (twice).

22. See J. E. Fitting, *The Development of North American Archaeology* (University Park: Pennsylvania State University Press, 1973), 4–11; cf. Gene Sterud, in *The Explanation of Culture Change: Models in Prehistory,* ed. Colin

Renfrew (London: Duckworth, 1973), 14ff. Kuhn's book is cited in no fewer than six articles in *Mod* (e.g., by Hill, 61ff.) and by Sterud (4ff). Dunnell himself concludes that "the old archaeology is slowly being nibbled to death by ducks" (*AJA* 84 [1980]: 478).

23. J.-C. Gardin shows that the Old World, up to that date, was practically excluded; see *Revue Archéologique* (1974): 347.

24. Schiffer does indeed speak (see above, p. 8) of archaeology "preceding the 1960s."

25. Clarke, *Mod,* 54.

26. See Hill, in *Mod,* 63.

27. See South, *MT,* 13ff.

28. L. Binford in *The Conference on Historic Site Archaeology Papers,* no. 6 (1971): 121.

29. See Clarke, *An A,* 43; Binford, *AP,* 12.

30. Hill, in *Mod,* 64, 68.

31. See Binford, in *Mod,* and *NP,* 318.

32. See W. Shawcross, in *Mod,* 580, 583, 585.

33. Binford, *NP,* 318.

34. Schiffer, *BA,* 164.

35. See South, *MT,* 1, xiii, 5 (quotation).

36. Renfrew, *AJA* 84 (1980): 291; see Dunnell, *AJA* 84 (1980): 494–97.

37. See Schiffer, *BA,* 4, 13, 27.

38. Clarke, *AP,* xiii.

39. Binford, *Am Ant* 31 (1965): 209, quoted in Clarke, *An A,* 43; see L. A. White, *The Evolution of Culture* (New York: McGraw-Hill, 1959), 8.

40. Clarke, *An A,* 43; Renfrew, *Em,* 480, 485.

41. South, *MT,* 4.

42. See P. J. Watson, S. A. LeBlanc, and C. L. Redman, *Expl,* 88ff., 92.

43. Clarke, *Mod,* 12.

44. See C. G. Morgan, *World Archaeology* 4 (1973): 259ff.

45. See Binford, *NP,* 26.

46. Ibid., 25; Binford, *AP,* 6. Cf. Hill: "advancement of knowledge," "advance of knowledge" (in *NP,* 138, 140).

47. Binford, *TB,* 3, 5.

48. South , *MT,* 16, xiii (quotation).

49. Binford, *NP,* 26.

50. Quoted in South, *MT,* 14.

51. In *RT,* 47–58.

52. South, *MT,* 14.

53. See Binford, *AP,* 70, 117.

Chapter 2

1. E.g., the work of Claude Bernard, or experimental medicine.

2. One should distinguish between the "starting" hypothesis and the "secondary" hypotheses that are deduced from it.

3. L. R. Binford, *AP*, 26, 29.

4. Binford elsewhere calls this an argument "of relevance"—between the hypothesis and its test implications. See J. N. Hill, in *Mod*, 84.

5. See Binford, *NP*, 19ff.

6. See Binford, *AP*, 33: "Such a postulate should . . . serve as the foundation of a series of deductively drawn hypotheses."

7. See, e.g., Binford, *NP*, 324, concerning post-Pleistocene adaptations.

8. D. L. Clarke, *An A*, 642.

9. J. M. Fritz and F. T. Plog, *Am Ant* 35 (1970): 410.

10. See Hill, in *Mod*, 79ff.

11. See, e.g., Hill, in *NP*, 140.

12. Binford, *AP*, 60, 61.

13. Ibid., 62, 71–72 (referring back to 34–37).

14. Ibid., 70, 121.

15. Ibid., 117.

16. Ibid., 118.

17. See Fritz and Plog, *Am Ant* 35 (1970): 410ff.

18. P. J. Watson, S. A. LeBlanc, and C. L. Redman, *Expl*, 49; Hill, in *Mod*, 82; see also 138.

19. See Clarke, *An A*, 643; Binford, *NP*, 17; my emphasis.

20. Binford, *NP*, 11, 13, 17, 22.

21. Binford, *AP*, 90.

22. D. H. Thomas, in *Mod*, 674.

23. See Binford, *AP*, 29–32; my emphasis.

24. Binford, *NP*, 20.

25. Binford, *AP*, 41, 45ff., 48ff.

26. See P. J. Munson, *Am Ant* 34 (1969): 83–85.

27. Binford, *AP*, 53–56. Binford misspells the name as Munsen throughout.

28. Ibid., 41, 57. D. W. Read and S. A. LeBlanc clearly showed the error of logic (the same result due to other causes); see *CA* 19 (1978): 308.

29. See L. A. White, *The Evolution of Culture* (New York: McGraw-Hill, 1959), 285; Binford, *NP*, 325.

30. Binford, *NP*, 321 (*Scientific American* 203 [1960]: 134).

31. Binford, *NP*, 332, 334.

32. Ibid., 335ff.

33. Ibid., 336.

34. Binford, *AP*, 117.

35. Ibid., 192; see Binford, in *Mod*, 109–66.

36. Binford, in *Mod*, 133; see also S. R. Binford, *NP*, 54, and L. R. Binford, *Am Ant* 43 (1978): 357.

37. See ibid., 156–61.

38. Binford, *Am Ant* 43 (1978): 359ff.

39. See S. R. Binford, *NP*, 53, 54.

40. Ibid., 58.

41. See L. R. Binford, *TB*, 5ff., in which he takes up one of Flannery's points of view in *RT*.

42. See K. V. Flannery and M. D. Coe, in *NP*, 276, 281.

43. See Thomas G. Cook, *Koster: An Artifact Analysis of Two Archaic Phases in Westcentral Illinois* (Evanston, Ill.: Northwestern University Archeological Program, 1976), 122, v.

44. See M. B. Schiffer, *BA*, 15, 17: "very few inferences are completely justified in the literature."

45. See S. South, *MT*, 113–18.

46. Ibid., 120, 234ff.

47. David L. Clarke, *Beaker Pottery of Great Britain and Ireland*, 2 vols. (Cambridge: Cambridge University Press, 1970).

48. Arthur H. Bulleid and Harold St. George Gray, *The Glastonbury Lake Village* (Glastonbury: Glastonbury Antiquarian Society, 1911–17), 45.

49. Clarke, *Mod*, 826.

50. See Bulleid and Gray, *Glastonbury*, 114.

51. See Clarke, *Mod*, 829 (date), 830 (demography—sixty, seventy-five, and 120 people, as opposed to two to three hundred [see Bulleid and Gray, *Glastonbury*, 65]).

52. Ibid., 827.

53. Ibid., 837.

54. Ibid., 838, 839.

55. Ibid., 839, 851.

56. Ibid., 854.

57. Ibid., 856.

58. Ibid., 860, 861.

59. Ibid.

60. Ibid., 867.

61. Ibid., 854, 856, 858, 863.

62. See C. Renfrew, *Em*, xxv.

63. Ibid., 37.

64. Ibid., 488.

65. Ibid., 18, 480.

66. Ibid., 44; my emphasis.

67. Ibid., 482 (first model), 484 (second model).

68. Ibid., 480; unlike Binford, *AP*, 116ff.

69. Ibid., 482.

70. Binford, *NP*, 319.

71. J.-C. Gardin, *Une archéologie théorique* (Paris: Hachette, 1979), 271.

72. See R. C. Dunnell, *AJA* 84 (1980): 471, in connection with ethnoarchaeology: "The virtually unanimous call for 'testing'" is only matched by "the equally ubiquitous lack of such tests."

73. J. M. Fritz and F. T. Plog, *Am Ant* 35 (1970): 411.

74. See Y. Fomine, *Bulletin de Correspondance Hellénique* 90 (1966): 32–47; J. Bousquet, *Revue des Etudes Grecques* 93 (1980): xff.; J.-P. Michaud and J. Blécon, *Le temple en calcaire* (Paris: Diffusion de Boccard, 1977).

75. See Paul Courbin, in *Etudes archéologiques*, ed. P. Courbin (Paris: SEVPEN, 1963), 98–100.

76. See L. Woolley, *Journal of Hellenic Studies* 58 (1938): 1–30.

77. See André Leroi-Gourhan, *Préhistoire de l'art occidental* (Paris: Mazenod, 1965); see also review in *L'Homme* 7 (1967): 126ff.

78. See M. P. Leone, *Am Ant* 36 (1971): 222.

79. See, e.g., Binford, *NP,* 17, 34 and *AP* 19, 102, 121, 342; Fritz and Plog, *Am Ant* 35 (1970): 412; Clarke, *Mod,* 1041 (index); Plog, *A Study of Prehistoric Change* (New York: Academic Press, 1974), 14, 17, 19; Redman, *RT,* 359ff.

80. The concept is taken up by Clarke, *Mod,* 54.

81. Bernard's name never seems to figure in the index. Colin Renfrew quotes Comte (*Em,* 16) in connection with the analogy of archaeological data and the data of the natural sciences.

82. See Binford, in *Mod,* 134ff.

83. Ibid., 132ff.

84. See Clarke, *Mod,* 802: "The objective was simply to explore the old data in a variety of new ways."

85. See Clarke, *An A,* 643.

86. Renfrew, *Em,* 484.

87. See Colin Renfrew, ed., *The Explanation of Culture Change: Models in Prehistory* (London: Duckworth, 1973), 539–58.

88. See C. G. Morgan, *World Archaeology* 4 (1973): 269–72; Schiffer, *BA,* 23; Binford, *TB,* 3ff.; D. E. Dumond, *Am Ant* 42 (1977): 336ff. Besides, there are occasions when Hill himself also postpones certain tests: see *NP,* 140.

89. See Hill, in *NP,* 104, 107, 114.

90. Ibid., 116.

91. Ibid., 134. Moreover, they modify the picture derived from modern pueblos (undecorated jars not intended for storage, medicinal plants less indispensable: see 140, 137).

92. Ibid., 139.

93. Ibid., 133. Which, it should be said in passing, any "classic" archaeologist would have noted systematically.

94. Ibid., 104, 146.

95. See Binford, *TB,* 8.

96. See Schiffer, *BA,* 12–17, 18–22 (since the three implications are confirmed, the model is too).

97. See South, *MT,* 106–12.

98. Signal Hill (1800–1860).

99. See South, *MT,* 116, 103ff.

100. *Sic:* Watson, LeBlanc, and Redman, *Expl,* 46–48.

101. See Plog, *Study of Prehistoric Change,* 23ff.

Chapter 3

1. L. R. Binford, *AP,* 8; see also 121: "We seek to replace these inadequate propositions by laws."

2. Binford, *NP,* 27; quoted in S. South, *MT,* 14.

3. L. R. Binford, *CA* 19 (1978): 631.

4. J. M. Fritz and F. T. Plog, *Am Ant* 35 (1970): 405, 408, 411.

5. P. J. Watson, S. A. LeBlanc, and C. L. Redman, *Expl,* 23.

6. However, see J. N. Hill, in *Mod,* 89 ("scientific law"; "lawlike answer").

7. See M. B. Schiffer, *BA,* 4ff.

8. S. South, *MT,* xiii, 122.

9. However, see D. L. Clarke, *An A,* 638 ("low level laws"). The word *law* is not in the index; see below, p. 50.

10. See C. Renfrew, *Em,* 16.

11. Moreover, Gene Sterud quotes, in support, the search for covering laws, the "revelation" of which is one of the subjects covered in the seminar (in *The Explanation of Culture Change: Models in Prehistory,* ed. Colin Renfrew [London: Duckworth, 1973], 15). See L. Klejn, *CA* 18 (1977): 25.

12. Republished in Binford, *AP,* 70.

13. Fritz and Plog, *Am Ant* 35 (1970): 408; Watson, LeBlanc, and Redman, *Expl,* 27, 5.

14. See Fritz and Plog, *Am Ant* 35 (1970): 406ff.

15. C. Hempel, *Aspects of Scientific Explanation* (New York: Free Press, 1965), 232.

16. Hill, in *Mod,* 89 (see below, p. 49): see also K. V. Flannery, *RT,* 51 (natural laws, low-level generalizations).

17. Binford, *AP,* 334. See also Fritz and Plog, *Am Ant* 35 (1970): 409 (ideas, beliefs functioning as laws); Schiffer, *BA,* 5 ("function as laws"); D. W. Read and S. A. LeBlanc, *CA* 19 (1978): 312 ("lawlike statements").

18. See G. Gjessing, *CA* 19 (1978): 632. For A. C. Spaulding, see *NP,* 34 ("general law or at least empirical generalization").

19. See Fritz and Plog, *Am Ant* 35 (1970): 408ff; Watson, LeBlanc, and Redman, *Expl,* 26–28.

20. Binford, *AP,* 117 (cf. above, n. 12).

21. See Binford, *CA* 19 (1978): 631–32.

22. Clarke, *Mod,* 3.

23. See Gjessing, *CA* 19 (1978): 632.

24. See Watson, LeBlanc, and Redman, *Expl,* 28; South, *MT,* xiii.

25. See South, *MT,* xiii.

26. Binford, *AP,* 117.

27. *Ibid.* Cf. Fritz and Plog quoting Hempel, *Am Ant* 35 (1970): 407.

28. Binford, *NP,* 27.

29. See below the examples from Schiffer and from Read, pp. 52–56, 65–68.

30. See Spaulding, in *NP,* 34, 36.

31. See Clarke, *Mod,* 15–20; cf. G. L. Isaac, in *Mod,* 185.

32. See Klejn, *CA* 18 (1977): 23.

33. See, e.g., J. Mehler or current criticisms of "behaviorism," an "outmoded philosophy."

34. Quoted in Binford, *AP,* 20; see also Renfrew, *AJA* 84 (1980): 295, where the formula is inverted ("Fellows, if it is evolution you are interested in, anthropology is *archaeology* or it is nothing").

35. Binford, *AP,* 32; Fritz and Plog, *Am Ant* 35 (1970): 411; Binford, *AP,* 118.

36. Hill, in *Mod,* 101; Isaac, in *Mod,* 172.

37. See Redman, *RT,* 6 (human behavior per se); Flannery, in *RT,* 50.

38. See Binford, *NP,* 321.

39. Binford, *AP,* 8; Schiffer, *BA,* 4.

40. Clarke, *Mod,* 57.

41. Spaulding, in *NP,* 36.

42. Binford, *AP,* 335.

43. See Binford, *NP,* 331.

44. See Fritz and Plog, *Am Ant* 35 (1970): 409ff.

45. Watson, LeBlanc, and Redman, *Expl,* 33.

46. Renfrew, *Em,* 16.

47. C. G. Morgan, *World Archaeology* 4 (1973): 274; Klejn, *CA* 18 (1977): 23.

48. Flannery, in *RT,* 51.

49. Ibid. For the same type of ideas, see Schiffer's two examples quoted below, pp. 51, 56.

50. See Watson, LeBlanc, and Redman, *Expl,* 51ff.

51. Ibid.

52. The critique of this type of "demonstration" has been made, in connection with W. A. Longacre, for example, by Read and LeBlanc (though the latter was a coauthor of *Expl*): see *CA* 19 (1978): 308.

53. See Schiffer, *BA,* 59–65.

54. See the example quoted by R. C. Dunnell, *AJA* 84 (1980): 470, of a present-day woodcutter who had never seen or used a stone ax, and a tree that was already cut into by a metal saw.

55. See Schiffer, *BA,* 59, 65.

56. See ibid., 63–65. It even reaches the point where the same equation gets two different numbers (18 and 24), and there seems to be a contradiction between equation (28) and the last (unnumbered) equation, which give the same value for durations of discard and of use when these were said to be unequal.

57. Ibid., 58.

58. South, *MT,* 122.

59. Schiffer, *BA,* 66.

60. Ibid., 67.

61. See Renfrew, *Em,* 25, 27; or again, the law of diminishing returns, ibid., 37.

62. See Klejn, *CA* 19 (1978): 163. For natural selection, see Read and LeBlanc, *CA* 19 (1978): 310.

63. Renfrew, *Em,* 16.

64. Dunnell, *AJA* 84 (1980): 471.

65. South, *MT*, 16. And Hempel already in 1965: see quotations in Binford, *CA* 19 (1978): 358, 631–32.

66. Read and LeBlanc, *CA* 19 (1978): 310; see also 312: "The only goal" of archaeologists is not "to produce [covering] laws."

67. See Fritz and Plog, *Am Ant* 35 (1970): 410.

68. See Binford, *CA* 19 (1978): 631–32; Binford, *Am Ant* 43 (1978): 358.

Chapter 4

1. See L. R. Binford, *AP*, 21ff.

2. Ibid., 120.

3. D. L. Clarke, *An A*, xiiiff.

4. Clarke, *Mod*, 1.

5. C. Renfrew, *Em*, 8.

6. See J. N. Hill, in *Mod*, 73–77. Cf. P. J. Watson, S. A. LeBlanc, and C. L. Redman, *Expl*, 61–88; it is especially the ecological form of systems theory that they stress.

7. See Binford, in *Mod*, 110–19.

8. See L. R. Binford, *CA* 19 (1978): 631–32.

9. D. W. Read and S. A. LeBlanc, *CA* 19 (1978): 310. The quotation is taken from Ernst Nagel.

10. Binford, *TB*, 7.

11. Ibid., 6.

12. Binford criticizes the article harshly; see *CA* 19 (1978): 631–32.

13. See Read and LeBlanc, *CA* 19 (1978): 310ff.

14. Ibid., 314.

15. The line joining the centers (= $l + 2r$) is proportional to the chord of arc L; in fact the calculation gives $L = \dfrac{C(l + 2r)}{C - r}$ if r = radius of a "residence location."

16. Let's recall, if need be, that a circumference of radius A has a surface area of πA^2; if $A \times 2$, the surface area becomes $\pi(2A)^2 = 4\pi A^2$.

17. See comments following Read and LeBlanc, *CA* 19 (1978): 317–30, with the reply, 330–33. Certain comments are very interesting, but none of them raises this problem. See also Binford, *CA* 19 (1978): 631–32; and E. G. Stickel, *CA* 20 (1979): 621–24.

18. $\beta = 2$ according to equation (21). But if one supposes $n = 4$, $\beta = 0.59$. It is Wiessner who says $\beta = 1.96$, according to her data. Both D. T. Bayard and M. P. Leone (*CA* 19 [1978]: 318, 324) throw in the towel in the face of these calculations.

19. See John E. Yellen, *Archaeological Approaches to the Present: Models for Reconstructing the Past* (London: Academic Press, 1977).

20. Binford, *Am Ant* 43 (1978): 330.

21. See M. B. Schiffer, *BA*, 193.

22. See Lewis R. Binford, *Nunamiut Ethnoarchaeology* (New York: Academic Press, 1978), and esp. *Am Ant* 43 (1978): 358.

23. Binford, *Am Ant* 43 (1978): 358.

24. Ibid., 353, 354.

25. Ibid., 354.

26. Ibid., 357.

27. Ibid., 359.

28. Ibid., 357.

29. Ibid., 360.

30. Ibid., 358 (*sic*).

31. Ibid., 335.

32. Ibid., 358.

33. Ibid., 360; see above, p. 27.

34. See, e.g., P. A. Larson, *CA* 20 (1979): 230ff. See also comments in *CA* 19 (1978): 318 (D. Bayard), 325 (C. G. Morgan), 326 (M. J. Rowlands), 327 (M. H. Salmon); and D. E. Dumond, *Am Ant* 42 (1977): 347.

35. See comments in *CA* 19 (1978): 318 (J. B. Bertram), 319 (M. Borillo), 322 (J.-P. Demoule), 327 (B. A. Segraves), 329 (A. Voorrips: absence of "formal theory"); see also Stickel, *CA* 20 (1979): 621.

36. See Read and LeBlanc, *CA* 19 (1978): 310.

37. R. C. Dunnell, *AJA* 84 (1980): 478.

38. See Bayard, *Am Ant* 34 (1969): 382.

Chapter 5

1. L. R. Binford, *TB*, 9.

2. See above, p. xxiv, concerning L. Klejn.

3. Binford, *AP*, 46.

4. See C. Renfrew, *Em*, 488.

5. See W. A. Longacre and J. N. Hill, in *NP*, 89–102, 103–42.

6. See D. L. Clarke, *Mod*, 22ff.

7. See, among others, Joseph V. Noble, *Techniques of Painted Attic Pottery* (New York: Watson-Guptill, 1965), xii–xv; hand-thrown Greek pottery has been attributed to women. Hesiod advises against the winter months for sea voyages, etc.

8. Binford, in *Mod*, 142; Hill, in *NP*, 140. Cf. "I do not pretend to have presented many substantive conclusions that have not already been believed for a number of years" (ibid.).

9. See Clarke, *Mod*, 847.

10. See Fred T. Plog, *A Study of Prehistoric Change* (New York: Academic Press, 1974), 144.

11. See D. W. Read and S. A. LeBlanc, *CA* 19 (1978): 317.

12. See Clarke, *Mod*, 53.

13. See G. Kushner, *Am Ant* 35 (1970): 127, which takes up the defense of diffusion, innovation, and acculturation.

14. See Binford, *NP*, 330ff.

15. See Clarke, *Mod*, 27.

16. F. Bordes and D. de Sonneville-Bordes, *World Archaeology* 2 (1970): 61–73; see esp. 66, 68, 73.

17. See Thomas G. Cook, *Koster: An Artifact Analysis of Two Archaic Phases in Westcentral Illinois* (Evanston, Ill.: Northwestern University Archeological Program, 1976), 13.

18. See D. E. Dumond, *Am Ant* 42 (1977): 337 (about Longacre).

19. Ibid., 343 ff.

20. Binford, *TB*, 3.

21. M. B. Schiffer, *BA*, 2.

22. On chalcedony, see Schiffer, *BA*, 159, 164. It is not exactly earth shattering.

23. See J. D. Muhly, *AJA* 84 (1980): 101 ff.

24. Ibid., 101: "Unfortunate[ly]," this publication "will, in the minds of many scholars, confirm a deeply felt belief that the 'New Archaeology' . . . is an archaeology of last resort . . . [that] you do when you do not find anything."

25. Schiffer, *BA*, 189.

Chapter 6

1. See L. R. Binford, *AP*, 117.

2. Binford, *NP*, 27.

3. Binford, in *Mod*, 163.

4. J. N. Hill, in *Mod*, 101.

5. Binford, *AP*, 455. See again, in 1976, his preface to S. South, *MT*, xi: "I anticipate a major change in the character of historic sites literature."

6. Binford, *Am Ant* 43 (1978): 354, 359 ff. See what I said above, pp. 22, 28, about nonconfirmed validations.

7. Binford, *TB*, 5.

8. M. B. Schiffer, *BA*, 78.

9. Among many other examples, see Clarke, *Mod*, 56; James E. Fitting, *The Development of North American Archaeology* (University Park: Pennsylvania State University Press, 1973), 288.

10. South, *MT*, 14, 121.

11. Gene Sterud, in *The Explanation of Culture Change: Models in Prehistory*, ed. Colin Renfrew (London: Duckworth, 1973), 14–15. The second quote is from Binford.

12. Clarke, *Mod*, 57.

13. Binford, in *Mod*, 161 ff.

14. See Thomas G. Cook, *Koster: An Artifact Analysis of Two Archaic Phases in Westcentral Illinois* (Evanston, Ill.: Northwestern University Archeological Program, 1976), 13.

15. See Binford, *AP*, 13; L. Klejn, *CA* 18 (1977): 11.

16. R. C. Dunnell, *AJA* 83 (1979): 444.

17. K. V. Flannery, in *RT*, 50. See also Renfrew, *AJA* 84(1980): 293 ("cult").

18. Quoted in Dunnell, *AJA* 83 (1979): 445.

19. M. P. Leone, *CA* 19 (1978): 664ff.

20. See Schiffer, *BA*, 49, 55, 87 (three times).

21. See Binford, *NP*, 27; *TB*, 1, 9; see also J.-C. Gardin, *Revue Archéologique* (1974): 341.

22. Renfrew, *AJA* 84 (1980): 294.

23. See Binford, *AP*, 330ff.

24. Ibid., 339.

25. See Renfrew, *Em*, 285; Schiffer, *BA*, 2–4.

26. See Binford, *TB*, 3ff.

27. L. R. Binford, *CA* 19 (1978): 631–32; see M. A. Jochim, *Am Ant* 43 (1978): 137ff.

28. See above, p. 5. To explain this attitude, the Vietnam war has been invoked (see Glyn E. Daniel, *A Short History of Archaeology* [New York: Thames and Hudson, 1981], 191), as have demographic factors (see Dunnell, *AJA* 83 [1979]: 440).

29. With regard to John E. Yellen, see Binford, *Am Ant* 43 (1978): 359.

30. See Binford, *NP*, 321ff.

31. See Binford, *Am Ant* 43 (1978): 358–60 (quotation on 359).

32. See Binford, *CA* 19 (1978): 631.

33. See Clarke, *Mod*, 53ff.; likewise G. L. Isaac, in *Mod*, 171, admits that he doesn't consider the old prehistory ridiculous. See also D. W. Read and S. A. LeBlanc, *CA* 19 (1978): 312.

34. Binford, *AP*, 450; Schiffer, *BA*, 3.

35. See Binford, *TB*, 9. See also P. A. Larson, *CA* 20((1979): 230.

36. See L. Klejn, *CA* 18 (1977): 24.

37. See J.-P. Demoule, *CA* 19 (1978): 323.

38. Flannery, in *RT*, 49, 53.

39. E.g., "Delumley, une cabane . . . Dan la grotte," "DeLumley" (Binford, *Am Ant* 43 [1978]: 357). Or even for American names—e.g., "Hodges" for "Hogers" (*Michigan Anthropological Papers* 19 [1963]; see also chap. 2 n. 27, above). J. B. Griffin himself calls Binford "L. H." (ibid., iii).

40. See Binford, *AP*, 10: "inevitable" suggestions.

41. See Renfrew, *Antiquity* 43 (1969): 243.

42. Dunnell, *AJA* 83 (1979): 439.

43. Binford, *AP*, 23. See ibid., 17: "they poked fun."

44. E.g., "societial" (Webster's : "societal") (*NP*, 85); "a necessary criteria," (in *Mod*, 124); "militaristic" (*AP*, 120); "systematic" (ibid., 117); "hypothetico-deductive-inductive" (see below, p. 129); "eluded" for "alluded" (*TB*, 9)—all of which do not seem to be typographical errors (like "casuality" for "causality"); similarly, the "empirical experience" (*Am Ant* 43 [1978]: 358).

45. Schiffer, *BA*, 57. See also S. Régnier, in *Raisonnement et méthodes mathématiques en archéologie*, ed. M. Borillo et al. (Paris: Centre National de la Recherche Scientifique, 1977), 150. In the same order of ideas, "homo nationalisus" (nationalized) (*Le Monde*, 23 September 1981).

46. See Renfrew, *Antiquity* 43 (1969): 242ff.

47. Clarke, *Mod*, 14, 18, 49.

48. Binford, *AP*, 6: for us too, alas.

49. Ibid.

50. Binford, preface to South, *MT*, xii, in connection with South's "formula."

51. Binford, *Am Ant* 43 (1978): 343. See above, p. 72.

52. See, e.g., Binford, *NP*, 328, where he compares the leisure time of hunter-gatherers with that of professors of archaeology.

53. Clarke, *Mod*, 24, 29.

54. Ibid., 55.

55. Renfrew, *AJA* 84 (1980): 293.

56. Ibid. See also Dunnell, *AJA* 83 (1979): 439.

57. E.g., J. D. Clark and J. G. D. Clark, cited by Isaac, in *Mod*, 195ff; Desmond Clark, then Clark, (184), etc.

58. E.g., G. L. Isaac, in *Mod*, 167, cites "Piggott, 1959; Renfrew, 1968, 1969; Trigger, 1969, 1970; Clarke 1968"! And "1968b" differs from one article to another in the same book.

59. It is true that often they are articles published in journals. This makes for an extra "detour"; there are simple, recognizable abbreviations for journals.

60. E.g., Clarke, *Mod*, 35, quotes in support J. E. Doran, ibid., chap. 10, who is particularly negative on this point. Or see Moberg, in *Arch Auj*, 308, quoting Binford, *AP*, 18–20, which upholds the opposite point of view.

61. See, e.g., Clarke, *Mod*, 49: "Fig. 18.2, 20.1, 21.9." But the chapter numbers are not given at the top of the page. So one has to hunt out these illustrations on pages 717, 758, and 844!

62. D. T. Bayard criticizes the absence of any drawings or even photographs in Binford's work (*Am Ant* 34 [1969]: 380). However, Hill gives four photos in *NP*, 111ff.: unless I'm mistaken, they are the only ones in the whole book. There are six plates in *Models in Archaeology*'s 1,055 pages.

63. See, e.g., Jean-Claude Gardin, in *Archéologie et calculateurs: Problèmes sémiologiques et mathématiques*, ed. J.-C. Gardin (Paris: Centre National de la Recherche Scientifique, 1970), 361.

64. See South, *MT*, 6; C.-A . Moberg, *Introduction à l'archéologie*, trans. Alain Schnapp (Paris: Maspero, 1976), 36, 38, 58, 62.

65. See South, *MT*, 15, fig. 2.

66. See D. H. Thomas, in *Mod*, 679, fig. 17.3.

67. See Clarke, *Mod*, 50, fig. 1.18.

68. Binford, about himself, *AP*, 12, 128.

69. See Daniel, *Short History*, 192.

Chapter 7

1. See C.-A. Moberg, *Introduction à l'archéologie*, trans. Alain Schnapp (Paris: Maspero, 1976); L. Klejn, *CA* 18 (1977): 16 and n. 3; or C.-A. Moberg, in *Arch Auj*, 308. Or see B. Soudský, whose "summary" of the paper given to the Marseilles colloquium (1969) fortunately corrects some points of

view that were far more disputable (B. Soudský, *Archéologie et calculateurs: Problèmes sémiologiques et mathématiques,* ed. J.-C. Gardin (Paris: Centre National de la Recherche Scientifique, 1970), 45.

2. See Gardin, *Revue Archéologique* (1970): 117–22.

3. See Gardin, *Revue Archéologique* (1974): 341–48. Gardin has the honesty to refer back to the previous review. "Refractory minds will have every opportunity to answer" that there is nothing new here except "jargon . . . the pedantry of which is often more striking than its fruitfulness" (344).

4. See L. R. Binford, *AP,* 11.

5. Serge Cleuziou et al., in *Annales Economies, Sociétés, Civilisations* (1973): 35–51 (republished in full in *Archéologie et calcul,* ed. M. Borillo [Paris: UGE, 1978]). On the other hand, one of them has finally—albeit temporarily—obtained the administrative post he coveted.

6. Ibid., 40.

7. Ibid., 50.

8. See ibid., 46ff. See below, p. 160. The "labeling" methods are very characteristic—instead of a refutation, or an attempt at refutation, they content themselves with "He merely expresses clearly the positions of traditional archaeology," or "We find here a language that we 'know well'" (one might be tempted to add, "me, too!"); or the methods of "pseudorefutation" (bad practice "takes nothing away" from the theoretical value; and Wheeler himself is summoned to the rescue—with no page numbers given—whereas all of his thinking strongly denies this position). There is an appeal to the Pavlovian reflex. See chap. 6, n. 60, and p. 138.

9. See Klejn, *CA* 18(1977): 8. The journal *Hephaistos* appeared only in 1979.

10. See R. Bucaille, *Cahiers d'Anthropologie Médiévale* 1 (1978): 36ff., in which medieval anthropology, with its walls and its texts, is compared (I kid you not) with prehistoric archaeology—with anything rather than "classical" archaeology which, as everyone knows, has not evolved for a hundred years.

11. Alain Schnapp, in *Faire de l'histoire,* ed. Jacques Le Goff and Pierre Nora, 2:3–23 (Paris: Gallimard, 1974), in which the example given of the hypothetico-deductive method is a classic circular argument. One should add that the site of St-Jean-le-Froid (Aveyron) is illustrated by an excellent photograph—of the site of Montaigut (Tarn)! It is always risky to do work at second hand.

12. See S. Cleuziou and J.-P. Demoule, in *Arch Auj,* 114–28. The authors, however, display a cheering reticence on other points. But the dendrogram of fibulae at Münsingen (114), which did not teach us anything new about the cemetery, the inevitable Broken K (125; Plog's criticism is only cited on p. 129 and is called "constructive"), the model of the Shoshone (this word seems to be taken as an adjective), despite the meagerness of its results (126), and the "Solcem" program, which Doran and Hodson found to have some very negative aspects (128), are all given as examples, as they stand.

13. Alain Schnapp, in *Arch Auj,* 20.

14. S. Cleuziou and J.-P . Demoule, in *Arch Auj*, 87, 89.

15. S. Cleuziou et al., *Annales* (1973): 49, 50.

16. Alain Schnapp, in *Faire de l'histoire*, 2:9. The term is not even defined. Although there have been many variations, it seems to connote the functioning of causes, the production of their effects, in short, the "dynamics" of a system (see Binford, *AP*, 117). One can see that the alleged new concept is only a word.

17. Alain Schnapp, in *Arch Auj*, 21. Compare below, p. 153.

18. Ibid., 20.

19. Jean-Paul Demoule, in *Nouvelles de l'Archéologie*, no. 2 (May 1980): 50 (distributed free); see Alain Schnapp, in *Arch Auj*, 16: the "logical procedures" ("true innovation" of 1973) are the same.

20. S. Cleuziou and J.-P. Demoule, in *Arch Auj*, 108 n. 13.

21. "The failure of . . . triumphalist . . . systems . . . of which we have heard nothing since"—Is this autocriticism? See S. Cleuziou and J.-P. Demoule, in *Arch Auj*, 104.

22. S. Cleuziou and J.-P. Demoule, in *Arch Auj*, 129. To note "too many failures" can only be the deed of a "peevish" mind: this is Chaplinesque stuff.

23. S. Cleuziou and J.-P. Demoule, *Nouvelles de l'Archéologie*, no. 3 (August 1980): 7.

24. S. Cleuziou and F. Pradeau, *Nouvelles de l'Archéologie*, no. 5 (March 1981): 49.

Chapter 8

1. For example, *AP* republishes several old articles by Binford who, the same year, presents the same article (on paradigms and Paleolithic research) in *Mod*, chap. 3; the posthumous book *Analytical Archaeologist* repeats several articles by Clarke, some of them admittedly scattered, but two of them already in *Mod* (chaps. 1 and 21); almost half of *Arch Auj* reproduces articles published between 1974 and 1977; the article by S. Cleuziou et al., as I have noted, reappeared in M. Borillo, ed., *Archéologie et calcul* (Paris: UGE, 1978). Certain books summarize, others adapt or translate, or contract into "digests," or both. Curiously, these authors are often among the most keen to preach economy in matters of archaeological publications.

2. See D. T. Bayard, *Am Ant* 34 (1969): 379ff. See also R. J. Braidwood, *Antiquity* 55 (1981): 24ff.; W. W. Taylor, *Science* 165 (1969): 382–84.

3. See C. G. Morgan, *World Archaeology* 4 (1973): 259–76, and, for the quotation, 275. This judgment is one of the most severe.

4. D. W. Read and S. A. LeBlanc, *CA* 19 (1978): 307, 309.

5. D. E. Dumond, *Am Ant* 42 (1977): 331.

6. P. A. Larson, *CA*, 20 (1979): 230.

7. See M. H. Salmon and W. C. Salmon, *American Anthropologist* 81 (1979): 61–74; R. C. Dunnell, *AJA* 84 (1980): 477.

8. See Bayard, *Am Ant* 34 (1969): 378–80.

9. See D. J. Meltzer, *Am Ant* 44 (1979): 644–57. See also Dunnell, *AJA* 83 (1979): 439, and *AJA* 84 (1980): 477; G. E. Daniel, *A Short History of Archaeology* (New York: Thames and Hudson, 1981), 191ff.

10. See L. Klejn, *CA* 18 (1977): 20.

11. For A. C. Spaulding, see *NP*, 38: "cogent premises."

12. See S. South, *MT*, 2–5.

13. Cf. the interplay of *cause* and *effect* in "processes."

14. Cf. the measurable aspect of behavior.

15. See M. B. Schiffer, *BA*, 4–10; L. R. Binford, *Am Ant* 43 (1978): 330, 353ff.; B. Trigger, *Time and Traditions* (New York: Columbia University Press, 1978), 12; Dunnell, *AJA* 84 (1980): 477 (with reservations, *AJA* 83 [1979]: 442).

16. See P. J. Watson, S. A. LeBlanc, C. L. Redman, *Expl*, 5.

17. See S. Struever, *Northwestern Archeology Report* 1 (1977): 6.

18. For Edward O. Wilson, the "pope" of sociobiology, all social behavior, hierarchical structures, conflicts, struggles are under genetic control. See J. Ruffié, *Le Monde*, 11 September 1979.

19. Ruffié, *Le Monde*, 28 September 1980, xv, xvii.

20. Questionnaire, 1980.

21. Ruffié, *Le Monde*, 28 September 1980, xv, xvii.

22. See Ruffié, *Le Monde*, 11 September 1979; 12 September 1979.

23. J. Monod, *Le hasard et la nécessité: Essai sur la philosophie naturelle de la biologie moderne* (Paris: Editions du Seuil, 1970), 127. Cf. François Jacob, *Le jeu des possibles* (Paris: Fayard, 1981), 64–66, 119–27.

24. C. Renfrew, *Em*, 18–19.

25. D. L. Clarke, *Mod*, 22.

26. Bayard, *Am Ant* 34 (1969): 377. See P. Bruneau, *Annales* (1974): 1478ff.

27. W. Shawcross, in *Mod*, 578ff.

28. Klejn, *CA* 18 (1977): 23.

29. Binford, *TB*, 9.

30. Renfrew, *Em*, 16. See above, p. 60.

31. Larson, *CA* 20 (1979): 231.

Chapter 9

1. C. L. Redman, *RT*, 5.

2. J. N. Hill, in *Mod*, 67.

3. See Gene Sterud, in *The Explanation of Culture Change: Models in Prehistory*, ed. Colin Renfrew (London: Duckworth, 1973), 10. However, see M. B. Schiffer, *BA*, 3. See n. 7 below.

4. See S. South, *MT*, 120ff.

5. See Hill, in *Mod*, 70. See also J.-C. Gardin, *Une archéologie théorique* (Paris: Hachette, 1979), 25–32.

6. G. L. Isaac, in *Mod*, 167.

7. South, *MT,* 15; see M. B. Schiffer, in *Research Strategies in Historical Archaeology,* ed. Stanley South (New York: Academic Press, 1977), 18.

8. See Lucien Febvre, *Combats pour l'histoire* (Paris: A. Colin, 1953), 431.

9. See L. R. Binford, in *Mod,* 121ff., 128ff., 135.

10. See S. R. Binford, *NP,* 51, 55.

11. See above, p. 11.

12. Hill, in *Mod,* 71. Likewise, K. V. Flannery, in *RT,* 49: "The way data are collected . . . may make it impossible to do processual studies later."

13. Binford, *Am Ant* 43 (1978): 138. And see M. A. Jochim, *AJA* 84 (1980): 472. For Isaac, see *Mod,* 188.

14. South, *MT,* 115, 124.

15. Hill, in *NP,* 133.

16. See D. L. Clarke, *Mod,* 803: "given," or "no archaeological study can be any better than the reliability of the observations upon which it is based."

17. See D. H. Thomas, in *Mod,* 674.

18. See Clarke, *Mod,* 10; Serge Cleuziou et al., *Annales* (1973): 45.

19. Hill, in *Mod,* 71, 96.

20. See Binford, *AP,* 118ff.

21. See Binford, in *Mod,* 121, 119 ("big surprise," in the singular), 111ff. F. T. Plog qualifies these as "ah-hah experiences" (*The Study of Prehistoric Change* [New York: Academic Press, 1974], 161).

22. Excavations by J. Deshayes at Dikili Tach.

23. Throughout the world, office construction, motorways; in France, the standardization of the depth/width of the Saône or the Rhine-Rhône canal; in the United States, "cultural resource management" (CRM).

24. Hill, in *Mod,* 72, 94, 96.

25. Hill, in *NP,* 133; see above, n. 15.

26. Hill, in *Mod,* 69, 96.

27. See Renfrew, *AJA* 84 (1980): 295: "[the selection of data] may be all very well for single period sites . . . but anyone who has dug on a deeply stratified site . . . with research problems in mind primarily relating to a specific phase, has had to face squarely the dilemma of what to do with the other material." This is perfectly obvious.

28. See Binford, in *Mod,* 159.

29. See Binford, *AP.*

30. Hill, in *Mod,* 70.

31. See Renfrew, *Em,* xxvi, *AJA* 84 (1980): 290 ("basic material"); E. Zubrow, *CA* 19 (1978): 330; Clarke, *Mod,* 35 ("real material"), 47 ("raw material"); South, *MT,* 85.

32. See Hill, in *Mod,* 70: one cannot collect data that will be useful to others; this goes against everyday experience, and he acknowledges it himself (96).

33. See Binford, in *Mod,* 137ff., 143.

34. See Binford, *NP,* 20.

35. See Plog, *Study of Prehistoric Change,* 163; South, *MT,* 89: it "may take . . . years" (*sic*).

36. By multiplying by three. See Renfrew, *Em,* 249.

37. Schiffer, *BA,* 49.

38. See South, *MT,* 114. See above, p. 115.

39. See ibid., 116. One can understand his procedure very well: there are many tailoring objects, weapons, buttons from military tunics, or toys. But what would one do in an archaeological situation where all the detail is less well known?

40. See ibid., 238ff. ("Dates-index").

41. See M. A. Jochim, *Am Ant* 43 (1978): 138.

42. Binford eliminates a composite category (in *Mod,* 136ff.); South groups together drinking glasses and glass plates (*MT,* 114); S. Régnier postulates a "homogeneous" terrain (Is that ever the case?), exact percentages, the absence of "eclipses" in the use of objects, and that the lowest layer is the oldest (which sometimes is wrong) (in *Raisonnement et méthodes mathématiques en archéologie,* ed. M. Borillo [Paris: Centre National de la Recherche Scientifique, 1977], 146). J.-C. Gardin deliberately adopts a "crude" view of things (*Mesopotamia* 13–14 [1978–79]: 106, 116, 124): he doesn't take into account the fine chronology of Ai Khanoum, the only one available, and he uses chronological periods that sometimes reach eight or nine centuries in a way that is as conscious and logical as it is paradoxical (see 141: period K). In addition, concerning a single site, see South (*MT,* 82: elimination of three-dimensional localization) or Schiffer (*BA,* 70–78).

43. See Schiffer, *BA,* 178ff.

44. D. W. Read and S. A. LeBlanc, *CA* 19 (1978): 312; Borillo, *CA* 19 (1978): 322.

45. See South, *MT,* 16.

46. Engineers, technicians, administrators, who, as everyone knows, are often authentic underpaid researchers.

47. Binford himself, *TB,* 9.

48. Interview given to a weekly publication.

49. See Binford, in *Mod,* 121–30, 135ff.

50. One can quote, for example, among others, the prytaneum at Thasos, or the Mycenaean pseudo-pretelesterion of Eleusis. See P. Darcque, *Bulletin de Correspondance Hellénique* 105 (1981): 593–605.

51. See Binford, in *Mod,* 119ff. D. E. Dumond saw this clearly: without the "old" archaeology, the "new" "would be woefully short both of data and of the chronological background that is so necessary to any sophisticated diachronic study" (*Am Ant* 42 [1977]: 346).

52. For example, in Argolid, for the former course of the Charadros in the Middle Helladic period, see Paul Courbin, *Etudes Archéologiques* (1963): 96–98. Or the excavations at Isthmia for marine transgressions; likewise on the Syrian coast, the researches of P. Sanlaville, and more generally the NIVMER program (P. Pirazzoli).

53. See Binford, *NP,* 17; *AP,* 117. Binford has not forgiven Braidwood for accusing him of incompetence. See also Read and LeBlanc, *CA* 19 (1978): 307.

54. See John D. Beazley, *Attic Black-Figure Vase-Painters, Attic Red-Figure Vase-Painters,* and the *Paralipomena,* published in 1942, 1956, and 1971 by Oxford University Press. Renfrew cites it, all the same, in connection with a recent book on prehistory that mentions it twice (*AJA* 84 [1980]: 297).

55. See Clarke, *An A,* 642ff.

56. See Binford, *NP,* 19ff. See also Schiffer, *BA,* 20.

57. See Hill, in *Mod,* 72. One often has the impression that, if need be, something false but explicit is better than something true but implicit.

58. Schiffer, *BA,* 23.

59. F. Bordes and D. de Sonneville Bordes, *World Archaeology* 2 (1970): 72.

60. See Schiffer, *BA,* 3.

61. See Hill, in *NP,* 137, on ways of "generating" hypotheses from archaeological data, ethnographic data, etc. These procedures are typically intuitive: see, for example, K. V. Flannery and M. D. Coe, in *NP,* 269, 277: "A number of colleagues have drawn to our attention some interesting parallels . . ."; "one reference which comes immediately to mind." Examples abound.

62. See Binford, *CA* 19 (1978): 632.

63. See ibid., 631.

64. Read and LeBlanc, *CA* 19 (1978): 332.

65. Ibid.

66. See Hill, in *Mod,* 64–68; Binford, *AP,* 116, 119: "unacceptable scientific procedure." See above, p. 9.

67. See above, pp. 68, 72, concerning Yellen.

68. Renfrew, *AJA* 84 (1980): 294.

69. Binford, *AP,* 133. Dunnell points out the contradiction between the deductive method and the inductive statistical method that Spaulding had compared (*NP,* 34).

70. See Hill, in *Mod,* 95, 94.

71. J. M. Fritz and F. T. Plog, *Am Ant* 35 (1970): 410; R. J. Mason, in *Mod,* 872.

72. D. H. Thomas, in *Mod,* 673, fig. 17.2.

73. See Thomas G. Cook, *Koster: An Artifact Analysis of Two Archaic Phases in Westcentral Illinois* (Evanston, Ill.: Northwestern University Archeological Program, 1976), 123; for Binford, see above, n. 66.

74. See South, *MT,* 15ff.

75. Read and LeBlanc, *CA* 19 (1978): 309.

76. S. Cleuziou et al., *Annales* (1973):43; Alain Schnapp, in *Arch Auj,* 20.

77. Hill, in *NP,* 139. On the model of explanation by covering laws, see C. G. Morgan, *World Archaeology* 4 (1973): 260ff., or more recently, the Salmons, *Am Anthr* 81 (1979): 61–74. For the circular nature of this type of explanation, see Read and LeBlanc themselves, *CA* 19 (1978): 308.

78. Deduction of implications and their verification repeat the same procedure and arouse the same criticism. In most cases, the implications are formulated only for the sake of form. In claiming to deduce these hypotheses from

modern pueblos, Hill acts as if he hadn't already excavated Broken K, as if he didn't already know what the rooms contained! It's eyewash. He himself answers this objection in a very curious and significant way: it's not always true, and the order of operations has no importance (cf. *Expl,* 14)! Hill, in *Mod,* 99. The only two cases where he says there is a discrepancy between the modern and the ancient must (or in any case could) have been established from the prehistoric pueblos, on seeing modern pueblos: (1) no jars in the small prehistoric rooms; (2) jars in the small modern rooms. And not vice versa: (a) jars in the modern pueblos; (b) there must have been some in the small prehistoric rooms, where there are none. It is a trick of presentation. See above, p. 42.

79. See J.-C. Gardin, *Revue archéologique* (1974): 343.

80. South, *MT,* 120 (in connection with the Carolina material).

81. Hill, in *Mod,* 97.

82. See Georges Daux, *Les étapes de l'archéologie* (Paris: Presses Universitaires de France, 1948), 14, 109.

83. See Hill, in *Mod,* 94.

84. See Binford, *NP,* 38, or N. Hume (quoted in South, *MT,* 8) who nevertheless had quite rightly said, in 1969, "The only skill that is peculiar to the archaeologist is his ability to study the artifacts."

Chapter 10

1. Spatial archaeology: David L. Clarke, ed., *Spatial Archaeology* (New York: Academic Press, 1977), and Ian Hodder and Clive Orton, *Spatial Analysis in Archaeology* (New York: Cambridge University Press, 1976); geoarchaeology: Donald A . Davidson and Myra L. Shackley, eds., *Geoarchaeology: Earth Science of the Past* (Boulder, Colo.: Westview, 1976); ethnoarchaeology: Richard A. Gould, ed. *Explorations in Ethnoarchaeology* (Albuquerque: University of New Mexico Press, 1978).

2. See chap. 9, n. 2.

3. Notably with the help of photogrammetry.

4. See, e.g., R. C. Dunnell, *AJA* 83 (1979): 445.

5. J. W. Mueller, *Am Ant* 39 (1974), memoir no. 28, ix, 45ff.

6. For example, J. N. Hill at Broken K, or J.-C. Gardin in Afghanistan (see Gardin, *Mesopotamia* 13–14 [1978–79], or J.-C. Gardin and P. Gentelle, *Bulletin de l'Ecole Française d'Extrême-Orient* 63 [1976]: 99).

7. See S. South, *MT,* 122. Where he dug—but he didn't dig *everything.*

8. See D. H. Thomas, *Am Ant* 43 (1978): 231–44 ("The Awful Truth about Statistics in Archaeology").

9. A die with twenty sides, of which only half are used (see Ralph M. Rowlett, in *Am Ant* 35 [1970]: 491). Random numbers are also generated by computer.

10. See Robert J. Sharer and Wendy A. Ashmore, *Fundamentals of Archaeology* (Menlo Park, Calif.: Benjamin-Cummings, 1979), 105, 204.

11. Hill, at Broken K, excavated eight additional rooms "as the importance of doing so became apparent" (*sic*), as well as the forty-six chosen by random

sampling: in total, a fraction of 60 percent (in *NP*, 104 and fig. 1). Likewise, see M. B. Schiffer, *BA*, 79–91. The attempt not to "falsify" things by shifting the workers around a site in successive rotations is not lacking in comedy (see S. Daniels, in *Mod*, 216ff.).

12. S. Cleuziou et al., *Annales* (1973): 39, 47. However, see J. Deetz, *Invitation to Archaeology* (Garden City, N.Y.: Natural History Press, 1967), 11–19, or P. J. Watson, S. A. LeBlanc, and C. L. Redman, *Expl*, 117, 125.

13. For example, South, *MT*, 113.

14. See M. A. Jochim and L. R. Binford, *Am Ant* 43 (1978): 137ff.

15. See Schiffer, *BA*, 69. Or Hodder and Orton, *Spatial Analysis*, 244ff.: "The realisation of the full potential of these techniques . . . will go hand-in-hand with the collection of better data . . . careful excavation of sites with detailed recording of percentages of types present . . . painstaking recording on sites of the position of artifacts and their relationship to other features. . . . It is really the slow collection of large bodies of reliable data, whether these concern neolithic axes or Romano-British pottery, that will allow spatial processes to be better understood."

16. D. T. Bayard, *Am Ant* 34 (1969): 380.

17. Binford, *AP*, 2.

18. See Schiffer, *BA*, 83–91.

19. See chap. 9, n. 27.

20. See chap. 7, n. 8.

21. Alain Schnapp, in *Arch Auj*, 19.

22. The aim seems to be an "ethnographic vision": of a totally original type like Pompeii, Medinet Habou, Ras Shamra, Mohendjo Daro, Taxila, etc.?

23. See Alain Ferdière, in *Arch Auj*, 51, 55ff. Curiously, this method is presented as an alternative to continuous clearance. On its novelty, see W. Müller and F. Oelmann, *Tiryns*, 1, no. 2 (1912) (on the excavation of 1907)—it's "beginning of the century" archaeology.

24. For example, at Kalapodi, in Boeotia, at Philia in Thessaly, and at Samos.

25. This is not always the case. Currently there are proposals for recording procedures (of stratification or artifacts) whose simplicity is not their primary characteristic. See Henri Galinié, in *Arch Auj*, 78, fig. 3, or 68: a wooden spoon designated "3.1214.1.12"! The role of recording is to record the data of an excavation: to make the excavation subordinate to the recording (see p. 63) is to put the means before the end; the to-ing and fro-ing of p. 104 seems preferable.

26. See the work of Peter Reynolds in England.

27. See W. Rathje, *Archaeology* 27 (1974): 236–41.

28. See J. G. D. Clark, *Prehistoric Europe: The Economic Basis* (London: Methuen, 1952), 3.

29. See Clarke, *Mod*, 10–40.

30. See Ian Hodder, ed., *Simulation Studies in Archaeology* (New York: Cambridge University Press, 1978).

31. See Schiffer, *BA*, 70–73.

32. Ibid., 67: "The constant ratios are not always so constant. For present purposes, it is assumed that this factor is negligible." See above, p. 59.

33. J. D. Muhly, *AJA* 84 (1980): 102.

34. For example, on a little site in the Loiret (Jean Chapelot, *Bulletin de la Société Archéologique et Historique de l'Orléanais*, n.s. 6 [1970]: 49–72), where potters' installations had been found accidentally, magnetic prospecting was carried out before the excavation: for the first time, the archaeologist didn't work blindly, the report's author suggests. Yet the numerous parallel trenches that were then cut by the bulldozer are remarkable for their emptiness, or near emptiness, three times out of four: so what use was the survey?

35. See South, *MT,* 120.

36. For example, for the choices of a pot's "segmentation," see Jean-Claude Gardin, *Code pour l'analyse des formes de poteries* (Paris: Centre National de la Recherche Scientifique, Roneo, 1956 [republished 1976]). See below, n. 43.

37. See below, pp. 146ff. H. Leredde and F. Djindjian, *Archéologia*, Dossier 42 (1980): 69ff., give an excellent account that is clear and adapted to the archaeological public.

38. Other examples in Schiffer, *BA,* 63–65 (on process duration). A somewhat comical example, on the pressure of a point ($p = \dfrac{F}{s}$ where F represents the force exerted and s the "surface" of a needle's point!)—see G. Delcroix and C. Tortel, *Méthodologie de la sauvegarde des biens culturels* (Paris: Centre National de la Recherche Scientifique, 1973), 133.

39. See Hodder and Orton, *Spatial Analysis,* 241, 243.

40. See South, *MT,* 112ff.

41. See above, p. 57, and chap. 3, n. 55: the total discard differs from the total discovered, $T_d \neq T_e$.

42. See E. B. Begler and R. W. Keatinge, *World Archaeology* 11 (1969): 208, 226. Similarly, in enology, a "mustimeter" gives the degree of alcohol in the must but obviously tells you nothing about the bouquet, the "body," etc., of the future wine.

43. See L. Fariñas del Cerro et al., in *Méthodes classiques et méthodes formelles dans l'étude des amphores,* Collection Ecole Française de Rome 32 (Rome: Ecole Française de Rome, 1977), esp. 179–94. The fault with all attempts of this type is that, contrary to the principle set out—that is, that a description corresponds to one object and one alone, and vice versa—in reality, a single description can correspond to similar but different objects; and furthermore, that objects, which ought to be distinguished to a fine degree, in fact receive the same descriptive formula. It is clear that the principle has to be modified radically: some attempts have been made in this direction (see 250ff.).

44. See above, p. 114. Similarly, J. E. Doran uses the previous classifications of fibulae from the Münsingen cemetery (in *Mod,* 443).

45. It is clear that certain publications of "crockery" content themselves with qualifying, measuring, and illustrating the material, without contributing

any new studies, and simply repeat knowledge that has already been acquired: I shall not be so cruel as to give examples. Similarly, certain architectural publications seem to be founded on the illusion that, failing anything else, the architectural "members" are at least "published": but the interesting characteristics have not been seen, and thus not indicated.

46. J. M. Fritz and F. T. Plog, moreover, themselves make classifications into an application of Hempel's method; see *Am Ant* 35 (1970): 470ff.

47. Jacques Bertin has specialized in all the techniques grouped under the name sémiologie graphique (*Sémiologie graphique: Les diagrammes, les réseaux, les cartes* [Paris: Gauthier-Villars, 1967]).

48. Schiffer, *BA,* 80, criticizes an alleged "peak" in the demographic curve. One of the most obvious requirements would be that the dots in "clusters" should be identifiable individually, unlike what is too often the case (however, sometimes they are replaced by very useful inventory numbers).

49. See Clarke, *An A,* 438 (trend surface analysis), 551–67, 548.

50. See *ibid.,* 548.

51. See Binford, in *Mod,* 136–55, in which J. D. Clark's data are used and his conclusions rediscovered, but not his explanations.

52. See Hill, in *NP,* 108ff.

53. J. E. Dumond, *Am Ant* 42 (1977): 337, 339ff.: Hill's analysis could not be "repeated." Hodder and Orton assure us that the opposite applies to "trend surface analyses" (*Spatial Analysis,* 242).

54. See D. Stiles, *CA* 20 (1979): 126–29; A. Voorrips, *CA* 21 (1980): 529–32.

55. See S. Cleuziou and J.-P. Demoule, *Arch Auj,* 92, 114, 119. Let me recall what I said about simulations above, pp. 120, 141.

56. Clarke, *An A,* 548. See Binford, *TB,* 5: "Statistical . . . statements . . . are simply complex empirical facts."

Chapter 11

1. See A. C. Spaulding, in *NP,* 34.

2. Ibid., 37.

3. Ibid., 35.

4. See C. D. Dollar, in *The Conference on Historic Site Archaeology Papers* (1968), 11.

5. See C. Renfrew, *Em,* 496, in which the importance of the individual is stressed.

6. See ibid., 16.

7. For example, S. South.

8. See M. B. Schiffer, *BA,* 4; see above, p. 49.

9. See above, p. 16.

10. Renfrew, *AJA* 84 (1980): 292.

11. Ibid., 293.

12. See Spaulding, in *NP,* 35.

13. E.g., P. Fougeyrollas; see below, p. 153.

14. Bruce Trigger, *Time and Traditions* (New York: Columbia University Press, 1978), 50.

15. See P. A. Larson, *CA* 20 (1979): 231.

16. Spaulding, in *NP,* 38; see also 33: "the abandonment . . . of the notion of historical explanation as a valid category of intellectual activity and, with even more force, of scientific activity."

17. See above, n. 10.

18. J. N. Hill, in *Mod,* 67.

19. Binford, preface to South, *MT,* xi.

20. See above, n. 13.

21. Marguerite Yourcenar, *Mémoires d'Hadrien* (Paris: Plon, 1956), 22.

22. Jean Lacouture, *Pierre Mendès-France* (Paris: Le Seuil, 1981), epigraph.

23. See Lucien Febvre, *Combats pour l'histoire* (Paris: A . Colin, 1953), 422ff.

24. See Lacouture, *Pierre Mendès-France,* 416.

25. B. Chapuis, in a recent interview.

26. See Spaulding, in *NP,* 36.

27. As is the case with the American New Archeologists.

28. For example, in France, the "school" of Jean-Pierre Vernant, Marcel Détienne, etc.: see, among others, P. Vidal-Naquet, *Revue Historique* 260 (1978): 3–21, or E. Will, *Korinthiaka* (1955).

29. E.g., Yvon Garlan, *Thasiaca,* supplement 5 to *Bulletin de Correspond-ance Hellénique* (Paris: de Boccard, 1979), 213–28, 256ff. (in which you will see a spontaneous application of the hypothetico-deductive method, with a "test"—a real one this time!). For anthropology one can quote, for example, J. Garanger, *Cahiers de l'ORSTOM,* Sc. Hum., 13 (1976): 147–61, etc.

Conclusion

1. C. G. Morgan, *World Archaeology* 6 (1974): 135; D. T. Bayard, *CA* 19 (1978): 318.

2. See L. R. Binford, *AP,* 120.

3. J. Ruffié, *Le Monde,* 12 September 1979, 12.

4. See Binford, *TB,* 9ff.

5. See Glyn E. Daniel, *A Short History of Archaeology* (New York: Thames and Hudson, 1981), quoting R. J. Braidwood: "Some of the writings of the 'new archaeologists' may have brought confusion to students and younger colleagues beyond North America and western Europe."

6. See W. W. Taylor, *A Study of Archaeology,* Memoir 69 (Washington, D.C.: American Anthropological Association, 1948), 44; Spaulding, in *NP,* 38.

7. Taylor, *Study of Archaeology,* 44.

8. Claude Lévi-Strauss, interview given to a weekly publication in July 1980.

Index

Abductive reasoning, 129
Abstraction, 100
Acheulian culture, 147
Aegean, 33–34, 77, 118
Afghanistan, 82, 125, 134
Africa, 4, 19, 23, 39, 68–69, 73, 77, 114, 145, 147, 153
Agora, 133
Agrarian archaeology, 125
Agriculture, 13, 25–26, 33, 34, 51, 59, 79, 89, 112, 114, 139
Ai Khanoum, 82, 182n.42
Aisne valley, 139
Akrotiri (Thera), 83
Alalakh, 37
Alaska, 4, 28, 69, 73
Al Mina, 37, 117–18
Amazonia, 166n.9
Americanist archaeology, 4, 10, 73, 91
Amoud (Ouadi), 115
Amphorae, 144–45
Amplification of deviation, 59
Analogy. *See* Ethnographic analogy
Analytical archaeology, 62, 64, 87, 146–47
Anarchy, 11, 121
Angkor, 82
Anthropology, 8, 14, 48–50, 59, 62, 75, 91, 110, 112–13, 123–25, 132, 148, 150–55, 159–60
Arbitrariness, 136, 140–41, 143, 145, 147
Archaeology. *See* New Archeology; Traditional archaeology
Archaeometry, 141–42
Architecture, 14, 37, 41, 43, 59, 112, 115, 123–24, 135, 143

Arctic, 69, 133
Arizona, 40. *See also* Broken K; Tucson
Armchair archaeologists, 12, 112
Asia Minor, 37
Assemblage, 6, 27–28, 69, 76, 79, 139, 146
Astrophysics, 14, 48, 107
Athens, 133
Atkinson, Richard, xiii
Australia, 4, 25, 133, 166n.9
Authority, 11, 126
Auxiliary, archaeology as, 121, 159–60
Axiom, 61, 63–65, 67

Bayard, Donn T., 101, 105, 107, 136, 160, 173n.18, 177n.62
Beakers, 4, 29
Bear, Rupert, 95
Beazley, John D., 126, 145
Beer cans, 69, 83, 87
Behavior, 13, 60, 85, 104, 106, 121, 139, 150, 152, 160
Behaviorism, 13, 48, 106, 108, 154
Bernard, Claude, 38, 167n.1, 170n.81
Bertin, Jacques, 187n.47
Bezerra de Meneses, Ulpiano, xi
Bibliography, 6, 95, 100, 116, 128, 144
Binclarke, Lewis D. L., 3
Binford, Lewis R., xiii, xix–xx, xxii, 3–6, 8–9, 11–14, 16, 18, 20, 23–29, 34–35, 38–39, 42, 45–47, 49–50, 59–60, 62–63, 67–80, 84–94, 99, 101–2, 105–6, 108, 114–16, 119–20, 127–29, 134, 136, 145, 147, 152–53, 158, 160, 166n.2, 168nn.4, 27, 173n.12, 177n.52, 182n.53
Binford, Sally. *See* Schanfield, Sally

Biology, 14, 18, 48, 60, 106, 108
Black Sea, 26
Boas, Franz, 12
Boileau, N., 94
Bordes, Denise, 79, 127
Bordes, François, 27, 79, 88, 114, 127, 147
Botany, 134, 141, 144
Bourdieu, Pierre, 152
Braidwood, Robert, 12, 25, 35, 49, 88–90, 99, 114, 182n.53
Breuil, Henri, 114
Brodbeck, May, 150
Broken K, 40–41, 77, 81, 87, 101, 127, 130, 137, 147, 184nn.78, 11. *See also* Hill, James N.
Brownian motion, 76, 107
Brunswick, Carolina, 43, 59
Bulldozer, 138
Bulleid, Arthur H., 30–31, 77, 114–15
Bushmen, 50, 64, 66–68, 71, 89, 166n.9
Butchering, 27–28, 77, 79
Butser Farm, 139

Calculation, 57, 124, 135, 140, 144, 146
Calligrams of Apollinaire, 95
Cambodia, 125
Camp, base, 64
Campsite, modern, 69, 87, 152
Captions, 95
Careerism, xxii, 96, 103
Carolina, 29, 43, 45, 60, 86, 115, 120, 144
Catalogs, xxii, 100, 145
Cause, 71, 73, 80, 147, 153
Central theory, 62
Chalcedony, 81, 175n.22
Chang, K. C., 46, 88
Charlatanism, 89, 147, 160
Cherokee Indians, 24, 40
Chicago, ix, 81
Childe, Vere Gordon, 13, 25, 35, 114
Chinese box model, 93
Chi-square test, 40, 146–47
Chorley, Richard J., 15
Chronology, 9, 52, 87, 112–13, 120, 125, 130, 134, 136, 143, 145–46, 153
Clark, J. Desmond, 27, 77, 114–15
Clarke, David L., xix–xx, xxii, xxv, 3–4, 7–8, 11–12, 14–15, 19, 21, 27, 29–

34, 39, 46–50, 60, 62, 76–77, 79–80, 85, 87, 90, 92–94, 96, 98, 107, 114–16, 119, 127, 139, 145–46, 148
Classic archaeology, 37, 81–82
Classification, 7, 9, 139, 142, 145, 148
Clusters, 139, 146
Codes, 143–44
Coe, J. L., 136
Coe, Michael D., 28
Coefficients of variation, 85
Colonization, 125
Competence, 113, 123, 126–28, 146, 148, 160
Computers, xxii, 15, 75, 86, 100, 102, 113, 132, 136, 146–48, 159
Comte, Auguste, 38, 170n.81
Conned, 98–103, 111, 121, 159
Contempt, 9, 88, 111, 114, 141, 150, 161
Contradiction, 84, 114–15, 118–20, 128–29, 144, 157
Control, 5, 139, 142. *See also* Validation; Verification
Cook, Thomas, 29, 79, 86, 129
Correlation matrix, 30
Covariance, 39, 113, 146–47
Covering law, 48, 90, 105, 130, 150–51, 171n.11
Creativity, 7, 60, 69, 128, 160
Creek Indians, 40
Crete, 34, 37, 116–18
Cybernetics, 14, 33, 80, 139
Cyclades, 33–34, 80–81, 117, 120, 123
Cyrene, 116

Daniel, Glyn E., ix, xv, 165n.15
Darwinism, 14, 106–8
Data, 6–9, 11, 21, 34, 39–41, 43, 92, 100, 113–32, 140–41, 144, 147, 154
Data bank, 100, 128, 144
Dating, 30, 120, 124–25, 131, 142–44
Decoration, 124
Deduction, 19, 27, 38, 42, 65, 73, 127, 129–30
Deductive method, 21, 48, 119, 128–30. *See also* Hypothetico-deductive method; Logico-deductive method
Deductivo-nomological method, 46
Deetz, James, 79, 147
Delphi, 82, 116

Demography, 25, 67, 120
Demonstration, 14, 18, 23, 26–28, 30, 39, 42, 44, 51, 56, 65, 78, 80–81, 84, 89, 105, 122, 126, 128–31, 146–47, 153
Denver, Colorado, 19, 49, 81
Description, 104, 142–45, 148
Determination, 9, 130, 142–44, 151, 154, 160
Determinism, 13–14, 47–48, 66, 93, 106–8, 152–53, 159
Diagrams, 95, 113, 146
Diffusion, 33, 76, 79–80
Discards, 29, 52–59, 92, 127, 140
Disciples, 22, 28, 38, 45, 47, 85, 87, 94
Disposal modes, 70
Distance, social, 51
Domestication, 25–26
Dominance, cultural, 59
Donor system, 79
Doran, James E., 3, 186n.44
Dumond, Donald E., 105, 147, 161, 182n.51
Dunnell, Robert C., 4, 13, 60, 74, 91, 105, 167n.22, 172n.54, 183n.69
Dynamics, 15, 47–49, 63, 72, 101, 121, 139, 150

East, 126. *See* Far East; Near East
Ebla, 82
Ecology, xxi, 14–15, 25, 62, 74, 133, 158
Ecosystem, 15
Egypt, 116–17
Einstein, Albert, 121
Elaboration, 75, 142–43
Electronics, 15, 146
Empirical philosophy, 7, 21, 47, 49, 62–63, 69, 71–73, 90, 92, 121
Empiricist approach, 6–9, 12, 18
Endogamy, 32, 51
Energy sources, 13
England, 29, 91, 122, 139
Environment, xxi. *See also* Ecology
Epistemology, xiv–xv, 7, 12–13, 22, 29, 52, 74–75, 83
Eretria, 139
Eskimos, 89, 139. *See also* Nunamiut
Ethnoarchaeology, xiii, xxii, 28, 60, 69, 133–35, 139, 142, 152, 157, 169n.72

Ethnographic analogy, 20, 23–25, 31, 73, 139, 158
Ethnography, 14, 27, 40, 65, 69, 71, 152–53, 157
Ethnology, 14, 106, 112, 132, 134, 161
Ethology, human, 13, 133
Euboea, 37, 82, 123
Euphrates, 87
Europe, 26, 38, 48, 77, 81, 86, 110, 117, 126, 133, 145, 150
Evolutionism, xxi, 13–14, 106, 108, 110
Excavation, 5–6, 36, 82, 93, 100–102, 112, 114, 116, 124, 132–33, 135–36, 138–39, 142–43
Exceptions, 141, 148, 151
Excommunication, 87
Exogamy, 32
Experience, 73, 127
Experiment, 11, 38, 47, 56, 63, 89, 92, 139
Explanation, 7, 12, 15, 18, 21, 23–24, 44–46, 48, 71–72, 75, 79, 104–6, 108–9, 121, 128, 150, 158
Explicitness, xxii, 11–12, 14, 16, 47–48, 50, 54, 59, 63–64, 84, 88, 100–101, 105, 108, 114, 126–29, 136, 138, 143, 147, 151
Extrapolation, 120, 161

Fabrication of facts, 120
Factor analysis, 27, 80, 140–41, 146–47
Facts, establishment of, xiv, 7, 12, 111–26, 131–32, 135, 139, 141–44, 148, 154, 159–60. *See also* Data
Fakes, identifying, 124
Falsifying, 85, 112, 120, 136
Far East, 77, 108
Fatalism, 153
Fauna, 28, 134
Febvre, Lucien, 114, 153
Feedback, 34, 106
Fibula, 30, 32, 39, 145, 186n.44
Fitting, James, 10
Flannery, Kent V., xiv, xvii, xxv, 3–4, 16, 28, 50, 80, 86–87, 91, 94, 110, 115, 168n.41
Flora, 134
Flow chart, 93–95
Followers, 4, 33, 35, 84, 90, 102, 136, 145

Form, ceramic, 123, 143
Formalization, 105, 144, 152
Foucault, Michel, xxii, 152
Fougeyrollas, Pierre, 153
Founding fathers, 3–4
Freedom. *See* Liberty
Fritz, John M., xviii, 4, 6–7, 11, 19, 21, 35, 46, 49–50, 60, 86, 129, 187n.46
Functional differences, 25, 28
Functionalism, 106
Furnace, 37
Furtins, Grotte des, xii

Gallay, Alain, xi
Galley Pond, 47
Garbage Project, 139, 152
Gardin, Jean-Claude, xi, 35, 98–99, 129, 134, 167n.23, 178n.3, 182n.42
Garrod, Dorothy, 115
Gaussian curve, 101
Generalization, 5–6, 9, 11, 47, 49, 62–63, 69, 71–73, 89, 90, 128, 150, 152, 160
Geography, 106, 158
Geometric period, Greek, 117
Geomorphology, 15, 93
Germans, 101, 138
Glastonbury, 4, 30–31, 33, 39, 77, 114, 145
Glycogenic function, 38
Graham, John A., 5–6, 88
Gray, Harold St. George, 30–31, 77, 114–15
Great Britain. *See* Glastonbury; Maesbury; Wessex
Greece, 37, 82, 92, 94, 120, 123, 138. *See also* Cyclades
Grinders, manos, 51–52
Gunn, Joel, xiv

Haggett, Peter, 15, 87
Hatchery West, 114
Hawkes, Jacquetta, x
Hebrew, 92
Heizer, Robert F., 5–6, 88
Hempel, Carl, 6–8, 18, 35, 38, 46–47, 69, 86, 105, 128
Hesiod, 174n.7
Hide smoking, 24, 81, 87
Hill, James N., xiv, 3, 7, 11–12, 19–21,

40–42, 45, 47, 51, 62, 76–77, 79–80, 85–87, 93, 101, 115–16, 118–19, 127, 129–31, 136, 147, 153, 170n.88, 177n.62, 184nn.78, 11
Hissarlik, 37
Histogram, 113, 146
Historians, 113, 122–24, 132–33, 154–55, 159–60
History, xxi, 75, 77, 85, 110, 112, 122, 132, 148, 150–51, 153–54, 159–60
Hodder, Ian, xiii–xiv, 3, 144
Homer, 37, 178n.5
Humanism, 5, 8–9, 100–102
Hume, I. Noel, 184n.84
Humor, xiii, 9, 93
Hunting stand, 69–72
Hypotheses, 18–44, 60, 68, 70, 75, 77–79, 87–89, 93, 100–101, 104–5, 109, 113, 116–19, 121, 127–31, 139, 144, 148, 157–58, 160, 167n.2
Hypothetico-deductive method, xiv, 8, 11, 18–44, 46, 60–61, 80, 99–102, 104–5, 121, 129, 158

Ibn Hani, 82
Iconic model, 93
Illustrations, 91, 94–97, 113, 146
Imagination, 9, 69, 78, 128, 132, 140, 160
Immigration, 25, 125
Implication, 21, 27, 35–37, 42, 130
Implicitness, 11, 27, 47, 50, 59, 100, 126, 150, 159
Impressionism, 143, 146
Incense, 86, 157
Independent data, 21, 39, 119
Indians, American, 24, 139
Induction, 11, 47, 105, 128–29
Inductive method, 6–7, 18, 48, 69, 71–73, 88, 116, 121, 129, 147
Industrial archaeology, 133
Inference, 5, 8, 18, 128, 160, 169n.44
Inferiority complex, 103
Innovation, 10, 16, 26, 80, 98, 153, 157
Intangibles, 8, 126
Interdigitation, 79, 87, 131
Interdisciplinary assistance, 148, 160
Interpretation, 6, 24–25, 27–28, 36, 87, 101, 122, 138–39, 142, 148, 154, 160
Intuition, 66, 126–29, 146–47

Invalidation, 105, 113, 130, 135
Invasion, 76, 79, 125
Invention, 60, 122, 128, 146
Iran, 4
Isaac, Glynn Ll., xix, 49, 113, 115, 176n.33
Isimila, 39
Isolationism, 11, 94

Jabrud, 28, 115
Jacob, François, 108
Jagerhaus cave, 120
Jargon, xiii, 11, 91, 94, 102, 104, 158
Jarry, A., 91
Jelks, Edward, 43
Jochim, Michael A., 88, 115, 120
Joint Site, 81
Julliard, Jacques, 122

Kalambo Falls, 39, 120, 131
Kemeny, John G., 96, 129
Kenya, 39
Kidder, Alfred, 77
Kiln, 37, 57
Kition, 82
Kiva, 41
Kleindienst, Maxine, 115
Klejn, Lev, xix, xxiv, 4, 50, 60, 86, 108
Koster, 29. See also Cook, Thomas; Struever, Stuart
Kuhn, Thomas, 9, 85–86, 167n.22

Laborit, Henri, 107
Larson, Paul A., 105, 108
Latin, 91–92, 94
Law and order archaeologists, 60
Laws, xiv, 6–8, 12, 16, 29, 44–61, 63, 68–69, 73, 75, 82–83, 87–90, 101, 104, 106–10, 121–22, 128, 151–54, 158
Leakey, Louis S. B., 27, 114
Leakey, Mary D., 27, 114
LeBlanc, Steven A., x, 16, 21, 44–46, 50–51, 60, 62, 63, 64, 68, 74, 87, 105, 120, 128–29, 168n.28, 172n.52
Lefkandi, 82
Leone, Mark P., 51, 86, 173n.18
Leroi-Gourhan, André, 38
Le Roy Ladurie, Emmanuel, 133
Lévi-Strauss, Claude, xiii, 188n.8

Lewontin, R., 106–7
Lexicography, xxii
Liberty, 106–7, 151, 153, 159
Linguistics, xiii, 14, 106, 111
Logic, xxii, 12, 18, 20, 26, 36, 46, 63, 84, 97, 102, 105, 109, 128–29
Logico-deductive method, 19–20, 46
Longacre, William A., 3, 51, 76, 79–80, 93, 115, 147, 172n.52

McLuhan, Marshall, 96
Macroarchaeology, 134
Maesbury, 32
Mafia, 3, 86
Magdalenian culture, 38, 123
Magnetism, 141–42
Mallaha, 26
Manipulation, 114, 119–20, 147
Mardikh, Tell, 82
Mariotte's law, 48
Markov chains, 147
Maruyama, Magoroh, 60
Marxism, xiii, xxi, 74, 106, 108, 153
Maryland, 115
Mason, R. J., 129
Materialism, 13–14, 74, 106, 108
Mathematics, 14, 48, 52, 58, 64–65, 67, 93, 97, 100, 108, 148
Mathematization, 56, 58, 143
Matrix, 14, 113, 146
Measurements, 37. See also Quantification
Mechanistic approach, 13, 153
Medicine, 18, 167n.1
Meltzer, D. J., 105
Mendès-France, Pierre, 153
Meso-America, 29
Mesopotamia, 77
Messenia, 4, 82, 138, 141
Messianism, 84
Metaphysics, 7, 13, 105
Metate, 41
Methodology, 12, 75, 80, 82, 86, 102, 105, 110, 126, 130, 135, 147
Mickey Mouse laws, 50–51
Middle-range theory, 62–63, 73, 122
Migration, 76, 79–80, 125
Mineralogy, 32, 39, 141
Mississippi, 24

Moberg, Carl-Axel, 98
Modelization, 99
Models, 19, 21, 26, 33–35, 42, 46–49,
   65, 67, 75, 86, 88, 90, 93, 95, 100,
   105, 113, 139–41, 145
Monod, Jacques, 107
Monte-Carlo model, 79, 147
Montelius, Oscar, 8
Moon, xiv, 15, 81, 114, 158
Morgan, Charles G., 15, 50, 105, 161
Mousterian culture, 4, 27–28, 79, 87,
   123, 127, 131
Mueller, J. W., 135
Multiplier effect, 34, 60
Munsell Code, 143
Münsingen-Rain, 178n.12, 186n.44
Munson, Patrick J., 24–25, 168n.27
Mureybet, 82
Mussolini, Benito, 90
Mutation, 28

Nagel, Ernst, 173n.9
Nautical archaeology, xxi, 133
Nazca lines, 123
Near East, 26, 28, 37, 49, 98, 118
Neolithic period, 26, 39, 77, 107
Neologisms, 92
Neutron activation, 141, 148
New Archeology, ix–xiv, xvii–xx, xxii–
   xxiv, 3–16, 20–44, 45–60, 63, 68,
   72–88, 90–96, 98–101, 103–11, 113–
   14, 118–19, 121–22, 125–26, 128–32,
   134–36, 138, 141, 145, 148, 151–52,
   157–60
Newfoundland, 43, 115, 120
Nichoria, 4, 82, 138, 141
Nominalism, 133
Nomological approach, 48, 106, 150
Nomothetic approach, 12, 45, 106
Novelty, 9, 121–22, 143, 157, 160
Nunamiut, 28, 68–71, 87, 93, 108, 114,
   152. *See also* Eskimos

Objectivity, 11, 110, 113, 143–44, 146–
   47
Observation, 28, 45, 63, 69, 71–72, 89,
   112, 114, 118–19, 122, 125, 127,
   130–31, 134, 143, 147
Oceania, 133
Oldowayan, Olduvai, 82, 147

Olorgesailie, 39
Omo, 77, 82
Oppenheim, Paul, 38, 105. *See also*
   Hempel, Carl
Orton, Clive, 144

Paleobotany, 134, 141
Paleogeography, 110, 134
Paleolithic period, 4, 27–28, 38, 79, 87,
   123, 127, 131, 147
Palynology, 41, 134, 141, 148
Para-archaeologists, 132
Paradigm, 10, 39, 77, 85, 87, 92
Particularism, 8, 11–12, 121, 150, 153
Pata-archaeology, xxii, 3, 91
Peacock, David P. S., 32, 39
Pedantry, 127
Peloponnese, 37
Pennsylvania, 115
Percentages, 43, 60, 81, 85, 113, 120,
   140, 143–44
Periodization, 146
Perrot, Jean, 26
Philip of Macedon, 82
Phillips, Philip, 48, 110
Philosophy, 7, 11–12, 14, 97, 105–6,
   108, 118, 148, 151–52, 159
Photography, 95, 123, 125, 134, 136,
   141, 148, 158
Physics, xviii, 14, 18, 48, 106–7, 142,
   148, 154, 160
Pincevent, 82
Pipe stems, 87, 93
Pits, 24–25, 50, 81, 87, 131. *See also*
   Hide smoking
Plausibility, 12, 34
Plog, Fred T., xvii, 4, 6–7, 11, 19, 21,
   35, 44, 46, 49–50, 60, 77, 80, 86, 93,
   105, 115, 120, 129, 187n.46
Polymorphism, genetic, 107
Polynesia, 25, 29, 40
Pomranky, 114
Popper, Karl, 44, 84–86
Population, 23, 25–26, 32, 50, 63–68,
   80, 125
Positivism, 13, 15, 106, 129
Postdepositional, 134, 140, 157
Potassium-argon dating, 141
Potential, 23, 85, 146
Pottery, 24–25, 30, 41, 51, 77, 80–81,

101, 112, 115–16, 119, 123–24, 126–
    27, 135
Power, 85, 103
Praxis, xxv, 110–11
Prediction, xxiv, 12, 19, 26, 33–35, 37,
    41, 50, 54, 71, 81, 85, 87, 99, 106,
    121, 127
Prehistoric period, 4, 8, 49, 69, 78, 81,
    93, 107–8, 110, 115, 130, 139, 142,
    150–51
Presupposition, 88, 140–41, 145, 159
Problems, approach to, xxiv, 9, 11, 75,
    83, 112–19, 121, 132–35, 142, 144,
    148, 152, 154, 157
Process, xiv, 9, 12, 28, 47, 72, 80, 91–
    92, 116, 121, 151, 158
Professionalism, xv, 36, 155
Prospection, 138
Publications, xxiii, 99
Pueblo, 4, 40–42, 44, 51, 77, 80–81,
    130, 137, 184n. 78

Quantification, 8, 11, 51, 58, 86, 107,
    127, 140, 143–44, 146, 157
Quina culture, 127

Radiocarbon dating, 141
Ragir, Sonia, 6
Read, Dwight W., x, 60, 63, 64–68, 74,
    77, 87, 105, 120, 128–29, 168n. 28,
    172n. 52
Reality, agreement with, 56, 64, 113,
    116, 118–20, 131, 133, 136, 141,
    159–60
Reconstruction, 9, 21, 27, 108, 123, 125,
    139
Rectification, 82, 120
Redman, Charles L., 16, 21, 44–46, 50–
    51, 62, 105, 110
References, 94–95, 128
Refutation, 24, 89. See also Falsifying
Regression, linear, 65, 146
Regularity, 47, 62
Renfrew, Colin, xi, xiin, 3, 9, 13, 15, 33–
    35, 39, 46, 50, 59–60, 62, 76, 80, 85,
    87, 91–92, 94, 96, 107–8, 115, 119–
    20, 129–30, 138, 151, 153, 170n. 81
Rescue operations, 117
Retro-archaeology, xiin

Revolution, in archaeology, xxii–xxiii,
    62, 75, 85–86, 99, 161
Ridgway, David, x
Ritual, 86
Ruffié, Jacques, 107–8, 158
Russia, 26
Rust, Alfred, 115

Sabloff, Jeremy A., 129
Sahara, 19, 23
Sahlins, Marshall, 29
Salmon, M. H., 105
Salmon, W. C., 105
Sampling, xxiv, 6, 21, 40, 76, 86, 93,
    113–14, 128, 135–36, 144
Santa Monica, California, 47
Sartre, Jean-Paul, 153
Satellite, 125, 134, 159
Schanfield, Sally, 3–4, 28, 115
Schiffer, Michael B., xix, 4, 8, 13, 29, 42,
    45, 49, 51–60, 63, 69, 77, 80, 83, 85–
    87, 90, 93, 106, 115, 120, 127, 136,
    140, 147, 152, 167n. 24
Schliemann, Heinrich, 37
Sciascia, L., xxii
Science, xiv, xxii, 5, 8, 13, 15–16, 18,
    22, 76, 78, 84, 86–87, 100, 104, 106,
    108, 121, 144, 152, 157–59, 161
Scientific archaeology, 12, 16, 20, 33,
    46–49, 60, 75, 79–80, 82, 84–86, 97,
    101, 104, 106, 108, 121, 128, 132,
    141–42, 150
Seasons, 26, 73, 76–77, 79, 82, 87, 115,
    131, 134, 157
Sectarianism, 86, 96
Selection, natural, 60, 107
Shawcross, Wilfred, 107
Shoshonean Indians, 22, 96
Shubbabiq, 28, 115
Siceliot, 123
Simplification, 120, 135
Simulation, 29, 43, 120, 139–41, 147
Skinner, B. F., 106
Sneath, P. H. A., 87
Snodgrass, Anthony, xi
Sociobiology, 106–7, 158
Sociology, xiv, 48, 50, 60, 112, 148,
    152–53, 159
Sociotechnic significance, 19, 23
Sokal, Robert R., 87

Somerset, 30–31
Soudský, Bohumil, 98, 177n.1
South, Stanley, 4, 8, 12–13, 16, 29, 43, 45, 59–60, 85–86, 93, 96, 106, 115, 119–20, 129, 144
Spatial relations, xxi, 29, 69, 71–72, 80, 124, 133, 140–41, 146
Spaulding, Albert, 47–49, 93, 106, 132, 150, 153, 160
Specialization, 28, 70, 85, 88, 145, 148, 154
Spectrometry, X-ray, 141
Statistics, xxii, 14–15, 42, 48, 53, 56, 70, 75, 79, 87, 107–8, 132, 136, 139, 145–48, 152, 159
Sterud, Gene, 85, 171n.11
Steward, Julian H., 115
Stiles, Daniel, 147–48
Stipulations, 29, 42, 127
Stochastic models, 48, 108
Stock rearing, 13, 89, 139
Stratigraphy, 5, 9, 15, 136, 138
Structural differences, 25, 28
Structuralism, xiii, xxi, 74
Struever, Stuart, 3, 29, 79–80, 106, 115, 138
Style, 76, 80, 93
Surface collections, 135
Survey, 134–35, 138, 141–42
Susa, 123
Swartz, B. K., 6
Symbiosis, 29
Symbols, xiii, 11, 93
Synthesis, 6, 10, 139
Synthetic theory of evolution, 14, 107
Syria, 28, 37, 82, 115
Systems theory, xxi, 3, 12–15, 33, 49, 62, 74, 87, 92, 106, 108, 152, 157

Tabaczynski, Stanislaw, xi–xii
Tailors, 43
Tanzania, 39
Tasmania, 166n.9
Tautology, 58, 68, 104, 130, 158
Taxonomy, 8, 92, 153
Taylor, Walter W., 8, 160
Technical problems, 6, 121, 124, 126, 132, 136, 138, 141–42, 147, 159–60
Technomic, as term, 19, 23, 92
Tell Halaf, 4

Terrorism, intellectual, 109, 160
Tests, 5, 6, 12, 16, 20–44, 46, 48, 60, 73, 75, 87–88, 93, 113, 128, 135, 139–40, 147, 158, 169n.72
Theory, xiv, xviii, xxiii, 12, 16, 22, 28, 61–75, 81, 83, 87–89, 100, 102, 104–6, 108–9, 113–14, 117, 119, 121–22, 124, 128, 132, 135–36, 138, 140, 153, 158
Thera, 83
Thermodynamics, 107
Thermography, 141
Thermoluminescence, 141
Thomas, David H., 22, 29, 86, 97, 115, 129, 135
Thracian site, 117
Tiryns, 138
Traditional archaeology, xvii, xxi–xxiii, 5, 7–12, 17, 27, 33, 35–36, 38, 47, 59, 62, 76, 78–80, 84–85, 87–88, 90, 94, 96, 99–102, 104, 114, 118–20, 127, 131–32, 150
Transformations, 42, 52, 63, 134, 140
Trigger, Bruce, 152
Trojans, 37, 117
Truth, 7, 9, 46, 84, 131, 141, 152
Tucson, Arizona, 139, 152

Underwater archaeology, 133
United Arab Emirates, 138
United States of America, 4, 9, 19, 24, 81, 86, 91. *See also* Arizona; Carolina; Maryland; Mississippi; Pennsylvania; Virginia
Universal laws, 48–49, 60, 63, 92, 108, 128, 144
Urban archaeology, xxi, 112, 133
Uselife, 52–56

Vacuum, theoretical, 74
Vacuum-cleaner technique, 7
Validation, xiv, xxii, 20–22, 35, 37, 43–44, 47, 60, 63, 75, 78, 89, 101–2, 104–5, 109, 113, 121, 128, 130, 158; pseudo-, 38–42
Variability, 27–28, 40, 51, 60, 69–70, 76, 79–80, 93, 102
Variables, 139, 147
Verification, 5, 12, 20–21, 27, 29, 31,

36, 39–40, 43, 111, 128, 131, 135, 154
Virginia, 115
Voorrips, Albertus, 147

Waste production, 57–58
Watson, Patty Jo, 4, 16, 21, 44–46, 50–51, 62, 105
Weathering, 139
Webster's Dictionary, 92
Wessex, 39
Whallon, Robert, 3

Wheeler, Mortimer, 138, 178n.8
White, Leslie, 13–14, 25, 106
Wiessner, Polly, 66, 77, 173n.18
Willey, Gordon R., 48, 110, 129
Wilson, E. B., 20
Wilson, Edward O., 107, 180n.18
Woolley, Leonard, 37, 118

Yellen, John E., 68–69, 71–73, 89
Yourcenar, Marguerite, 153

Zubrow, Ezra, 119